THE
CHRISTIAN
COLLEGE

A History of Protestant
Higher Education
in America

WILLIAM C. RINGENBERG

Christian
University
Press

A Subsidiary of Christian College Consortium

and

WILLIAM B. EERDMANS PUBLISHING COMPANY
Grand Rapids, Michigan

*Dedicated
with
appreciation and affection
to
seven Ringenbergs:
my parents, Loyal and Rhoda
my wife, Becky, and
our four children,
Matthew, Mark, Peter, and Melodie*

Available from Wm. B. Eerdmans Publishing Co.
255 Jefferson Ave. S.E., Grand Rapids, Mich. 49503

Library of Congress Cataloging in Publication Data

Ringenberg, William C., 1939–
    The Christian college.

    Includes index.
    1. Church colleges—United States—History.
2. Protestant churches—United States—History.
I. Title.
LC621.R56   1984   377'.8   84-8025
ISBN 0-8028-1996-6

Contents

Preface

This work seeks to trace the history of the Protestant college in the United States from its beginning at seventeenth-century Harvard to the present day. Before deciding to undertake this study, I consulted a variety of scholars, asking among other things their judgment on the need for it. Frederick Rudolph, who generally is considered the dean of historians of American higher education, advised: "The idea is a good one. In working on my recent book, *Curriculum: A History of the American Undergraduate Course of Study Since 1636*, I ran into nothing that came near being what you have in mind." Additionally, Charles R. Bruning, a Lutheran scholar who has studied extensively the literature in the field of Protestant higher education, observed in his book, *Relationships Between Church Related Colleges and Their Constituencies* (1975), that "there is no comprehensive history of church-related higher education in the United States."[1]

Lacking a history of the American Protestant college, the continuing Christian colleges are limited in their ability to appreciate fully their own tradition. As Carl Henry wrote recently, "The problems faced by evangelical colleges . . . increasingly include [that of] the presence of faculty who though competently trained, are not deeply informed in the evangelical heritage because their training was secular."[2] The purposes, then, of this book are both to assist Protestant colleges in increasing their understanding and appreciation of their educational and spiritual heritage and to help fill a void in the historiography of American higher education.

One could use many themes in tracing the history of American higher education (e.g., the increase in the number of colleges and the size of their enrollments as the country expanded westward, the growing democratization of the student bodies, the evolution of the curricula, the growth of the extracurricula, and the increasing role of the state and federal governments). The most significant theme, however, is the changing influence of the Christian worldview in the intellectual life of the colleges.

The founding of private colleges in America has been primarily a Christian endeavor. Religiously motivated individuals and church organizations led in the creation and early operation of nearly all colleges—private and public—before the Civil War and in the great majority of private institutions since 1865. Yet only a minority of these colleges remain avowedly Christian today. Most state universities became largely secularized by 1900; however, not until this century did the Christian religion lose its dominant intellectual position in those institutions which began as private Protestant colleges. The degree of secularization in the liberal arts colleges has increased steadily since 1900, so that by 1966 the authors of a major study on the small private colleges in America could conclude that "the intellectual presuppositions which actually guide the activities of most church colleges are heavily weighted in the secular direction."[3]

In the 1980s several types of colleges operate as church-related institutions. They include the type which was once in the Protestant camp but is now becoming—or has become—a secular college. The other two major models still wish to be called Protestant; however, theologically one is liberal and the other conservative.

While my attempt in this book is to be as fair as possible in presenting the history of the several varieties of Protestant institutions of higher education, my greatest sympathy is with those institutions which promote an open search for truth (i.e., every question may be asked and every perspective may be analyzed) and which require of the faculties both intellectual competence and Christian commitment. Whether he recognizes it or not, every historian starts from a set of assumptions or values, and from these he tells his story. My assumption is that of the several approaches to Protestant higher education during the last 350 years in America, the orthodox/evangelical model represents the best approach in the search for truth.

Books which are general surveys of a broad topic usually depend heavily upon the work of other scholars, and such is the case with this study. Although I have used college catalogs and other types of primary source material, I have relied for my information primarily upon books and scholarly articles, especially those which discuss in detail a single aspect of the history of Protestant higher education (e.g., curricula, student activities, financial support, religious activities, admission procedures, and academic freedom); studies of higher education among specific groups (e.g., denominations, Bible colleges, women, blacks, fundamentalists); and contemporary studies in the philosophy and practice of higher education. I used histories of specific institutions primarily for the purpose of locating appropriate illustrations of broad trends. The most useful of the many journals and magazines contributing to this study were the *History of Education Quarterly,* the *Harvard Educa-*

tional Review, the *Teachers College Record,* the *Journal of Higher Education,* the *College and University Journal, Religious Education, Liberal Education, School and Society, Christianity Today,* and the *Christian Century.*

The majority of the material for this book was obtained through the highly effective Taylor University Inter-library Loan Service. In addition I have worked in the Fort Wayne Public Library, the Library of Congress, and the libraries of Ball State University, Michigan State University, and Wheaton College.

I am indebted to many people for their contributions to this book. David Dickey, Timothy Sutherland, and Lois Weed were unusually generous with their time in bringing books and articles from libraries across the country to Upland where they could be studied conveniently. Gregg Holloway, Jill Lawrence, Deborah Minnick, Alane Messersmith, Alberta Miller, Jo Ellen Nelson, Ruth Osenga, Sherri VanBelkum, and Doris Wallace typed the manuscript. Gregg Holloway prepared the index. Robert C. Andringa, Thomas A. Askew, Randall E. Bell, Lawrence Cremin, John R. Dellenback, Edward E. Dinse, Edward E. Ericson, Jr., Gary Greinke, Arthur F. Holmes, Roger L. Jenkinson, Carl Lundquist, Robert W. Lynn, David O. Moberg, Tom Mullen, Edward M. Panosian, Charles Ramsay, Milo A. Rediger, Loyal R. Ringenberg, Douglas Sloan, Richard Solberg, John W. Snyder, W. Richard Stephens, Kenneth D. Swan, Gerald C. Tiffin, D. Elton Trueblood, Arthur L. Walker, and Alan H. Winquist shared helpful insights, bibliographical suggestions, and encouragement. Also, much earlier, Robert H. Ferrell and Harry J. Brown provided instruction and inspiration in historical inquiry and literary expression for which I will be forever grateful. Harold Z. Snyder, who in many ways is a wise steward in support of Christian higher education, provided financial assistance for much of the research expenses; and a grant from the Institute for Advanced Christian Studies and a Taylor University sabbatical leave allowed time to devote to the project.

I owe a special word of appreciation to Mark A. Noll, author of the introductory essay. To an unusual degree he possesses an informed and sympathetic understanding of the history of Christian higher education and a willingness to help promote such understanding. His is no ordinary introduction. He correctly identifies this work as a general history of the Protestant college; then after he calls for scholars to use it as a foundation for preparing more specialized studies, he responds to his own call by presenting a concise intellectual history of the Christian college. His introduction, therefore, provides both a conceptual framework for the general institutional history which follows and an exemplary model for the specialized studies he encourages.

Parts of the book appeared previously in article form in *Christianity Today,* the *Mennonite Quarterly Review, Michigan History,* and the *Taylor Magazine,* and are reprinted here by permission.

Finally, let me add a technical explanation. Many colleges currently carry different names from those with which they began. My usual practice, unless noted otherwise, has been to identify an institution by its present name.

Introduction:

Christian Colleges, Christian Worldviews, and An Invitation To Research

MARK A. NOLL

William Ringenberg's *The Christian College* is a well-researched and informative guide to the institutional history of Protestant liberal arts education in America. With the exception of a few Catholic colleges, this kind of higher education was virtually the only form of American collegiate instruction until the development of universities in the years following the Civil War. Since that time, the four-year liberal arts colleges which maintain a self-conscious religious orientation have become a distinct minority. Whatever else one might say about the changes in higher education over the last 120 years, these changes have at least made it possible to study such colleges as a distinct genre of educational experience. Particularly in recent decades, differences among the theologically conservative Protestant liberal arts colleges—arising from diverse denominational heritages, economic and social affinities or constituencies, or the simple barriers of geography—which once seemed to divide them into separate categories have receded in importance. This reflects the growing consciousness among the colleges themselves that within the general scheme of American higher education they share a great deal in common.

Until very recently, however, the full extent of that commonality has not received adequate attention, in part because of the absence of a general institutional history for this kind of college. Such an institutional history is necessary not because it can tell us everything we need to know about the Christian liberal arts colleges, but rather, as a framework for organizing the diffuse experience of these institutions and as a map for charting the educational landscape they occupy. Such an institutional history can do for its subjects what political history does for a nation. The modern British historian G. R. Elton once commented that "political history must come before any other and has always done so. The study of history began as political history . . . It need not stop there, but unless it starts there, it will not start at all."[1] In these terms, Professor Ringenberg's general institutional history of American Protestant education offers a "start," a beginning, for self-understanding among the Christian colleges. By itself it is an interesting and important work, but it also constitutes a summons for examining many other interesting and important questions related to Christian higher education in America.

Professor Ringenberg has focused his research on the predominately white Protestant colleges which have maintained a theologically conservative, or evangelical, position. He has wisely recognized that this is a somewhat nebulous designation, and so he has also made fruitful use of a wide variety of sources for closely related institutions: histories of Southern Baptist, black, and Lutheran colleges whose development overlaps that of the "evangelical" colleges in so many ways; histories of Catholic colleges and universities which often reveal a similar story to their Protestant counterparts; and histories of the many nonsectarian or theologically liberal colleges which came into existence with the same commitments that the evangelical schools continue to espouse. The sensitivity with which these different historical traditions are interwoven enriches Professor Ringenberg's particular concentration on the evangelical colleges.

His work stands on its own. It should become a widely read resource on the campuses of the Christian colleges themselves, and it should serve as a valuable fount of information for the general study of American higher education. It should also constitute an important foundation for further research, inasmuch as it touches on matters of interest to all of the subdisciplines that today constitute historical study. The Christian colleges offer an especially fertile field for research in ethnic history (because of the overseas heritages of many sponsoring groups), the new intellectual history (because of the interplay of ideas and behavior at such institutions), ecclesiastical history (because of the role colleges have played in the history of many denominations), social history (because of interlocking connections among family, vocation, economic influence, and professionalization which can be studied at each of the schools), and political history (because of the opportunity to see how college education interacts with the known political preferences of delimited constituencies). In particular, Ringenberg's work is an open invitation to study more carefully the graduates of Christian colleges. Does attending such an institution make a difference in long-term religious allegiance, political participation or convictions, vocational preference, or in other measurable areas? With this book as a foundation, those who pursue such issues will have a reliable guide to the general patterns which have characterized the entire history of Christian higher education in America.

Now, in this introduction, it is appropriate to address most particularly the historical role of the Christian colleges in the formation of distinctly Christian approaches to the life of the mind and to the world. These questions, which concern the sometimes precarious fate of Christian worldviews in the unfolding of American history, provide the essential context for understanding the rise of Christian colleges and their pathway through American history. They are also the key questions for evaluating the success of these colleges in fulfilling their educational purposes and for prognosticating their fate in the future.[2]

CHRISTIAN WORLDVIEWS AND CHRISTIAN COLLEGES

Christian thinking in America has passed through several distinct stages, with alternating periods of stability and change. These stages have reflected the developing nature of America's religious and intellectual culture, the culture which has always provided the setting for Christian higher education. To understand more generally the relationship of Christian worldviews and the Christian colleges, it is helpful to have a sketch of the historical terrain. Before roughly 1925, it is clear that American Christian thinking experienced two long and relatively stable periods of synthesis and two great and tumultuous periods of transition.[3] Since 1925 the picture is not as clear, but even in more recent times it is possible to note some general tendencies.

The Puritan worldview provided the first relatively stable period of American Christian thinking. For the sake of convenience, we can date the prominence of this perspective from the founding of Harvard College in 1636 to the death of Jonathan Edwards in 1758. Then from about the mid-eighteenth century to the period of the Second Great Awakening (roughly 1795-1820), great changes took place in American society, affecting not least the nature of Christian thought. This transitional period was succeeded by another relatively stable time which stretched from the Second Great Awakening to the beginning of the academic revolution that created the modern American university (1869 and 1876 are both useful chronological pegs at the end of this stable period, the first being the year when Charles Eliot began his momentous tenure as president of Harvard, the second the year in which John Hopkins began operation as a graduate university based on the German model). From that time until early in the twentieth century (the Scopes Trial over evolution in 1925 is another convenient date), there was once again a great tumult in American thought and religion which profoundly affected the shape of education generally and Christian higher education particularly. Since 1925 several forces have seemed to be at work within the thinking of theologically conservative Protestants. An effort to roll back the clock to the early nineteenth century (i.e., to deny or repudiate the great changes at the end of the century) coexists alongside careful efforts to incorporate some of the ideas set in motion during the late nineteenth century into a Christian picture of the world. Terms to describe these general directions are slippery, but it might not be amiss to suggest that modern "fundamentalists" favor the first, while contemporary "evangelicals" favor the second. There are even indications that some evangelicals are more generally dissatisfied with the shape of Christian thinking in America and wish to recreate something closer to a Puritan approach, although without necessarily replicating the specific content of the Puritan worldview.

These very general chronological divisions beg to be clarified. Each of the stages in American Christian thinking witnessed the development of complex intellectual problems. Each had major implications for the shape of Christian higher education. And each contributed significantly to the present issues facing those who desire to develop a Christian worldview appropriate for both modern culture and the students at Christian colleges.

Puritanism.   The Puritans remain an object of discomfort for modern Americans, Christians no less than secularists. Some of this discomfort is warranted, for these energetic and sober Englishmen who set out to tame "the howling wilderness" could be an intimidating group. They would tolerate few concessions to human weakness and precious few alternatives when considering the path to the "city on a hill."

At least from modern Christians concerned about the life of the mind, however, the Puritans deserve much better.[4] They remain, more than two centuries after the passing of their communities, still the only significant group of theologically conservative Protestants in American history who attempted both a Christian and an academic reconstruction of formal thought. Their colleges, of which seventeenth-century Harvard was most representative, were the most self-conscious practitioners of the integration of faith, life, and learning in the history of Christian higher education in America.

The magnitude of the Puritans' accomplishment is suggested by the breadth of their reforming interest. This included not only the spiritual renovation of individuals and the systematic renewal of church and society, but also the reconstruction of the mind. Drawing upon ideas of covenant, which they traced back to Scripture but which also reflected the creative jurisprudence of Elizabethan England, the Puritans formulated relatively sophisticated theories of political and social cohesion. More than piety knit the Puritans together who ventured into the New World during the 1630s, just as more than enthusiasm inspired the continuing struggle for reform by Puritans who stayed in England. Their covenantal theology, extrapolated into theories of church, state, and society, provided a potent intellectual balance to what Oliver Cromwell once called "the heart of the matter," the soul's personal attachment to God. To be sure, Puritan theories of social order were not overly successful: England's "Puritan Revolution" lasted less than two decades and came to an end conclusively with the restoration of the monarch in 1660; America's "Holy Commonwealths" in Massachusetts and Connecticut exchanged Puritan piety for Yankee profitability before a century had gone by in the New World. Yet the very presence of these experiments, not to speak of the lingering impact which so many Puritan ideas have exerted in America, distinguishes Puritan thought as a rare commodity in American history.[5]

Puritan thought was also notable for its explorations in psychology and rhetoric. Its emphasis on conversion, witnessed in diaries, sermons, and formal treatises, went much further than either Luther or Calvin had gone in charting the migration of a soul from darkness to light. So careful could this reflection become, as illustrated in the diaries of Thomas Shepard or the sermons of Thomas Hooker and John Cotton, that it is fair to regard the revivalistic and evangelistic thinking of Americans since the seventeenth century as but abridgments, popularizations, or simplifications of the Puritan standard.[6] Puritans reflected with similar seriousness on the style of public speech appropriate to their messages. The development of the "plain style" sermon and the other forms of direct public address which the Puritan sermon encouraged was a result of self-conscious strategy. Rhetorical analysis, in this rare case, preceded argumentive speech. Even more rare was the fact that Puritans designed this rhetorical style to meet the needs of their larger commitments, rather than letting instances of rhetorical success dictate the shape of the larger commitments.

The most ambitious efforts to shape a distinctly Christian worldview came in the Puritans' attempts to restrict or even supersede the philosophy of Aristotle. Not surprisingly, Puritans were never entirely successful in this attempt. Aristotelian structures had guided university instruction in Europe since the thirteenth century and had continued to be the basis for instruction in the Protestant academies and universities, in spite of fulminations by Luther and Calvin against the authority of Aristotle. The Puritans most spectacular contribution was their use of the discussions on logic and rhetoric by Peter Ramus.[7] Ramus (1515–1572), a French scholar who would eventually die a martyr to the Calvinist cause on St. Bartholomew's Day in 1572, had proposed new methods for classifying and arranging the propositions of arguments which he thought came closer to the common-sense reasoning of normal human discourse than did Aristotle's syllogisms. These proposals became very important guidelines for the Puritans who constructed the theory of a plain-style sermon. Ramus was also an inspiration generally for encouraging the conviction that Christians, with the divine authority of Scripture at hand, should not be so closely tied to the conclusions of the non-Christian Aristotle.

Puritanism's sharpest questioning of the Aristotelian heritage came, however, not in rhetoric but in ethics, where the precepts of Aristotle had shaped formal thought for several hundred years. Aristotelian ethics were rational and intellectualist. They taught that action flows from the dictates of the understanding. The Puritans who sought self-consciously to flesh out their biblical, Augustinian, and Reformed understanding of theology in the wider worlds of thought could not accept those conclusions. Rather, they proposed ethical theories which they felt reflected more accurately biblical teaching on human nature and the doing of good. For these Puritans, morality was at bottom volitional and affectional. They held that behavior arises from, and reflects, the dispositions of the heart—and the state of the heart depends on the free exercise of God's grace. William Ames (1576–1633), among the early Puritan intellectuals who remained in the Old World, stated the distinctly Puritan conclusions most expansively in his book, *The Marrow of Theology*. In America, however, nearly a century after Ames, Cotton Mather (1663–1728) still expressed the same distrust of Aristotle's natural moral philosophy. To Mather, since Aristotelian moral philosophy did not comprehend the fact that truly good behavior flows from a heart renewed by God's grace, it remained "*a sham*" that "pretends to give you a Religion without a CHRIST, and a *Life* of PIETY without a *Loving Principle; a Good Life* with no other than Dead Works filling of it. . . ."[8]

The tradition for which Ames and Mather stood reached its culmination in Jonathan Edwards (1703–1758), who faced a more difficult task than had William Ames a century before. By the early eighteenth century, a new form of ethics had emerged which grounded virtue in the state of the inner being much as Puritan ethics did. This "new moral philosophy" differed from Puritanism, however, in its assertion that people possessed *by nature* the capacity to nurture goodness. For the Cambridge Platonist Henry More (1614–1687), the British sentimentalist Lord Shaftesbury (1671–1713), and the Scottish moral philosopher Francis Hutcheson (1694–1746) there was no need for the specific activity of God's grace to prepare the heart for virtuous behavior. Edwards was, consequently, faced with the task of defending a volitional and affectional ethics against the Aristotelian tradition and a Reformed and Augustinian theology against the new moral philosophy.

Edwards's treatise, *The Nature of True Virtue* (published posthumously in 1765), was his major attempt at performing this task. In this book Edwards praised the new moral philosophers for certain aspects of their work. On the basis of a belief in common grace, Edwards held that natural conscience did have a prudential value in regulating conduct, that sentiments of beauty provided insights into the nature of morality, that pity and familial affection helped stabilize society, and that the natural "moral sense" revealed some truths about the world. Edwards went on to assert, however, that these useful products of natural virtue fell far short of true virtue, which had its basis only in the saving grace of God. "Nothing is of the nature of true virtue," Edwards wrote, "in which God is not the first and the last."⁹

Edwards went on to demonstrate that the supposed virtue which arises from natural capacities is not really virtue at all, however valuable it might be for smoothing life in society. He set about this task by arguing that pity, the natural moral sense, the natural passions, natural familial affection, and conscience were no more than species of prudence, self-seeking, and self-love.

Edwards's work did not convince everyone who read it in his day, nor had it ever enjoyed widespread approbation in American intellectual history. Nevertheless, modern Christians should be impressed with Edwards's effort, even if they may not approve its specific details. Modern Christian academics especially ought to be able to learn valuable lessons from Edwards as they plan their own strategies for effective use of learning. The importance of Edwards lies in the example he set by carefully dissecting and analyzing the intellectual discoveries, assumptions, and reflexes of his age. Edwards not only possessed a strong belief in God's particular grace, he also respected the wisdom which God had given to believers and nonbelievers alike. He thus studied very carefully not just the spokesmen for his own basically Puritan positions, but also Locke, Newton, the philosophers Samuel Clarke, Shaftesbury, and Hutcheson, and many more beside. In fact, Edwards's ability to mount effective counterarguments against the "new moral philosophy" depended upon his capacity to take the best thinkers of his day with utter seriousness. For Edwards, total dependence upon the Holy Spirit pushed him *toward* contemporary intellectuals, not *away* from them.[10]

Edwards was virtually the last of his breed. After his time, even the best American Christian thinkers gave in readily to the idea that people possessed by nature the mental capacities to understand the deepest secrets of the world and the moral ability to act in accordance with conscience or the demands of the gospel. Yet even though Edwards had few heirs, his efforts deserve attention from those in our day who labor in Christian higher education. They hold up the vision that a Christian education may exist which is at once open to the world's finest wisdom and fully consistent with biblical orthodoxy.

Edwards himself played only a very minor role in higher education during the colonial period. While he did take young men into his home to assist in their preparation for the ministry, he was not even among the most notable pastors of his day in this kind of training. Edwards did accept the presidency of the College of New Jersey (later Princeton University) in 1757, but he served only a few short weeks at that post before being felled by an inoculation for smallpox. In addition, by Edwards's day the earlier Puritan position on Christian thinking was beginning to give way to other convictions, of which the "new moral philosophy" was the most obvious example. Harvard College, after entertaining a mixture of Puritan/Augustinian teaching (mostly in the form of William Ames's works) and Aristotelianism during its first century, had accepted the new moral philosophy as its guiding light by the early part of the eighteenth century. Yale College (founded in 1701) and Princeton (founded in 1746) both retained more of the old Puritan synthesis, but only until the 1760s, when the ideology of revolution hastened the exchange of Augustinian Puritanism for a perspective which was more optimistic about innate human abilities.

Before the changes of the mid-eighteenth century, the earliest American colleges had done their part in promoting the Puritan intellectual synthesis. College authorities assumed that students would matriculate with a full knowledge of Scripture, which then would mark the conceptual boundaries of collegiate instruction. At least until the tumults of the colonial Great Awakening in the 1740s made officials skeptical about "enthusiastic" religion, they encouraged students to look for the conversions which were so much a part of the Puritan tradition. In addition, they provided instructional materials from the Reformed communities of England

and the continent which depicted education as a practical service to God. They encouraged students to master the classical European curriculum (especially the grammar, rhetoric, and dialectic of the traditional university) because they regarded this curriculum as the distillation of the common grace which God had given to the ancients. But college authorities also taught the students that the classics could not provide the essential orientation to the world which came by God's grace alone. A student, in the words of Harvard's earliest set of "Rules, and Precepts," was to "be plainly instructed, and earnestly pressed to consider well, the maine end of his life and studies is, *to know God and Jesus Christ which is eternall life* . . . and therefore to lay Christ in the bottome, as the only foundation of all sound knowledge and Learning."[11] The result was wholistic education which gave nature its due while reserving the essential framework, in both personal lives and academic instruction, for grace.

Colonial colleges were never in the forefront in articulating these views. The most influential Christian thinkers were not professional scholars but ministers like Cotton Mather and Jonathan Edwards. Expectations for college graduates were set by the influential leaders of the colonies—governors, magistrates, major land holders, and (eventually) merchants. The colleges were training grounds for the colonial elite and for the New World's ministers. Instructors were pedagogues rather than scholars. They handed on what they had been given but were rarely innovators themselves. All of this meant that while the colonial colleges reflected the Puritan worldview, they did not do much to shape it. Only after the Civil War would those who were most influential in articulating worldviews teach in colleges and universities, but by then the colleges themselves had undergone great changes from their Puritan beginnings.

The Revolutionary Generation.

The Revolutionary Generation. From the end of the French and Indian War in 1763 to well beyond the turn of the century, America's cultural values were in flux.[12] Within the space of a half-century, Americans threw over the rule of the world's most powerful nation, they dallied with several forms of the European Enlightenment before coming to embrace a conservative expression of that great movement. They embarked on a love affair with the idea of liberty which had both bracing and unsettling consequences, and they reestablished Christian thinking and the churches on new foundations. It is hardly surprising that in this rapid realignment of values, the nature of instruction at the country's colleges, and the colleges themselves, also changed dramatically.

Intellectual change had much to do with the consuming passion of the American Revolution. Edmund S. Morgan has summarized perceptively the long-term intellectual results of the Revolutionary era: "In 1740 America's leading intellectuals were clergymen and thought about theology; in 1790 they were statesmen and thought about politics . . . One may properly consider the American Revolution . . . to mean the substitution of political for clerical leadership and of politics for religion as the most challenging area of human thought and endeavor."[13] This intellectual revolution had immediate implications for the new nation's colleges. Most obviously, with the excitement of politics in the Revolutionary age, the number of graduates choosing the ministry declined rapidly in favor of careers in law, business, and public service. Princeton's experience was not atypical when it saw the percentage of its graduates entering the ministry decline from 47 percent during the period 1748-1775 to 13 percent for the period 1776-1806.[14] Thereafter, American colleges have never trained as high a proportion of ministers as in the colonial period.

The changes underway in the new United States, however, involved much more than a mere shift in the vocational preference of college graduates. In simplest terms, the entire Revolutionary generation represented the abandonment of tradition, history, and hierarchy in favor of innovation, the future, and egalitarianism. It was a time when the heady wine of liberty communicated an intoxicating message to almost every sphere of American life.[15]

The ideology which lay behind the War for Independence certainly played an important part in the change. Stress on the corruption of the Old World, insistence upon "natural rights" in the face of Parliament's "tyranny," and a vision of history as never-ending struggle between forces of oppression and freedom shaped perceptions not only for politics but for every sphere of American life. Thus, upstart religious bodies broke from the settled traditions of established denominations, the older denominations themselves were forced to reconstitute on American principles, formerly respected professions like the law came under attack as unjustly privileged sanctums, and politicians began to make much of "the people."[16] In general, the forces which led both to DeTocqueville's *Democracy* and to Andrew Jackson's "age of the common man" were set in motion.

Perhaps even more important than the specific ideology of the Revolution were the general intellectual guidelines which Americans embraced at this time. In order to justify resistance to Great Britain, in order to challenge the heavy hand of encrusted tradition, and in order to strike out confidently on behalf of liberty,

Americans turned enthusiastically to the ideals of the conservative European Enlightenment. Americans knew about all the major forms of the eighteenth-century Enlightenment: the moderate and balanced work of Newton and Locke, the skepticism of David Hume and Voltaire, the radical proposals of Rousseau and William Goodwin. They took to their hearts particularly, however, the principles of what Henry May has called a "didactic" Enlightenment with origins in the universities of Scotland.[17] This form of Enlightenment made it possible to mount a tradition-free, scientific defense of natural law, social liberty, and the innate powers of human intellect and morality. This didactic Enlightenment was vital for America's politicians in the Revolutionary era because it provided a means to hold in check the centrifugal forces of liberty without having to fall back onto the hierarchical authoritarianism of Europe. It was similarly important for America's Christians. The didactic Enlightenment enabled them to agree with the wider American culture in rejecting the corruption of the past while yet maintaining the truthfulness of historic Christianity. As might be expected, such a broad intellectual movement also had great impact on American colleges.

This form of the Enlightenment made its most notable advances in the colleges during and immediately following the War for Independence. Christian leaders like President John Witherspoon (1723–1794) of Princeton and President Timothy Dwight (1752–1817) of Yale faced two pressing needs. The theoretical task was nothing less than to defend the knowability and reality of the external world. The threat here was epitomized by the speculative philosophy of David Hume. How could Americans maintain liberty, justice, and order if a philosophical sophistry was unleashed which made such concepts meaningless? The practical need was to save Christian social morality from the threats of infidelity, French anarchy, and the wanton antinomianism released by the Revolution itself. Committed as they were to the freedom which the War for Independence had gained, leaders like Witherspoon and Dwight nonetheless looked for ways to restrain the instability evidenced by rioters in western Massachusetts under Daniel Shays, by Masonic-like conspirators passing under the banner of the Bavarian Illuminati, and by the suspect humanism of political theorists like Thomas Jefferson.

These two needs, furthermore, cried to be addressed with *scientific* responses, for the great influence of Newton and Locke had made its mark in America. It was an Englishman, Alexander Pope, who wrote, "Nature and Nature's laws lay hid in Night. / God said, Let Newton be! and all was Light," but the sentiment which these lines expressed spoke also for the New World. In addition, Americans possessed an exaggerated fondness for Francis Bacon and the methods of empirical and inductive science which he promoted.[18] They also had great admiration for John Locke, whose defense of English liberty in 1688 and his charting of "Human Understanding" had made his entire point of view extraordinarily influential in America. By the Revolutionary period, in other words, good "explanations" for Americans were those which could rest on a Baconian appeal to "the facts," which could reduce complex phenomena to Newtonian-like laws, and which could follow John Locke in basing knowledge on the orderly classification of sense experience.

In the two-pronged effort to overcome crises in the Revolutionary period and to exploit its enthusiasms, educated American Christians allied their own faith with the mentality of the didactic Enlightenment. In so doing they seemed to accept the underlying conviction of all who took part in the European Enlightenment that the fundamental reality was matter in motion and that fundamental truth depended upon human apprehension. The acceptance of these beliefs had momentous consequences for Christian higher education in America, both in the years immediately following the Revolution and in the century to follow.

President Witherspoon of Princeton, more than any other person, was responsible for bringing Christian higher education into line with the new cultural convictions of American society.[19] In providing solutions to the difficulties of the Revolutionary era, he also laid out the basic structure of the "moral philosophy" or "mental science" course which tied together the college curriculum through the time of the Civil War, and which influences the Christian colleges to this day. Witherspoon, a Scot who became president of the College of New Jersey in 1768, brought to America the philosophical perspective known as Scottish Common Sense Realism. This point of view began by *assuming*, in opposition to Hume, that the world we perceive really exists. It began by *assuming* that the normal perceptions common to humanity correspond to the way things really are. Hence, the epistemological dilemmas posed by skeptics of the Enlightenment were solved through an appeal to the universal, or common, sense of humankind.

In the hands of Witherspoon and then other Christian educators, Scottish Common Sense did even more—it went on to solve social and moral problems. If intuition can assure us of the reality of the natural world, these thinkers held, then surely it can teach us morality as well. What, in fact, do we find out about morality when we look at the common moral sensations of humanity, when we consciously reflect upon our own "moral sense"? According to this way of thinking, we certainly find that the principles of traditional morality are just as real as the existence of the external world. Scottish Realists held that when by intuition we look into our own consciences, we discover the idea of a supreme judge who rewards good and evil. To the Scottish Realists, this idea that God rewards good and evil reflects the reality of a just God as certainly as our perceptions of the physical world reflect the reality of that world. Intuition, thus, is not a phantasmagoria of the imagination but a scientific device capable of solving epistemological and ethical problems. The result was that intuitions, common sense, became just as valuable for knowing the truths of epistemology as sense observation was for learning about the material world.

In the creative hands of the Scottish philosophers and their American followers, this line of reasoning represented a *tour de force*. By scientific intuition—the systematic study of what humans hold in common—we can know certainly that the world exists and that traditional morality is valid. What the Scottish philosophers and the American educators had done was to restate Christian morality in a scientific form without having to appeal to the special revelation of Scripture or to the authoritative traditions of the church. In fact, Scottish Realism seemed to provide the only means in the Age of Reason for retaining a belief in scriptural authority and the usefulness of the church, since it could demonstrate their reality on the basis of common-sense perceptions of the physical world and the transmissions of the internal moral sense. Through these means, the Scottish philosophy reestablished the validity of natural science, reconfirmed traditional morality, and demonstrated the continuing truthfulness of historic Christianity. Its great triumph was the salvation of the reality of the physical world and the reality of the eighteenth-century Enlightenment. The great questions would eventually become whether Christian higher education, having wed the spirit of one age, would be widowed in the next.

Having set to rest theoretical problems about knowledge and morality, Witherspoon and like-minded Scottish Realists set about inculcating these principles into the nation's rising generation of leaders. In the colleges of the late eighteenth and early nineteenth centuries, teachers like Witherspoon and Dwight did their best to defend the respectability of traditional morality. They also did their best to impart a sense of duty to the graduates of Princeton, Yale, and other colleges. If the moral law was as scientific as the laws of nature, and if the moral law demanded Christian morality and good citizenship, then every effort could be bent to produce graduates inflamed with energetic zeal for God and country. When we remember the great influence eventually exerted in politics by Witherspoon students like James Madison or in religion by Dwight students like revivalist and social reformer Lyman Beecher, we begin to see how important the intellectual ideals of the college leaders actually were.[20]

So long as the United States remained overwhelmingly Protestant, Scottish Common Sense Realism remained the dominant perspective in American colleges, for it provided scientific support for traditional Protestant truths and for traditional Christian morality. So long as American popular culture remained under Protestant influence, no one would question the analogy which Scottish Common Sense drew between the mind and the universe; no one would question the way in which "science" (the unquestioned authority) had been used to defend the traditional morality whose moorings had been shaken in the Revolutionary period.

Almost without notice in the tumult of the times, however, a great change had taken place in Christian thinking and in the goals of Christian higher education. Puritans had grounded their thinking in special revelation and had worked to turn special revelation into a framework for all of learning. The educators of the new United States grounded their thinking in the Enlightenment and worked to give special revelation a place within that framework. Or to put matters another way, where Puritan education had proceeded from a Christian perspective which sought to dominate the shape, purposes, and structure of learning, leaders in America's Christian colleges after the Revolution allowed truths of the didactic Enlightenment to lay out the shape, purposes, and structure of knowledge, within which they were delighted to find a place for Christianity.

The triumph of Christian higher education in the Revolutionary era was its survival at a time when everything from the past had become suspect, when Americans were dispensing with one after another of the traditions which had been passed down to them. The dilemma of Christian higher education after the Revolutionary era was the principles on which it was grounded, for it no longer rested on self-consciously Christian thinking but on the Christian use of Enlightenment thought.

The triumph was everywhere more evident than the dilemma in the first century of the new United States. With justice, that period may be called the great age of Christian higher education in the history of the country.

A Christian-Cultural Synthesis.   In the years between the administrations of presidents Thomas Jefferson (1801–1809) and

Abraham Lincoln (1861–1865), Christian values and the values of American public life joined in a powerful cultural synthesis.[21] The Revolution had brought the United States into existence; its ideology of liberty provided a powerful impetus for constructing a new nation. Similarly, the Second Great Awakening had witnessed the conversion of many people; its twin engines of evangelism and reform also offered means to reconstruct society.[22] When these two influences came together—as they did so clearly for the great revivalists like Charles G. Finney, the great reformers like abolitionist Theodore Dwight Weld, the great organizers like Lyman Beecher, the great educators like Noah Webster, and the great politicians like Lincoln—the result was a singularly powerful set of cultural values which decisively shaped the character of America's Christian higher education.

Three central beliefs governed the synthesis. Antebellum America believed in America itself, it believed in individual freedom, and it believed in what could be called Protestant Newtonianism. The belief in America can be seen most clearly from a northern perspective during the years immediately before the Civil War. For many in both North and South, this struggle brought together reform, millennialism, and the sense of America's unique destiny under God. For northerners the preservation of the union meant no less than breathing life into Manifest Destiny, overcoming slavery (the greatest evil remaining in America), and perhaps even harbingering the millennium. "Stand up, stand up for Jesus, the strife will not be long," wrote George Duffield in 1858, one eye looking askance at the Dred Scott decision of the previous year which had treated slaves like property, the other cocked for the final kingdom of Christ. The words of the New School Presbyterians at their General Assembly of 1861 stood for many others: "Rebellion against such a government as ours . . . can find no parallel, except in the first two great rebellions, that which assailed the throne of heaven directly [Satan], and that which peopled our world with miserable apostates [Adam and Eve] . . . . We here, in deep humiliation for our sins and the sins of the nation, and in heartfelt devotion, lay ourselves, with all that we are and have, on the altar of God and our country."[23] For their part, southerners often looked at Yankees as lawless aggressors destroying the precious Christian heritage of the United States.

Christian America believed not only in itself as a nation, but in the individual freedom of its citizens. This second belief was compounded of much that was vital in America's young history: the stirring words of the Declaration of Independence, the convictions of Jefferson and Jackson, the philosophical individualism of John

Locke and the Scottish Realists, the accelerating influence of the Methodists, and even the newer theories of some Calvinists. In its extreme form the belief in individual freedom resulted in visions of human perfection—some coming from the Unitarian departure from Calvinism, others from the more advanced forms of Methodism. In its more usual forms, American individualism foresaw great social benefits arising from individuals organized against social evils—slavery, drunkenness, dueling, prostitution, the theater, and frivolous amusements. Although America's infatuation with the individual was not confined to Christian circles, Christians no less than non-Christians gave their whole-hearted commitment to the individual as the hope of the future.

Finally, the educated elite of nineteenth century America were committed to a worldview in which first principles were God-ordained laws and the human capacity to work with such laws. Apart from a few vastly overpublicized Transcendentalists, most Americans who thought at all before the Civil War thought in terms of a Protestant Newtonianism. Americans were Protestant in their convictions about Scripture, their commitment to an American understanding of the priesthood of believers, and their primitivistic allegiance to first-century Christianity. They were Newtonian, and hence of the Enlightenment, in their commitment to simplicity in ideas and in a corresponding distaste for intellectual ambiguity. They reflected this Newtonianism even more in their commitment to a concept of static law. It was, for example, as axiomatic as the law of gravity that national prosperity was a sign of God's blessing or that the exercise of correct stimuli in a revival would bring the correct results. Protestant Newtonianism was, that is, no more than the conviction that externally fixed laws governed the "facts" of national life and morality as surely as they did the "facts" of nature.

This then was the American Christian-cultural synthesis before the Civil War. It emerged when the content of a great revival was poured through the forms of a domesticated Enlightenment. It helps us understand how philosophies of life like Jacksonianism, Manifest Destiny, and voluntaristic reform could flourish. It enables us to make sense of social, political, and religious convictions in the nineteenth century. And it provides the proper context for understanding the education in America's Christian colleges.

Intellectual life in America's colleges before 1870 bears little resemblance to what we know today.[24] The curriculum of the old college consisted of a little mathematics; a great deal of praise for empirical science with, however, only meager opportunities to carry out actual experiments; much drill in the classics; and an exposure to systematic arguments for morality, civic virtue, and the existence of God. Modern languages and literature had no place in the curriculum, and history as a discipline was just beginning to be recognized. Instruction proceeded by recitation. The professor, acting more as scorekeeper than teacher, called upon the students to translate, parse, recapitulate, or summarize. Close discipline, extending well beyond the classroom, was the rule. Teachers were regarded as keepers of the peace. At Harvard in 1827 a financial crisis forced the college to increase teaching loads, consolidate positions, and also extend the parietal responsibilities of the faculty to nightly bedchecks of the undergraduates. Not surprisingly, the tedium of the classroom, the rigor of extracurricular discipline, and the natural feistiness of late adolescence led to student unrest. One of the less destructive ways in which students protested their lot was to disrupt the morning devotional by herding a compliant cow into the chapel. Student unrest often led to violence as well, including once or twice the murder of professors who had fallen from favor.

Some of the student exuberance noted in the frequent disturbances may have reflected their unconscious awareness of higher education's comparative lack of importance. Throughout the nineteenth century, a bachelor's degree in the liberal arts remained more an ornament of the upper middle class than a doorway to intellectual growth or economic success. It was not necessary to study the liberal arts before taking up a career in medicine or law, and only some of the country's new seminaries required ministerial candidates to stand a regular four-year undergraduate curriculum. The country's best engineers came not from the liberal arts colleges but from the military academy at West Point.

Nor were college faculty members the country's intellectual elite. The faculty at the nation's oldest and most prestigious college, Harvard, was not even the dominant intellectual force in Boston. Henry Adams, reflecting on the Harvard faculty in the years surrounding the Civil War, wrote that "no one took Harvard College seriously." One of the reasons may have been the college's casual regard for scholarship, an attitude seen, for example, when the same Henry Adams was in 1870 appointed professor of medieval history, a subject about which he professed himself "utterly and grossly ignorant."[25]

By 1870 it was clear that the old college was barely keeping pace with the intellectual needs of the country. In that year the nation's colleges enrolled about 52,000 out of a general population of 40 million (the equivalent of 300,000 students in our present population). Furthermore, the rate of growth in the number of college students was falling behind the rate of growth in the country as a whole.

For all of its weaknesses, however, the old-style American college had one important advantage: with very rare exceptions, it was founded and operated as an avowedly Christian institution. In the great westward expansion of the country before the Civil War, Protestant denominations exceeded one another in founding educational institutions.[26] Many of a denomination's schools were founded by the efforts of a single clergyman. Most struggled along with pitifully few students and a rapidly changing faculty. Most suffered from a surplus of competition and a deficit in financing. All sought to answer the Protestant need for a literate laity and a learned clergy and the democratic American need for informed citizens.

In 1821 Harvard was the largest college in the country with 286 students and 16 faculty members. By 1860 it had been joined by Yale and Dartmouth as the largest colleges, numbering 300-400 students and 15-25 faculty members. These schools and the many other smaller colleges led a precarious existence, but they did know why they existed. The founders of colleges, and the parents who sent their sons, saw them as places of "intellectual stability and order in a fluid society."[27] Edward Everett, president of Harvard, could speak in 1846 of the three purposes for colleges: to acquire knowledge, to train the mind, to prepare good citizens. He went on to say that of these the third was far and away most important.[28] Colleges before the Civil War offered one of the ways for exuberant American society to retain a measure of order and cohesion. Moreover, at the vast majority of colleges, where evangelical conviction was stronger than at Harvard, Christian beliefs significantly influenced the ideals of order, cohesion, and citizenship.

The capstone of the college experience in those days was a year-long course, often taught by the college president, in "moral philosophy" or "mental science." It was a course with vast horizons, much as Witherspoon had set it out, including everything having to do with human beings and their social relations (the subjects studied under this rubric would later become the separate disciplines of psychology, philosophy, religion, political science, sociology, anthropology, economics, and jurisprudence). The course almost always included an investigation of epistemology in general and the epistemological foundations of Christianity in particular. The purpose of the course was to provide final Christian integration for the college career and final exhortations concerning the kind of citizenship good Christians should practice.

In view of what would happen to college education later in the nineteenth century, it is worth pausing to sketch in greater detail the intentions and methods of this moral philosophy course.[29] From a modern Christian perspective, the instruction in moral philosophy had much to commend it. It represented an effort to perceive all bits of knowledge as parts of a comprehensive whole, and to do so within a Christian framework. It was, in modern jargon, a course seeking to integrate faith and learning. Moral philosophy provided college seniors with a respectable defense of God's existence and the moral law. It offered comprehensive exhortations to live morally in society, to support religion, to put public good above selfish interests, and to work for the coming of God's kingdom in America.

Moral philosophy was useful in holding back atheistic skepticism, promoting democratic republicanism, and encouraging social morality. It nonetheless had several deficiencies. First, the Christianity of moral philosophy was reductionistic. Textbooks in mental science by the Calvinistic Presbyterians Archibald Alexander and James McCosh, the Arminian revivalist Charles Finney, and the Harvard Unitarians James Walker and Andrew Preston Peabody shared the same commitments—to intuition as a defense of morality, to science as the royal road to truth, and to logical arguments as proof for the existence of God. The "Christianity" these arguments promoted was a pale form of belief looking more like the deists' convictions about a watchmaker God than Christian convictions about the God and Father of the Lord Jesus Christ. In addition, Protestant academics of all theological positions often left the impression that their ultimate concern was not so much the actual content of Christian beliefs as the preservation of established order in American society.

Second, the ethics of moral philosophy was individualistic. Moral philosophy could inspire collegiates and seminarians to organize individuals in the battles against slavery and drink, but it saw with less clarity that evil could be a property of institutions as well as persons. The ethics of moral philosophy called for the recapture of the nearly mythical virtue of the founding fathers or urged its adherents to bring in the millennium. In neither case did it look for more than personal exertion, however, nor did it encourage an examination of the social and economic structures of American life.

Third, moral philosophy was captive to the static categories of Baconian (after Francis Bacon) science. It was wholeheartedly committed to science, but its science was conceived in narrowly inductivist terms. "Facts" were unchanging elements of nature, perceived reliably by unbiased sense experience, organized inductively into generalizations, and summarized as natural laws. To suggest that the mind of the scientist predisposed him to see certain things and not others in the facts or to contend that the construction of scientific laws required hypothetical or unverifiable steps was to be scorned as promoting speculative, romantic, idealistic, and false ideas.

Finally, moral philosophy stood squarely in the intellectual lineage of the Enlightenment. Unlike Edwards, who rejected the naturalistic framework of Enlightenment thought while continuing to see much value in specific proposals by Enlightenment thinkers, Christian educators in the antebellum period largely accepted that natural framework while rejecting some of the specific conclusions drawn from it. That is, they agreed with the intellectual world at large in resting the Bible on natural proofs, in defending the supernatural by the material, and in grounding benevolence on a utilitarian sense of what God can do for the righteous. Yet these convictions did not lead to the abandonment of the faith, as it had for many in the Revolutionary generation like Jefferson and Tom Paine, because these same individuals continued to insist upon the reality of God's free activity in revival and reform and upon the truthfulness of a divine revelation.

Antebellum Christian educators, thus, possessed divided minds. They seemed to be saying intellectually that their faith rested on an ability to demonstrate its validity to the satisfaction of modern science and modern philosophy. At the same time they often acted as if revelation and God's activity provided its own best explanations. The difficulties in holding these contrasting convictions were not readily apparent in the years before the Civil War. Later, in the last third of the nineteenth century, however, they became the occasion of the greatest crisis in the American history of Christian higher education, when a series of major changes transformed the character of both public values and collegiate instruction. Before that time, however, evangelical Protestants had developed another institution, the theological seminary, which was destined to play a vital role in the story of American Christian thinking.

The Rise of the Seminary.   A number of different factors led, in the early nineteenth century, to the founding of schools devoted specifically to the training of candidates for the ministry.[30] Before this time ministerial education had been a random process. Among the older denominations like Congregationalists and Presbyterians, college graduates regularly studied as apprentices with older ministers for a year or two before seeking their own charges. The newer denominations like the Baptists and the Methodists did not require formal training in college or elsewhere but relied rather upon native intellectual ability and the more direct calling of the Holy Spirit. This diffuse approach to ministerial training changed first for Congregationalists and Presbyterians, but by the time of the Civil War, formal seminary education was standard for most of the major evangelical bodies. The effects on the Christian colleges, and on the effort to formulate Christian perspectives on the world, were considerable.

Andover Seminary in Massachusetts was the first of the new institutions. It came into existence in 1808 specifically as a trinitarian and evangelical protest against the appointment of a Unitarian to the professorship of Divinity at Harvard College. As with most of the other seminaries founded before the Civil War, however, larger concerns also lay in the background. Soon there were other seminaries. Princeton, established in 1812, was the first of many such schools founded by Presbyterians.[31] Yale created its own Divinity School shortly thereafter to serve primarily Congregationalists. Soon almost all of the major Protestant bodies possessed their own specialized institutions for training clergymen.

More than anything else, the cultural crisis of the Revolutionary period was responsible for the rise of the seminary. The Revolutionary picture of the past as a sink of corruption and its great stress on the rights of individuals created a situation in which authority had to be a function of individual ability and accomplishment. In addition, the rapid growth and spread of the population led to a desperate need for clergymen to minister in the new centers of population. As an indication of the dimensions of this problem, annual reports of the Presbyterian General Assembly during the 1790s and the first decade of the nineteenth century regularly showed more vacant "preaching stations" than churches with regularly settled ministers. To top it all, secularization (or "infidelity," in the terms of the day) seemed to be spreading much more rapidly than the gospel. At least until the full effects of the Second Great Awakening were felt in the 1820s, Christian leaders wondered if a Christian witness could be preserved in the country. In response to all of these needs, the theological seminary seemed to be an idea whose time had come. It offered a respectable certification for candidates against the threat of egalitarianism, single-minded attention to training for ministry against the threat of unreached people, and specialized study in the Bible and theology against the threat of infidelity.

The seminaries did meet these needs. In the process they went on to become the prototype for graduate education in the country and remained the most successful institutions for advanced study into the twentieth century. By the time Princeton Seminary celebrated its centennial in 1912, for example, it had trained over 6,000 students, far more than any other institution of graduate education in any field in the United States. The only competitors at that time were Andover Seminary, which had educated already nearly 3,600 students, and the Southern Baptist Seminary in Louisville with 4,500 alumni.[32] The seminaries also served as effective training grounds for Christian workers and were one of the reasons why American missions, home and abroad, possessed the personnel to accomplish its great tasks in the nineteenth century. In addition, the seminaries provided a setting conducive to serious academic work. Until the Civil War, journals from the evangelical seminaries were probably the most sophisticated general publications in America, and they retained some of their intellectual weight and cultural breadth into the twentieth century. The autonomous seminary, separate from college or university and often under the direct control of a denomination, was a singularly American creation. It has exerted a profound influence on the shape of the Christian faith in America.

Its existence, however, also created problems for Christian liberal arts education. If seminaries specialized in theology and encouraged systematic reflection on Christian interaction with the world, what theological role remained for the Christian colleges? This question did not loom as large in the antebellum years before the rise of academic specialization and professionalization, but it was still a difficulty. Should the colleges become miniature seminaries in focusing their curriculum on biblical and theological subjects? Is theological reflection, and the consideration of how revelation affects other areas of thought, to be left with the professors at the seminaries? Questions like these took on increased importance when it became clear that the most influential, and perhaps also the most intelligent, Christian commentary on science, and eventually the social sciences, on public ethics, and on the religious destiny of the United States came from the seminaries instead of the Christian colleges. To this day, professors at evangelical seminaries are the best trained of all professional academics identified with evangelical institutions, and their work is read far more widely in evangelical circles than work from professors in the Christian colleges.[33]

The problem does not involve the quality of seminary faculties, which was high throughout most of the nineteenth century and which again is high in the late twentieth century. The problem deals rather with connections between theology and other forms of learning. The rise of the seminary created a situation in which experts in Scripture and theology worked in different institutions from those who were trained in the wide range of academic subjects. Nothing exists in America like the universities of Britain and the continent where the most serious work in Bible and theology goes on right next to serious work in the other disciplines. In America, the threefold division of Christian liberal arts colleges, evangelical seminaries, and secular research universities has preserved many important values. Independent seminaries, for example, are less likely to be corrupted by the secularism of a university than is a divinity school attached to such a university. But a price must be paid for such gains.

As a result of these institutional divisions, there has been precious little cross-fertilization in the United States between first-level biblical scholarship and first-class thinking in the arts and sciences, especially since the dramatic professionalization of the last century. Evangelical seminaries have often enjoyed brilliant biblical scholars, but these scholars have been isolated from comparably brilliant Christians in the liberal arts and comparably brilliant non-Christians in all fields. Professional societies bridge some of the gaps between professors of religion in the evangelical colleges and professors at seminaries, but many chasms remain, and such professional groups hardly make up for sustained interdisciplinary concourse. In American religious history, biblical scholarship has lost the balance it could gain from advanced studies in astronomy, literary theory, and anthropology, and students in these fields have lost the balance they need from experts in biblical and theological studies. Such a situation will continue, moreover, so long as the Christian colleges, the evangelical seminaries, and the research universities go their own ways.

What has been lost specifically is an ideal of Christian intellectual life in which biblical scholars and scholars from other disciplines work in constant relationship to each other. In such an ideal, scholars in Scripture would provide the others with fruits of their labor in Bible study and theological reflection. The others would offer Bible scholars interpretations of modern learning and creative ventures in applying the results of their labors to Christian teaching. Both together would reflect on the foundational theological commitments and philosophical presuppositions which shape inquiry in every field of thought.

Portions of this ideal have been realized in American Christian thinking, but only as evangelical scholars from various sorts of institutions establish informal networks among themselves. In general, however, the divided structures of evangelical Christian thinking have nurtured divided mentalities, and attempts to integrate faith and learning have been frustrated by the very success of an approach to formal learning which maintains several mutually distinct institutions of intellectual life.[34]

The rise of the seminary was a phenomenon of the early nineteenth century which continues to have an influence on American Christian thinking to this day. Even more, the educational changes in the late nineteenth century still shape the intellectual world in which the Christian colleges attempt to accomplish their tasks.

The Emergence of Modern Higher Education. No historical event has been more important for contemporary Christian higher education than the reorganization of the colleges at the end of the nineteenth century.[35] This reorganization was itself a vastly significant event, and it will engage our attention here. We must not forget, however, that it was but one aspect of another broad crisis in cultural values comparable to that of the Revolution. The questions of this crisis, however, were more expansive than those of the previous century. Would America be able to offer her freedoms not only to Northern European Protestants, but to Southern European Catholics, to Jews, to Asians, and to the Afro-Americans who began to insist on civil liberties? How would the reconstruction of economic life in an industrial society affect perspectives on consumption, social status, and personal worth? How would America's emergence as a world power change its image of itself? Perhaps above all, how would American culture react to the momentous ideas of nineteenth-century Europe promoted by seminal minds like Marx, Freud, Nitzsche, and Darwin? The educational story, as it affects the Christian colleges today, is the story of a change so striking as to deserve the overworked term "revolution."

The years from 1865 to 1900 constituted the great period of transition for American higher education. When Charles Eliot became president of Harvard in 1869, he set that influential institution on a course of innovation and expansion. The Johns Hopkins University, founded in 1876, exercised leadership in the establishment of graduate education. Other major changes were also under way: new universities were founded like Cornell, Chicago, Stanford, and Clark; older private colleges like Yale, Princeton, and Columbia were transformed into universities with the addition of graduate and professional schools; major state universities like Michigan and Wisconsin grew up almost overnight in the Midwest and West.

It is of the greatest significance that the money for this academic explosion did not come from the Christian communities which had hitherto been the financial bellwether for American education. The federal government, for one, had begun to provide land and money for the practical arts through the Morrill Act of 1862. Much more important at this time were the large sums coming from the new industrialists, from those who had best exploited the postwar expansion of the American economy. Before citing names and numbers, it would be helpful to establish a standard of comparison from the old time college. Harvard enjoyed a $10,000 annual grant from the Massachusetts legislature for the ten years following 1814 and was the envy of struggling academicians everywhere. When Princeton a decade later audaciously sought $100,000 from its alumni, it created a sensation.

The sums contributed to establish the new universities, however, were on a different level entirely. Ezra Cornell, who made his money in telegraph construction and banking, donated $500,000 to the school which bears his name and managed a Morrill grant for $2,500,000 more. Johns Hopkins, a banker and investor in the Baltimore & Ohio Railroad, left $3,500,000 to the university and an equal sum to establish a teaching hospital. Cornelius Vanderbilt (steamships and railroads) gave an initial gift of $1,000,000 to establish a Harvard of the South and later followed this up with other generous bequests. Leland Stanford, who parlayed political office into control of the Central and Southern Pacific Railroads, left $20,000,000 to establish a university in honor of his son. James Duke, of the American Tobacco Company, assigned the largest part of the income from a $100,000,000 trust fund to the university that bears his name. John D. Rockefeller's gifts to establish a great Baptist university in Chicago eventually totaled $45,000,000. From a different but still dizzying perspective, private donors in the twenty years from 1878 to 1898 gave $140,000,000 to American colleges and universities. What this could do for an individual institution can be seen from the jump in Harvard's permanent endowment from $2,500,000 in 1869 to $20,000,000 in 1909.

The number of students attending colleges and universities grew almost as rapidly as the number of dollars going into higher education.[36] While the country's population nearly doubled (40 million to 76 million) from 1870 to 1900, the number of college students leaped nearly fivefold (from 52,000 to 238,000). In 1870, 1.7 percent of the 18-21-year-old population was in college. By 1930, the figure had reached 12.4 percent. To cite again the example of Harvard, it grew from 1,000 students in 1869 to 4,000 in 1909; during the same period its faculty grew even more rapidly, from 60 to 600. The surge in attendance was fueled by the growth in public high schools, by the growing numbers of women seeking higher education, and, very likely, by an increasing desire for higher education by individuals outside of the traditional Anglo-Saxon Protestant sources.

Almost unnoticed in the great influx of dollars and students was the decline of the Christian characteristics that had marked higher education by this time. Neither the new donors nor the new breed of administrators were overly concerned about the orthodoxy of their faculties. Visible signs of this change abounded. At Harvard compulsory chapel ceased in 1886. The opening ceremonies at Johns Hopkins in 1876 contained no prayer but did feature an address by British evolutionary theorist Thomas Huxley. As money from businessmen increased, so did their concern that boards of trustees and college administrators function in a businesslike way. Thus it was that businessmen replaced clergymen as trustees, and laymen replaced ministers as college presidents. In 1839, fifty-one of the fifty-four presidents of America's largest colleges were clergymen (forty of these being Presbyterians or Congregationalists). By the end of the century the number was greatly reduced. Princeton, always conservative, waited until 1902 to name its first lay president, Woodrow Wilson.

Another facet of the revolution in higher education was the growing appeal of the German model for academic life. Anglo-American higher education had traditionally stressed character as much as intellectual stimulation; it had paid greater heed to transmitting the old than to experimenting with the new; and it had favored discipline over creativity and novelty. In the last half of the nineteenth century, however, the German emphasis on specialized and advanced scholarship became increasingly attractive. Germany had early appealed to Americans as an academic mecca, with nearly 300 American scholars in German universities during the 1850s. In the 1900 edition of *Who's Who*, 300 of the 700 academics listed had studied in Germany. What appealed most to these scholars was the German emphasis on freedom: freedom for the students to choose their own studies in an elective system, freedom for the faculty to teach subjects of their own choice and to pursue sophisticated research. It is at least possible that the practice of laissez-faire in American economic life during this period was promoted by infatuation with the laissez-faire of German academic life.

Under the influence of this German model, the new university took shape rapidly. In the first instance, promoters of the new university stressed its freedom from sectarian and paternal control. It became increasingly common to regard the faculty as the essence of the university. Advanced study became the jewel in the university's crown. Undergraduate education also moved into a new era. The elective system, popularized by Eliot at Harvard, fostered competition among the new disciplines and stimulated a thirst for relevance which still remains unslaked a century later.[37] Science, particularly laboratory science, became an increasingly important part of undergraduate work, as did instruction in modern language and literature. The vocational and scientific requirements of the wider community also received more attention in the colleges. Cornell was one of the first of the new universities to offer agricultural and vocational courses in its regular academic curriculum. John D. Rockefeller was won over to a belief in the value of American universities at least in part because of practical improvements made at Yale in the refining of oil. The need to serve more, and more specialized, scholars led to a rapid growth in libraries as well. At Harvard the library grew from 20,000 volumes in 1820 to 900,000 in 1900. Earlier in the century debating societies often possessed more extensive libraries than their colleges, but this would no longer be the case. Taken as a whole, the German ideal promoted the beginning of professionalization in American higher education.

If the German example was the source of the university's professionalization, the new science was the source of its pride. This new science was popularly, if inaccurately, associated with the name of Charles Darwin, whose *Origin of Species by Means of Natural Selection* had been published in 1859. Darwinism, which one recent scholar has neatly summarized as "a scientifically credible theory of random and purposeless change," stood for an intellectual perspective which went well beyond questions in biology.[38] It is in fact possible to see three levels of Darwinism: a scientific method, a scientific result, and a philosophical system. At each level, Darwinism both undercut the antebellum scientific world of American higher education and offered the glowing prospect of unprecedented scientific progress.

Superficially considered, the scientific method of Darwinism closely resembled the science championed by American moral philosophers before the Civil War. Both made much of empirical observation, and both generalized from the results of empirical observation, though the newer science did question the earlier confidence in induction. At a deeper level the doxological character of the old science was being replaced by the agnostic cast of the new. Epistemological realism was giving way to idealism. Baconian inductivism was yielding to a science in which imaginative hypotheses played a larger role. Practitioners of the new science criticized advocates of the old for prejudging questions of scientific fact, for forcing the bedrock data of science into the comfortable but ultimately unscientific molds of the past. In Darwin, as they saw it, they possessed the shining example of a true scientist who dared to follow the data wherever they led.

The scientific results of Darwinism were no less offensive to the old scientists. Darwin's principle of "natural selection" contradicted all that moral philosophy had sought to prove over the previous century. Random change did not fit into a world where the moral law within, and the laws of nature without, were alike considered images of the law of God. The harmony among nature, man, and God was disrupted if nature operated according to no laws but its own. Darwinists shrugged at these charges and reminded the old scientists of their commitment to the results of sense experience. We must follow our observations, the Darwinists said, even if they lead us to a universe where the Bible's cosmology (at least as traditionally understood) passes into myth.

It was as a philosophy of life, however, that Darwinism caused the moral philosophers greatest pain. In the *Systematic Philosophy* (1862–1893) of Herbert Spencer, Darwinism appeared as a comprehensive, non-Christian explanation for all of life. According to Spencer, mankind was progressing from simpler to more complex forms, from worse to better modes of existence, from primitive to sophisticated states. One grasped best the nature of things not by delving into divine relevation but by understanding what it meant for the fit to survive.

To many academicians from old colleges and new universities alike, the three levels of Darwinism seemed bound together inextricably. Virtually all academicians in the new universities accepted one or more of Darwinism's meanings. While Darwinists gloried in the breathtaking discoveries opened up through the new scientific perspective, practitioners of the old science reeled in confusion. It was bad enough that God and the moral law were in danger from Spencer's social Darwinism. Even worse was the fact that this non-Christian worldview claimed to rest on the kind of scientific explanation that they themselves had championed for so long. Science, once the handmaiden of morality, seemed now to have become an ally of agnosticism. As science was rapidly coming to be understood, it seemed to have passed from defender of the faith to its prosecutor.

As moral philosophy collapsed, each of the many disciplines it had gathered in its skirts went its own way—psychology, epistemology, political science, sociology, anthropology, and others. The breakup of moral philosophy's integrating force, coming as it did when the appeal of German higher education was reaching its peak, led to a rapid growth of specialization in the new university. Almost overnight the Ph.D. became a new symbol of prestige and the ticket to advancement in university life. Yale had granted the first American doctorate in 1861; in 1880 American universities gave 54 doctoral degrees, and the flow would increase.

Not surprisingly the years between the Civil War and World War I saw the organization of professional societies to provide outlets for specialized research and extrainstitutional stimulation for specialized scholars. Of the forty-two professional societies currently members of the American Council of Learned Societies, twenty of them were founded between 1869 and 1912, including such prominent bodies as the Modern Language Association, the American Historical Association, and the Society for Biblical Literature. Professional journals proliferated. In the last third of the century, it also became the practice for medical and law schools to require candidates to hold B.A. degrees.

A whole new idea of the faculty member was also coming into existence. The new professional enjoyed certifiable training and he coveted standing in an academic specialty. He, and gradually she as well, normally went through a probation period as teacher-researcher-scholar. He sought employment at institutions offering specialized instruction. He was committed to publishing the results of his research for scholars outside his own institution. His scholarly functions and professional reputation became at least as important as his teaching responsibilities or his institutional loyalty. Befitting this new status, faculty members were spared some of the responsibilities they had traditionally exercised. One of the first of their traditional tasks to go was disciplinary responsibility for the students during their non-class hours.

The new professor also adopted a different role in society and in the world at large. Old time college leaders had spoken to society as a whole, but mostly as moral cheerleaders and defenders of a public faith. The new academicians achieved their recognition as experts, individuals with extraordinary competence in one or another of the new disciplines cultivated at the new university. The public pronouncements of Oliver Wendell Holmes on the law, Thorsten Veblen on economics, or William James and John Dewey on philosophy were not always followed, but they were heard. Worldviews were now coming from the university.

In sum, more than just thirty-five years separated the new university at the turn of the century from the old college at the close of the Civil War. The new university was professional; it offered technical training in a wide variety of separate fields; it was funded by large gifts from America's industrial giants; it had laid aside the external marks of Christianity; its professors sought to become well known in their fields and to speak expertly to society as a whole; its new science purported to illuminate a better way to truth, progress, and perhaps even happiness; and it was offering its wares to an ever-growing part of the American population.

In almost every way imaginable the new university undercut the traditional values of Christian higher education in America. Excess capital generated by the industrialists after the Civil War arose from a widespread exploitation of new scientific technology. This excess wealth was generated, furthermore, by individuals who had largely laid aside the constraints of Christian altruism which moral philosophy, for which the new capitalists had no time, sought to inculcate in college graduates. American industrialists, to one degree or another, seemed to have favored the kind of social Darwinism popularized by Herbert Spencer. One of the reasons this new class of wealthy Americans funded education was to encourage more of the practical science and managerial theory coming from the new universities and less of the moralism coming from the old colleges. Whether through the direct influence of the industrialists or not, clergymen were replaced by businessmen on college boards of trustees and ministers were replaced as college presidents by educators alert to management ideas and the demands of the new science. These new presidents, in turn, focused much more attention on scholarship than on orthodoxy. Furthermore, the new scholarship which these presidents encouraged had been "liberated" from the old orthodoxies of moral philosophy. It was frankly naturalistic in science and pragmatic in philosophy. In turn—and this brings the circle full—the new naturalistic science and the new pragmatic philosophy encouraged industrial giantism by providing training and technique to the capitalists while at the same time offering few criticisms of the new industrial wealth.

Against this combination of new money, social Darwinism, and naturalistic science, moral philosophy stood almost no chance. Its reductionistic Christianity had little guidance to offer industrialists or the new urban masses. Its individualistic ethics could not comprehend the magnitude of new economic and social developments. Its empiricism had been turned against the traditional orthodoxy.

The collapse of moral philosophy signaled the collapse of the effort to preserve a unified Christian worldview in America. From the point of view of the new university, the effort to view knowledge whole was abandoned under the assumption that discrete parts of truth, discovered through empirical science, could stand on their own. The effort to integrate religious faith with learning was abandoned under the assumption that the pursuit of science carried with it no antecedent commitments to a worldview. On another level, Scottish Common Sense Realism, which had bonded the old synthesis, lost its hold on the major centers of American learning.

There were, however, many places where the pursuit of Christian education continued. A few old-style colleges, a few institutions recently founded by Christian immigrants, a few newly created Bible schools, and a surprisingly large number of public institutions in the South and Midwest rejected Darwinism, agnostic science, and Spencerian evolution. If such institutions had American roots, it was likely that Scottish Common Sense Realism continued to provide the model for instruction. These institutions, however, had come to occupy a very different place from the colleges which held to such views had occupied before the academic revolution. Now the colleges which clung to Scottish Realism and pursued the formation of Christian character inhabited an intellectual backwater, relatively out of touch with the main stream of early twentieth-century academic life.

This transitional period in American higher education marked the demise of the nineteenth-century Christian-cultural synthesis as the dominant American worldview. The earlier alliance between Christian and Enlightenment values experienced notable strain. For many scholars in the new universities, an enlightened pursuit of learning led to the abandonment of historic Christianity. The crisis, however, did not lead as many conservative Protestants to break with the Enlightenment. American evangelical educators tended rather to insist upon the Enlightenment-Christian synthesis even as it slipped from dominance in the colleges and universities. Theologically conservative Protestants, in other words, were not returning to the model of Edwards or the Puritans, nor attempting to reconstruct the life of the mind on the basis of a new look at the categories of special revelation and common grace. They were rather digging in their heels and insisting upon the continuing validity of the earlier synthesis.

The fundamentalist-modernist controversy certainly exacerbated problems of Christian thinking in this transitional era.[39] So thoroughly had evangelicals internalized the values of the didactic Enlightenment into their Christian worldview that they reacted to both modernistic theology and new proposals in science, philosophy, and the arts as equally heretical. Fundamentalists, committed both to historic Christianity and to the thought forms of the early nineteenth century, were naturally suspicious of proposals which called either into question, especially when the new ideas were allied with assaults upon traditional theology or morality.

Many modern evangelical colleges are the heirs of this rear-guard action which preserved a Christian dimension in American higher education at the turn of the century. Much has happened since then to force rethinking of the distinctions which fundamentalists drew between historic Christianity and the new learning. By their continued confessions of faith, evangelical colleges today testify to their debt to the fundamentalist nay-sayers of the late nineteenth and early twentieth centuries. Just as surely, however, by their selective reengagement with modern forms of thought they testify to their implicit judgment that the reductionistic faith, the Baconian science, and the individualistic ethics of the nineteenth century Enlightenment-Christian synthesis had become a burden as much as a blessing in the pursuit of Christian higher education.

The Recent Past.   Since the academic revolution at the turn of the century and the fundamentalist-modernist controversies of roughly the same period, the evangelical colleges have returned at least part way to the educational mainstream. At the same time, they have also maintained many of the theological and ethical convictions of the nineteenth-century Christian colleges. Living between two worlds as they are, committed both to Christian values and to modern learning, the evangelical colleges have singular opportunities and singular difficulties as they attempt to encourage Christian perspectives on the world.

It is always precarious to write the history of the recent past, for living memory is at once more powerful and more impressionistic than the cold documents of bygone eras. Yet it is possible to chart a few general developments in Christian thinking as these have affected the colleges over the last half-century. In so doing, however, we run into a number of dimly perceived questions to which it is appropriate, at this early stage of historical self-consciousness, to draw attention as subjects for further research.

The most obvious characteristic of the evangelical colleges in recent American history is their institutional vigor. The last section of Professor Ringenberg's book provides detailed evidence for the relatively good health of the modern Christian liberal arts college. For our purposes now it is enough to note that a form of higher learning which seemed doomed by the educational revolution of the late nineteenth century has not only survived, but prospered.

Several distinct elements have contributed to that prospering. One is the colleges' ability to provide students with the necessary educational certification for entering the major vocations and professional schools. Another is their success in cultivating the support of Christian communities which had come to distrust modern higher education but which expressed confidence in institutions that retained Christian professions and traditional behavioral standards. A third is the capacity of faculties at the evangelical colleges to articulate to themselves, to college administrators, and to wider Christian constituencies the theoretical and practical necessity for distinctly Christian views of the world.

Merely to note these factors, however, does not take us very far into the many different histories represented by the various Christian liberal arts colleges. Although the evangelical colleges do share much in common, they also are products of many different strands in Protestant history. As such, the relationship between colleges and the constituencies which they serve can be very different in spite of the fact that they advertise nearly identical educational goals. Some of the colleges, founded by more recent immigrants, have never had to overcome the distrust of higher education which characterized the American fundamentalists. Others, however, wage a constant battle to convince their supporters of the values of the liberal arts and the virtues of an acquaintance with modern thought. A great deal of further research is necessary before it would be possible to say with certainty how the varying constituencies of the Christian college have affected the shape and purposes of the education they offer. Just to note that Baptists, Presbyterians, Reformed, Independents, Pentecostals, Nazarenes, Brethren, Mennonites, Lutherans, and still others work together in the Christian College Coalition and in other educational organizations is enough to indicate the varied traditions which participate in evangelical higher education. The most that can be said now is that distinctly different patterns do appear. Some evangelical colleges are the lengthened shadow of one person or one family. Others rest securely within a particular denomination, and still others serve complex interdenominational networks. These patterns, and wide variations within each, call for explication. It will not be possible to provide reasons for the survival of the evangelical liberal arts colleges until such research of the colleges and their constituencies is carried out.

Something of the same may be said for the question of faculty professionalization. Quite clearly the modern evangelical college expects its faculty to possess standard graduate training and to take some part in the ongoing professional activities of their academic disciplines. While the Christian colleges employ only a few professors who have become prominent in their disciplines, they are home to a goodly number of scholars who regularly read papers at academic conferences, review books for professional journals, and engage in some kind of continuing research. This pattern, however, is fairly recent; it seems to have developed only after World War II.[40] A number of factors contributed to this professionalization, among them a growing distance from the fundamentalist-modernist controversies and wider exposure to European forms of orthodox Christianity. Yet this is a subject needing more serious investigation. Faculty professionalization touches upon the recent history of the evangelical colleges at many points. One of the most interesting of these pertains to the renewed relationships which these colleges have established in wider worlds of American higher education. Especially at a time of increasing competition for government funds, Christian colleges are finding common cause with other private institutions. Relations established here, within the accrediting associations, and among administrators and faculty at many levels beg for insightful research and clarification.

Faculty professionalization also raises larger questions of self-identity. Do the evangelical colleges desire the presence of faculty with Ph.D.s only to be respectably certified? Do they mean their professors to affect the actual shape of the academic disciplines by encouraging faculty publication? Do they want students to have models of caring teachers who occasionally do a little research, or of the colleges and in their present operation militates against either the creation of Christian perspectives or their application to modern intellectual life.

They also, however, draw attention to those aspects of the recent past which relate especially to the promotion of a Christian view of the world. Commitment to a Christian worldview is the academic *raison d'etre* of the evangelical colleges. Yet much in the heritage of the colleges and in their present operation militates against either the creation of Christian perspectives or their appliction to modern intellectual life.

A series of conundrums can show the difficulties which the evangelical colleges face in this regard. In an age when the thinking which shapes worldviews comes regularly from research universities, evangelicals do not have a single research university or the serious prospect of one. In an age when secularism tugs at Christian thinking from one side and long-entrenched denominational shibboleths tug at it from the other, evangelical higher education retains the distinct college and seminary tiers of its heritage and the barriers to cohesive Christian thinking which that structure perpetuates. In an age when scholars (sometimes even Christian scholars) have called into question almost every settled intellectual tradition in the West, evangelicals remain surprisingly content with the intellectual synthesis of the early nineteenth century. In an age when sophisticated secular intellectuals set the tone for considerations of politics, economics, and secular values, evangelicals continue to set their course by popular preachers who are not reluctant to pronounce judgment on every facet of modern learning. In an age, finally, demanding forceful Christian responses to powerful secular ideologies, careful Christian probing of complex intellectual issues, and creative Christian initiatives for pressing contemporary problems, much of evangelicalism still retains a stultifying nineteenth-century suspicion of all thinking which does not rest on mythic views of America's past, egalitarian common sense, or popular interpretations of the Bible.

These conundrums speak as much to the broader evangelical culture as to the liberal arts colleges themselves. They are nonetheless the pressing problems which evangelical colleges face in attempting to articulate Christian views of the world. They are problems, moreover, rooted in the history of the colleges and their constituencies. With the insights and information supplied by William Ringenberg in the account which follows, those who are concerned about Christian higher education in the late twentieth century will be equipped both to see more clearly the path which has led to the present and the possibilities in the future for realizing both religious and intellectual goals of Christian higher education.

The Path Ahead.   The history which follows is in many ways a most inspiring one. The Puritans who established the colonial colleges, the intrepid ministers who created a vast network of higher education in the opened frontier, the doughty theological conservatives who founded Bible colleges or who maintained Christian distinctives during the academic revolution of the late nineteenth century, the hard-pressed immigrants who scraped together the means to preserve both Christian and Old World commitments, and the evangelical trustees, administrators, and faculties who guide Christian higher education through the perils of the late twentieth century have overcome great obstacles. Their vision, however inarticulate at times, has been to capture thinking for Christ, and by so doing to contribute also to good citizenship, the spread of the gospel, social harmony, and the general well-being of students and constituencies alike. Professor Ringenberg's account offers much in every way to those who would understand that vision and the many complementary strands of its expression.

At the same time, this book makes possible a clearer view of the challenges of the future. Most obviously, evangelical colleges face many of the problems which confront all private colleges in the late twentieth century. Financial pressure, the changing nature of governmental support, and uncertainties concerning the number of available students are difficulties as urgent on the campuses of the Christian colleges as elsewhere in private higher education. Yet these may be the least serious issues facing the Christian colleges.

Far more germane to the purposes for which these institutions exist are questions related to overall academic purpose and to relationships which the colleges sustain with their wider constituencies. The history of Christianity in America, not to speak of its worldwide history, testifies to the precariousness of penetrating Christian thinking. The tendency has ever been present for Christian academics to drift into the secularism of the wider culture or to relapse into the obscurantism of cultic sectarianism. Only an unambiguous loyalty to the hegemony of special revelation can check the propensity to secularism; only an unswerving commitment to the values of common grace can restrain the sectarian impulse. Against the children of the world, Christian colleges must stand for grace; against the children of grace, the Christian colleges must stand for the world.

More particularly, Christian colleges are poised between the demands of free academic inquiry and of committed theological loyalty. Without the first, it is hard to see the Christian colleges preserving intellectual viability, but without the second they will not retain their Christian character. Again, the evangelical tradition in America has had difficulty finding a place for intellectual freedom within the general framework of orthodoxy. The challenge for the future is to broaden expectations for creativity while at the same time heightening the value of theological commitment.

Finally, social and political factors pose a growing dilemma for evangelical higher education. The Christian Right has strong convictions about social and political questions and (often) the money to promote those ideas in the colleges. The Christian Left has less money, but its positions are generally argued with greater moral fervor. The challenge to evangelical higher education is to open doors wide to any political or social position which claims to rest on Christian foundations, but then to go on to rigorous scrutiny of the position and its supposed Christian base, never allowing the gospel to be equated with any changeable form of human conviction.

These challenges are only some of those facing the Christian colleges as they move past the midpoint of the fourth century of Christian higher education in America. It is impossible to discern whether Christian colleges—not to speak of the world as we now know it—will still exist to celebrate Harvard's early Christian heritage at its 400th anniversary in the year 2036. One of the ways to prepare for what lies between now and then is to understand how we have arrived here from there. That has been the burden of this Introduction, and it is even more an invitation to the pages which follow.

Chapter 1

The Colonial Period

The average American living in the late twentieth century finds it difficult to identify with the colonial period, for that era differs sharply from the present in many ways. The colonial population, even at its peak, never equaled 2 percent of today's census; those few million colonists lived in only that small section of North America between the Atlantic Ocean and the Appalachian Mountains; they found it very difficult to travel even moderate distances except by water; and nearly everyone was a farmer, while almost no one worked in an industrial or service occupation.

Higher education, then and now, also offers a study in contrasts. Only a very small percentage of colonial young men enrolled in college (the colleges awarded only 9,000 baccalaureate degrees between 1642 and 1800);[1] the professors had acquired little training beyond their own undergraduate courses of study and they usually cultivated additional professional interests such as the ministry or medicine; the curriculum placed primary emphasis upon the study of Latin, Greek, and mathematics; and the colleges were more, rather than less, religious than was society in general (by 1800 only 7 percent of the population had joined a church, although approximately twice as many attended without formal membership).[2]

THE PERVADING CHRISTIAN PURPOSE OF COLONIAL EDUCATION

The Christian worldview, more than any other system of thought, dominated American intellectual development during the colonial period. As clergymen were the leading representatives of the intellectual class, it is not surprising that they, and the denominations which they represented, took the lead in founding colleges and instructing the students. While religious leaders founded institutions of higher learning primarily to educate future ministers, these colleges never operated solely as ministerial training seminaries. They also sought to provide culture and breadth of thought for the other leaders of society.

Regardless of the vocation for which a student was preparing, the colonial college sought to provide for him an education that was distinctly Christian. At Harvard the original goal of higher learning was "to know God and Jesus Christ which is eternal life (John 17:3), and therefore to lay Christ in the bottom as the only foundation of all sound knowledge and learning." Yale in the early 1700s stated as its primary goal that "every student shall consider the main end of his study to wit to know God in Jesus Christ and answerably to lead a Godly, sober life." Similarly, President Samuel Johnson of Columbia, in a 1754 advertisement, declared that the primary purpose of his college was "to teach and engage the children to know God in Jesus Christ and to love and serve him in all sobriety, godliness, and righteousness of life with a perfect heart and willing mind; and to train them up in all virtuous habits and useful knowledge as may render them creditable to their families and friends, ornaments to their country, and useful to the public Weal in their generations." The Calvinist-related colleges probably promoted their religious goals more intensely than did the Anglican ones. Only Pennsylvania maintained primarily secular goals; perhaps it would have been more religious if the dominant denomination in its state, the Quakers, had desired during this early period to educate their clergymen. Even Pennsylvania experienced some Christian influence, however. For example, the first president was the Rev. William Smith, an Anglican clergyman who "gave the students all the Anglicanism the traffic would bear."[3]

Although Massachusetts Bay was not the oldest colony in the new world, it was the first to establish a college. The unusually well-educated and spiritually earnest Puritans waited only six years to found Harvard primarily because they feared that if they delayed much longer they would risk leaving "an illiterate ministry to the churches when our present ministers shall lie in the dust." Thirty-five of the university men in early New England, including a large majority of the Harvard founders, had attended Emmanuel College of Cambridge University. As a result, that "hot bed" of Puritanism became the institution after which Harvard modeled itself.

During the early years of Harvard, such a large percentage of its graduates entered the ministry that many referred to the college as "the school of prophets" and the students as "the sons of prophets." By the eighteenth century, however, a growing number of New Englanders believed that Harvard was no longer the school where true prophets taught, but rather had become an institution which true prophets denounced. Among the leading denouncers were Increase Mather (Harvard president, 1685–1701) and his son Cotton Mather, who hoped to prevent Harvard from moving away from its original Calvinist orientation in an Arminian direction.

Even though Increase Mather was the most distinguished president to serve Harvard during the colonial period, he could not check the declining influence of the old faith. During the eighteenth century, Harvard not only moved away from Calvinism, but to and then beyond Arminianism toward a Unitarianism that became its most characteristic theological expression by the early nineteenth century.[4]

What the Calvinists could not maintain at Harvard they sought to establish at Yale. Although the citizens of Connecticut had long wished for a college of their own, the actual establishment of Yale in 1701 was considerably encouraged by the belief of many New England Calvinists that Harvard was slipping from the true path. Yale also experienced early challenges to its Calvinism; however, it dealt with these threats differently from Harvard. For example, in 1722 a rumor circulated that Rector (President) Timothy Cutler, Tutor Daniel Brown, and a handful of influential citizens in the New Haven community were beginning to accept Anglicanism. The trustees conducted an investigation which confirmed their worst fears. Subsequently, they dismissed both Cutler and Brown. Also, the board determined that the students should be taught Calvinist theology and none other, and that every officer of the college must publicly subscribe to the Westminster Confession of Faith and the Saybrook Platform of the Congregational churches in Connecticut before receiving an appointment. As a further effort to protect its students, Yale forbade them from attending Episcopal church services in New Haven. By contrast, a 1747 oath bill proposed at Harvard to impose Calvinism upon the members of that community failed to advance beyond the talking stage.[5]

TABLE 1

COLONIAL COLLEGES
LISTED BY RELIGIOUS AFFILIATION[6]

College	Founding Date	Religious Orientation
Harvard (Mass.)	1636	Puritan/Congregationalist
William & Mary (Va.)	1693	Anglican
Yale (Conn.)	1701	Congregationalist
Princeton (N.J.)	1746	New Light Presbyterian
Columbia (N.Y.)	1754	Essentially Anglican
Pennsylvania (Pa.)	1755	Primarily Secular
Brown (R.I.)	1765	Baptist
Rutgers (N.J.)	1766	Dutch Reformed
Dartmouth (N.H.)	1769	New Light Congregationalist

While nine colonial colleges eventually appeared, to speak of them as a group is misleading because during most of the seventeenth century only Harvard existed, and until the generation before the American Revolution, only two more appeared (see table 1). Something must have happened, therefore, about the middle of the eighteenth century to stimulate the founding of six colleges during such a short period. More than any other factor, this active period of college founding is explained by the Great Awakening (or the First Great Awakening) of the 1730s and 1740s. This first major period of mass revivalism in American history swept through every colony and every denomination. As a result, several major religious groups which heretofore had not operated colleges quickly established such institutions in an effort to improve the quality of their increasing number of ministerial recruits. Therefore the Presbyterians founded Princeton; the Baptists, Brown; the Dutch Reformed, Rutgers; and the pro-revival Congregationalists, Dartmouth.[7]

While the four new colleges understandably sympathized with the emotional faith which had helped give them birth, the two oldest colleges in the North reacted strongly against what they saw as the Awakening's irrational approach to religion. The Harvard and Yale faculties recoiled particularly at the direct charges made against them by the leading preacher of the Awakening, the youthful and sometimes excessively exuberant itinerate minister George Whitefield. He charged, "As for the Universities, I believe it may be said, their light is become Darkness, Darkness that may be felt, and is complained of by the most Godly ministers. . . ." Even worse, the Harvard and Yale students sometimes echoed the charges of Whitefield.[8]

The major theological controversy resulting from the Great Awakening was the question of whether experiential and emotional factors or rational factors should play the prominent role in religion. Many Presbyterians, particularly those in the South and West, accepted the New Light (e.g., pro-revival) position and consequently became increasingly dissatisfied with Harvard and Yale. A major related problem for them was that ministerial candidates who grew up in the East and attended colleges there hesitated to leave their native homes to assume ministerial responsibilities for the needy parishes in the Appalachian Mountain regions. Consequently, the need for ministers in the West was met by several Presbyterian academies, the most famous of which was Rev. William Tennent's "Log College" at Neshaminy in Bucks County, Pennsylvania.

The Log College—actually a simple cabin "about twenty feet long and nearly as many wide," as remembered by George Whitefield—and the twenty or thirty other academies that were modeled after it were apprenticeship institutions that in level of instruction operated somewhere between a grammar school and a college. Groups of students, especially ministerial candidates, would move in with a learned minister and study divinity and related subjects with him. The ministers who conducted these schools tended to be of the New Light persuasion and included such able figures as Samuel Davies, Samuel Finley, Jonathan Dickinson, and Aaron Burr. Gradually, however, William Tennent grew older and the supply of preachers being furnished by the other academies became inadequate; as a result the New Light Presbyterians sought an alternate means of training their future ministers. Thus by the mid-eighteenth century, both the western log colleges and the older established eastern colleges, for different reasons, were becoming increasingly unable to provide the type of training desired by the New Light ministers. Consequently, they founded Princeton.[9]

While Dartmouth developed into the school for New Light Congregationalists, it did not begin that way. It came into existence in 1754 as an institution for teaching American Indians. Its most famous early Indian students included Joseph Brant and Sampson Occum. Brant became a Mohawk chief, a colonel in the British army, and a Christian missionary who translated the Episcopal Prayer Book and part of the New Testament into Mohawk. Occum was a Mohegan who could speak fluent English and deliver stirring sermons. Eleazar Wheelock, the Dartmouth founder, sent Occum to England to raise funds, and his appearance in that country caused a major stir. Englishmen, who at this time were experiencing the Wesleyan revivals, were moved by the sight of a devout and persuasive Indian seeking funds to convert and educate the members of his race in England's leading colony. Consequently, when Occum and Nathaniel Whitaker, who accompanied him, returned in 1766, they brought with them over £12,000 for the college. Although it was not the intention of Wheelock, the college quickly began to train many more whites than Indians, with the latter studying primarily in the preparatory department.[10]

The fact that the colonial institutions were religious in nature does not mean that they were private colleges in the modern sense of the term, for the twentieth-century distinction between public and private institutions did not exist in the colonial era. Although each of the three earliest colleges, Harvard, William and Mary, and Yale, was chartered by the established church in its colony, each also held a direct relationship to the state and served as the center for training civic as well as clerical leaders for its region. The governments in turn recognized the importance of the colleges and contributed significant amounts of financial aid to support them. For the most part, the colleges welcomed students and instructors of the several Protestant denominations, although usually they gave preference to members of the denomination sponsoring the college. Most of the new colleges founded in the mid-eighteenth century wrote into their charters specific provisions prohibiting denial of admission on the basis of religion. As a further reflection of their public nature, most of the new colleges named public officials as ex-officio members of their boards.[11]

If colonial higher education operated from a Christian foundation, it did so primarily because such an intellectual framework also characterized the European institutions that served as models for the colonial college founders. The essential characteristics of American church-related higher education can be seen as early as the fifth century in the palace, monastic, and cathedral schools, and during the middle ages in the continental universities and British universities and dissenting academies. In each of these periods, there was something about Christianity which stimulated people to inquire deeply about the nature and meaning of the universe.

The greatest influences on the colonial colleges, however, came from the universities of Cambridge and Oxford in England. The colonial colleges imitated the pattern of these two English institutions in several ways: religious groups largely controlled the institutions, the curriculum was narrow, the students resided as well as studied on the campus, higher education was primarily for the elite, and teaching youthful minds rather than discovering new knowledge was the primary purpose.[12]

During the eighteenth century, many of the new colleges looked more to the dissenting academies in Great Britain than to Cambridge and Oxford. Despite the vast emotional distance between the academies and the universities, they were very similar in structure and program. The academies came into existence in the late seventeenth century when following the period of Puritan rule, the restored Parliament dismissed all non-Anglican faculty members from the universities. Some of the released faculty members attracted a group of sympathetic students and founded dissenting academies for the primary purpose of providing training for the ministers of such groups as the Congregationalists and the Presbyterians. The academies were smaller but often better institutions than the universities; their quality was unpredictable, however, varying widely depending upon the ability of the master. Where

young men were able to study under an instructor like Philip Dodd-
ridge of Northampton, they probably received as good an education as was available anywhere in Great Britain at the time. The
curriculum of the academies was broader than that of the universities and supplemented the primary emphasis upon ancient
languages, philosophy, and theology with substantial work in
mathematics, natural philosophy, and even English literature and
public speaking. The founders of Princeton as well as those of the
other Presbyterian schools which began in the South shortly after
the Revolution knew well the work and nature of the dissenting
academies and were strongly affected by them.[13]

Beginning in the eighteenth century, influences from Scotland
became increasingly significant in shaping American higher education. The increasing number of immigrant Presbyterian ministers
who filled the pulpits in Scotch-Irish communities in the middle
and southern colonies usually had graduated from Scottish universities or academies, and a number of them operated similar
academies in their own manses. Also, some of the leaders of the
American colleges had received their training in Scotland. The first
president of William and Mary, James Blair, graduated from the
University of Edinburgh, and the first provost of Pennsylvania was
a graduate of the University of Aberdeen. John Witherspoon, who
received his education at the University of Edinburgh, migrated
directly from Scotland to become president of Princeton.[14]

Witherspoon was easily the most important force in bringing
Scottish thinking into American higher education. Not only did
his ideas dominate Princeton during the last third of the eighteenth
century, but the Scottish system of philosophy called Common
Sense Realism spread from Princeton to become the dominant
mode of philosophical thought in American colleges for the next
century. In essence the Scottish system replaced the abstract
idealism of George Berkeley, the pessimism of David Hume, and
the quasi-materialism of John Locke with a common-sense, easily
understood verification of the Christian ideals.[15]

INSTRUCTORS AND THE INSTRUCTION

Very few men served as college instructors during the colonial
period. The typical college hired a president and two or three tutors,
the latter being the approximate equivalent in status and function
of today's graduate assistants. Such was the case at Harvard
throughout the seventeenth century and at Princeton as late as the
1760s. The number of regular professorial appointees (to be
distinguished from those who served only as tutors) in all colleges

numbered only 10 as late as 1750, but grew sharply to 41 in the late 1760s and approximately 100 in the 1790s. This sharp increase during the late eighteenth century reflected both the increasing size of the faculties of the older schools and the growing number of new colleges that came into existence shortly after the Revolution. Altogether, between 1750 and 1800, there were approximately 200 different men listed in catalogs and college histories as holding professorial positions.[16]

The president was often the most distinguished instructor. When an institution was very small, especially in its beginning years, he sometimes did much of the teaching himself. One can even find examples of presidents—such as Samuel Johnson of Columbia and Jacob Hardenbergh of Rutgers—who taught every subject in the curriculum. Consequently, the president of a small developing college needed to know something about almost every area of learning; even such an unusually able scholar as Jonathan Edwards harbored serious doubts about his qualifications to be president of Princeton when he was called in 1757. (He thought himself deficient in certain parts of mathematics and Greek literature.) Usually, however, the president restricted his teaching activity to philosophy and theology instruction for the upper-division students. Once a college was established, the president was far too busy to teach more than this, for he also served as fund raiser, secretary, treasurer, purchasing agent, librarian, student counselor, college spokesman, and Sunday preacher.

A college tended to select as its president a man who had achieved distinction in education, the ministry, and public life in general. Usually he was selected from among the most widely respected ministers of the denomination supporting the college, and usually he had achieved something of a reputation for intellectual ability and theological orthodoxy. These college leaders normally emphasized a rational approach to religion and the importance of order and stability in society. Among the more noteworthy colonial college presidents fitting this description were Samuel Johnson of Columbia, Jonathan Edwards of Princeton, and Thomas Clap and Ezra Stiles of Yale.[17]

All the professors, president or not, usually came from families of high or at least middle social status, received their training at the most widely recognized colonial colleges, limited their teaching careers to a single institution, and pursued professional interests other than teaching. Approximately two-thirds of the colonial professors came from families in which the father was a clergyman, a large planter, or a wholesale merchant. Another one-third of the instructors grew up in farm, artisan, or retail business families. Most of the colonial instructors received their college training at

Harvard, Princeton, Yale, Pennsylvania, or Edinburgh. Almost invariably, professors limited their instructional careers to a single institution. Very few taught at two different colleges, and only three men taught in more than two institutions. No more than 20 percent of the late-eighteenth-century professors considered college teaching to be their major lifetime occupation, and less than one-half of them devoted all of their energies to teaching during the period of their college appointments. The great majority pursued a second vocation (usually the ministry or medicine) at some point during their working years.[18]

The role of the tutors in the early American colleges was an unenviable one. Most tutors had graduated recently from college and were selected because of exemplary records in piety and scholarship. Few thought of staying in the position more than a short time; frequently teaching offered the opportunity to pursue post-graduate work in divinity with the president prior to assuming a pastoral charge. The position offered neither financial reward nor great popularity with the students. The pay was sufficiently small that the tutors could not raise families on it. They roomed in dormitories with the students and served as first-line institutional disciplinary officials. Most of them found this disciplinary role very difficult; they lacked the experience and often the tact to perform it well. Consequently, the students resented—and sometimes hated—them, and, as one commentator noted, they "seldom lasted long enough to become experienced at anything but dodging stones thrown through their windows by unappreciative students." As instructors, the tutors each assumed responsibility for teaching all or nearly all of the subjects for one and in some cases two of the classes. The tutors tried, but the role demanded more experience and maturity than most of them possessed. The situation was unfair both to them and to the students they attempted to teach. This system of relying heavily upon the services of young, inexperienced tutors did cost very little, however, and perhaps the colonial economy could not yet support a more expensive system.[19]

If the tutors did not need to be experienced, both they and the regular professors did need to be religiously orthodox. For example, at Harvard the Massachusetts civilian authorities expected the college to hire as instructors only "upright Christians and not any that had shown themselves to be unsound in faith or scandalous in their lives." Even in the eighteenth century, the Harvard board of overseers insisted on examining on the subject of his religion every serious candidate for a teaching position.[20]

With some notable exceptions, the American instructors failed to acquire the authority to govern their own institutions. Only William and Mary followed the medieval practice of self-government after the manner of the guilds. Harvard adopted an intermediate position whereby the corporation of fellows (the internal group) and the board of overseers (the outside group) shared power. It was Yale that developed what was to become the typical pattern in America. At Yale, the Congregational clergymen who founded the college (in part because of their suspicion of Harvard) decided that it would be wise to keep the control of the institution in their own hands. In that way they hoped to protect the college's orthodoxy. By the early nineteenth century, even William and Mary and Harvard were joining the newer schools in adopting the Yale model.

Why did the instructors lose to the trustee boards in the contest to become the primary governing force in higher education? In addition to concerns about the college's orthodoxy, there was also the fact that during the colonial period many of the instructors were young men who held only temporary positions. Obviously, they were not in a strong position to seek increased authority. Also since the colleges then, as now, struggled to balance their budgets, the institutional leaders believed it financially advantageous to have wealthy businessmen and lawyers closely related to and responsible for the institution.[21]

As the single most important reason for founding the colleges was to provide ministerial training, it is not surprising that the early leaders designed a curriculum that would be broadly useful for aspiring clergymen. The New England churches expected a minister to be able to read the Scriptures in the original languages and to consult the large number of theological writings in Latin. They also expected him to be broadly learned, and, since the ancient classics were valued as a timeless source of wisdom and truth, it was important to have a sophisticated knowledge of Latin and Greek language and literature. It was also necessary for the minister to develop skill in public speaking and reasoning, thus the emphasis upon oral communication and philosophy. The early ministerial students met these goals better than did the divinity scholars of the eighteenth century.

The curriculum was also largely relevant for the aspiring lawyer and doctor. Law and medicine both assumed that their practitioners were familiar with Latin. Lawyers and other public officials needed the same public speaking skills that the clergymen sought to acquire, and societal leaders of all types found useful a careful study of the ancient classics.

The usefulness of the studies in divinity were obvious for the clergymen but also were considered important for the lay Christian leader. The extent to which the curriculum included studies in biblical content—in contrast to biblical languages—is not clear; however, at Princeton, at least, every student presumably "had to know his Bible from cover to cover." At Harvard, ministerial students often stayed beyond graduation for up to three years to pursue courses of independent study in divinity with the president, while perhaps teaching a course or two. As an optional program, Harvard ministerial students, following graduation, could live with practicing clergymen and read divinity with them as apprentices. Not until 1811 did Harvard organize classes in divinity for graduate students.[22]

One careful student of the colonial curriculum has attempted to translate the early Harvard courses into the modern system of granting an hour of credit for attendance at one class per week for a term. Under such a plan, he found that Harvard students in the 1640s would have earned 140 hours of credit in a three-year period with the curriculum divided as follows:

Logic and disputations (in Latin)	30 hours
Greek	24 hours
Hebrew, Aramaic, and Syriac	24 hours
Rhetoric and declamations	24 hours
Divinity	16 hours
Ethics and politics	8 hours
Arithmetic and geometry	6 hours
Physics	2 hours
Botany	2 hours
Astronomy	2 hours
History	2 hours

The most striking fact about this early colonial curriculum, in contrast with the pattern of the eighteenth and early nineteenth centuries, is its minimal emphasis upon science and mathematics. The eighteenth-century curriculum did not change dramatically from that of the earlier colonial period, but, in part as a result of Enlightenment thinking, there were some shifts of emphasis from ancient to modern languages, from divinity to the social sciences, and from metaphysics to the natural sciences.[23]

Although the seventeenth-century students and faculties appreciated science, they studied it only minimally. Before 1750, work in science included only tasks like memorizing the major commentaries on the physical world and performing simple arithmetic computations. By the middle of the eighteenth century, the colleges increased their emphasis upon science, and some institutions even appointed professors to chairs of science and mathematics. Other colleges, even as late as 1820, went through long periods of time without any science instructor. They delegated their meager science instruction to the tutors, who often operated without the help of any significant equipment for laboratory and demonstration purposes. William and Mary established the first professorship of natural philosophy (natural science) and mathematics in 1711; unfortunately, the first incumbent, a Mr. LeFevre, created controversy nearly the whole of his tenure because of the "idle hussy wife" who accompanied him from London and because of his own drunkenness, negligence of duties, and other irregularities which led to his dismissal in 1712. Of more lasting importance was the creation at Harvard in 1727 of the Hollis Professorship of Mathematics and Natural Philosophy, whose first important occupant was John Winthrop IV. Winthrop held the position for four decades after his 1738 appointment, and he became the most able science and mathematics instructor in the colonial period. He conducted research as well as taught, he was the first college instructor to lead an excursion for astronomical observations, and, during the American Revolutionary War, he assisted the colonial government in the design and development of armaments.[24]

The most common teaching method in the colonial colleges was recitation, in which the professor or tutor quizzed students individually to see how well they had studied the lesson for the day—or whether they had studied at all. On the occasions when the seventeenth-century tutors varied the routine by lecturing to their classes, it usually involved nothing more exciting than reading aloud from a prescribed textbook in Latin with the students taking notes or following in texts of their own. Gradually the more knowledgeable professors began to depart from the recitation method to offer lectures of the twentieth-century variety. This type of lecturing appeared earliest in the eighteenth-century science classes. In such disciplines as physics and chemistry, an illustrated lecture using the new scientific equipment was the natural teaching method. Gradually the colleges began to compete with each other in acquiring expensive scientific apparatus, including such devices as globes, barometers, thermometers, microscopes, telescopes, prismatic glass, air pumps, mirrors, lens, levers, pulleys, electrical machines, and orreries. Especially popular were the latter machines, which served to show the relative sizes and positions of the planets and other bodies in the solar system. David Rittenhouse built the most acclaimed orrery in 1767 and placed it at Princeton. Thomas Jefferson believed that in constructing this device Rittenhouse "approached nearer his creator than any man who has lived from the creation to this day."[25]

In the mid-eighteenth century, Princeton and then Harvard departed from the traditional instructional system, under which a tutor taught all of the subjects to one or two classes, by having tutors specialize in subject matter rather than in classes. For example, one tutor might provide all of the instruction in Greek and Latin. This increased degree of specialization represented only one step in the direction of improved instruction. Another, and more important, step was the declining instructional role of the young and inexperienced tutors as the colleges hired a larger number of older, more mature, and more learned professors. These professors, who possessed more knowledge about which to lecture, made greater use of the newer instructional method than had the tutors.[26]

The college library, then as now, offered students one of the greatest learning opportunities; however, it remained largely an untapped resource during the colonial period. The libraries were small; as late as 1775 Harvard owned only 4,000 volumes; William and Mary, 3,000; and Pennsylvania, Columbia, and Dartmouth, 2,000 each. Even more limiting was the narrow range of subject matter in the collections. As clergymen donated most of the volumes, the libraries emphasized theology. The colleges bought very few books and generally did not encourage the students to make use of their collections. Princeton claimed as highly unusual its invitation to the senior class to browse in the library.[27]

STUDENTS AND STUDENT LIFE

Most colonial college students came from the culturally and financially elite class. Other groups usually possessed neither the interest nor the time to send their sons to college or even to provide them with the necessary preparatory work to be able to gain admission. It was not impossible for a student from a poor and obscure family to enter college, but it was very difficult. An impoverished lad who showed unusual success in grammar school and then classical school might find a wealthy sponsor or some fund for assisting pious youths—especially if he wished to become a minister. Such a student was most likely to be attracted to Princeton and Brown, which had the lowest rates, or Dartmouth, which offered employment opportunities. Princeton and Brown represented denominations whose constituencies contained members of the lower class; therefore the institutions responded to pressure from their denominations to keep the rates as low as possible. Often Presbyterian and Baptist ministerial students came from the artisan and farmer classes. By contrast, Columbia and Pennsylvania were the most expensive institutions.[28]

Some correlation existed between the amount of fees charged by a college and the size of its student body. Costly Columbia and Pennsylvania attracted the smallest enrollments, and the relatively inexpensive Princeton enrolled the largest number of students in any of the colleges founded in the mid-eighteenth century. The 120 students who studied at Princeton in 1766 placed that institution on nearly the same level with the older Harvard and Yale, which, by the end of the colonial period, were enrolling about 150 students each. Most of the newer colleges other than Princeton attracted no more than forty or fifty students; consequently, by the eve of the Revolution the three oldest institutions still enrolled a majority of the students.[29]

Colonial students gained admission to college at an earlier age than do today's students. During the third quarter of the eighteenth century, the median age for admission was sixteen or seventeen at Yale, sixteen at Pennsylvania, and fifteen at Columbia. In some cases especially bright lads of eleven to thirteen might gain admittance. For example, Timothy Dwight enrolled in Yale at the age of thirteen in 1752, after passing the entrance examination with ease. Most applicants, however, took the admissions examination with much less skill and more fear than did the able Dwight. To gain admittance, applicants sat before the instructors to demonstrate their ability to translate elementary Latin and Greek. Also, after about 1750, a student often needed to demonstrate proficiency in lower-level mathematics. The specific examination at Rutgers in the late colonial period required the entering student to be able to translate into English Caesar's Commentaries, the Ecologues of Virgil or one of the Aeniads, and one of the four Gospels. An especially able candidate might gain placement in the sophomore or junior class, while an inadequate performance did not necessarily mean that the student could not attend the school. In this period when the skills of the applicants varied widely, a student might be allowed to study on the pre-college level to make up his deficiencies. When a college admitted applicants liberally, it might do so more to assure its survival than to show generosity to the students. As President Johnson found at Columbia, often the choice was either to admit students "very raw" or to have no students at all.[30]

The colonial college officials administered their institutions with an orderliness that they hoped would create disciplined Christian gentlemen. Many would have concurred with the statement of acting president Charles Inglis of Columbia to his students: "The sacred law of Order [is] Heaven's first Law." The Harvard rules identified eighty-three separate student offenses, and to the students

at Harvard and elsewhere it must have seemed that they were required to obtain permission for nearly every activity apart from
the normal daily routine. There were regulations governing such
things as hunting, sailing, spending money, and even lying down
on one's bed during daytime. The laws called for showing respect
for one's elders, including the lads in the classes ahead of yours.
The infamous "freshman laws" required first-year students to run
errands for all upperclassmen and to take off their hats when
approaching an upperclassman or a tutor. Even the system of collegiate architecture, in which the major hall contained dormitory
rooms and dining halls as well as classrooms, reflected the
philosophy of total student control.

The detailed list of college rules carried specific penalties for those
who chose to disregard them. For example, at Princeton a student
who failed to attend Sunday church faced a fine of four pence,
and if he left town without permission, he owed five shillings. Most
colleges imposed a similar system of fines for such minor offenses,
or perhaps confined the student to campus or his room or gave
him extra lessons to translate. Those who committed more serious
breaches of acceptable behavior (such as the Columbia student who
challenged the president, Myles Cooper, to a duel with pistols in
the middle of a recitation) faced expulsion with readmission
sometimes possible only following a public confession.[31]

A sharp change in student behavior occurred at Harvard between
the seventeenth and eighteenth centuries. In the earlier period, there
were few cases of misconduct, and these usually involved individual
students. The typical seventeenth-century Harvard student was
serious about his relationship with his God and with his studies.
The later group of young men, however, "came to be made
gentlemen, not to study," and they were more likely to enjoy their
sinfulness rather than to lament over it. The new students resulted
from a new admissions policy at Harvard in which the college
seemed willing to accept nearly everyone who applied, particularly
the sons of the newly rich merchants. Perhaps the new students
would have behaved better if the college had modified its program
to accommodate their interests, but it did not.

The college began to witness an increase in wild parties, pranks,
stealing, drunkenness, fighting, lying, swearing, and card playing.
One favorite nighttime activity began with a foray to a neighboring farm to steal geese, continued with a feast of the roasted fowl,
and ended with a drunken brawl.[32] Sometimes the more pious
students—especially those preparing for the ministry—organized
themselves into clubs (e.g., "The Association for the Suppression

of Vice") to protect themselves as well as to effect spiritual reform in the lives of the wayward students.[33]

Harvard changed in the eighteenth century in large part because New England was changing. After 1689, Massachusetts no longer operated as an official Puritan commonwealth, and subsequently Calvinism no longer completely dominated the approach to religious instruction at Harvard. Also, with the growth of the colonial population and with its increasing interest in acquiring higher education, Harvard began admitting young men who were preparing for a much broader range of vocations. Perhaps it was too much to expect that either the Massachusetts colony or Harvard would remain as religiously orthodox as they were at their founding. The original Puritan founders were a highly selective, especially pious group, which the law of averages would suggest could not be reproduced indefinitely, yet the authorities at Yale thought that Harvard did not try hard enough to continue the earlier religious traditions. Yale did try to continue the old Puritan piety, and it was more successful in the effort; for this reason it, together with Princeton, served as the model for most American colleges founded before the Civil War.

The colonial colleges chose to feed and house their students for several reasons. The students were young, the college wanted to exert the maximum possible religious influence upon them, and alternate housing was minimal. In addition, the residential plan was the model then in vogue in English colleges. The typical colonial college student compared in age to today's high school student; for that reason alone he needed considerable supervision. Also the deeply religious college officials viewed the student as more than a mind to be trained. Most of them would have considered themselves remiss in their duties if they had not educated soul and spirit as well, and they thought that they best could realize this goal by influencing the student's total environment. Some students could have lived off campus, but because the colonial communities were small, such opportunities were limited. Even if they had wanted to do so, most colonial colleges could not have relied upon their communities to house all of their students.

Probably the single most significant factor in explaining why colonial colleges adopted the residential pattern, however, is that it characterized English colleges of that day. English institutions served as the primary model for the colonial colleges, and the English philosophy of the residential college included bringing professors and students together for social and intellectual exchange outside the classroom. Unfortunately, the colonial institutions rarely realized this idea. Still, the residential pattern in America at least allowed the colleges to exert a greater influence over the lives of their students than did the universities in continental Europe, where students generally lived in the community rather than on campus.[34]

Some students preferred to eat their meals off campus even though it cost them more to do so, because in that way they could obtain a more attractive diet. The college dining hall, usually located in the basement of the main building, typically featured bread and butter for breakfast; meat, potatoes, and beer for dinner; and leftovers for supper. Although college students have always tended to criticize even the best dining commons offerings, reports of very bad food appearing in the colonial refractories occur with sufficient frequency to suggest that there must have been some truth to them. Occasionally the students went beyond complaining to rebelling over the situation, as during the late seventeenth century "butter rebellion" at Harvard. On that occasion, some students reacted to their diet with "A Book of Harvard," a protest written in a biblical style, containing such passages as:

> Behold! Bad and unwholesome butter is served unto us daily; now therefore let us depute Asa the Scribe to go unto our rulers and seek redress. Then arose Asa the Scribe, and went unto Belcher, the Ruler, and said behold our butter stinketh, and we cannot eat thereof; now give us we pray the butter that stinketh not . . . And Belcher the Ruler said, Trouble me not, but be gone unto thy own place. But Asa obeyed him not.[35]

The financing of colonial higher education depended more upon student fees and private philanthropy than is the case in the modern era, when most students attend publicly supported institutions. Yearly student expenses for room, board, and tuition in the late eighteenth century varied from £9 at Princeton to £18 at Columbia. Other expenses (e.g., firewood, candles, clothing, travel, and books) added significantly to the comprehensive costs. By the eve of the Revolution, even the cheapest institution cost £25-35, and Columbia charged its students £50-80. By comparison, the cost of a college year in England in this period was over £100. One can better appreciate the significance of such figures by noting that the average annual income for a skilled carpenter in America at this time was £50; for a college instructor, £100; for an army captain, £136; and for an able lawyer, £500.[36]

Harvard in the seventeenth century charged its students much less than the full cost of their education, thus setting the precedent followed thereafter in America of balancing the books by supplementing student charges with income from other sources. Public financial support was a significant factor in the early financing of only William and Mary, which received about £2,300 per year from such sources as export taxes on skins, furs, and tobacco, and export taxes on liquor; however Harvard, Yale, and, to a lesser extent, Columbia received a limited amount of aid from their colonial legislatures. Before 1726, Harvard received approximately £8,500 from the Massachusetts Assembly, but it raised nearly £20,000 from private donors.[37]

Not only did Harvard create the pattern of charging students much less than the total cost of educating them, it also developed many of the fund-raising methods used ever since by college agents to raise money from private benefactors. These methods included the following:

1. Preparing literature to state the case for giving to the college (Harvard's famous initial promotional piece was entitled "New England's First Fruits").

2. Convincing wealthy citizens—especially the merchants, who were the most affluent colonial group—that (a) they owed their fortunes to the blessings of God; (b) therefore they had an obligation to perform to society; and (c) aiding the education of Christian youth was one of the best ways to discharge this obligation.

3. Appealing to the pride of a donor by suggesting that his name be used for a college building or program, or perhaps for the institution itself.

4. Appealing to the longer established regions (in the colonial period this usually meant England) for aid in furthering the promotion of the Gospel by training future Christian leaders.

English philanthropy constituted more than 30 percent of all private gifts to Harvard before 1712. The greatest gift from England came after this date when Thomas Hollis, a London merchant, contributed more than £5,000 to establish endowed chairs in theology and science. The Hollis Professorship of Divinity was the first endowed chair of any kind established in the British colonies. Hollis was a Baptist, and his gift carried with it the condition that the chair thus endowed be open to qualified applicants of all orthodox Christian denominations. Curiously, however, the Board of Overseers initially restricted the holders of the Hollis chair to those who subscribed to orthodox New England Congregationalism.[38]

Other colleges quickly followed the Harvard example of sending agents to Great Britain to raise funds. In 1753–54, Samuel Davies and William Tennent raised £1,700 for Princeton. William Smith, provost of Pennsylvania, and James Jay, a representative of Columbia, together collected over £16,000 in the 1760s in what was probably the first cooperative college fund-raising effort. A year abroad by President Wheelock of Dartmouth produced £5,000, but unfortunately he lost it all—and nearly his life also—when the returning ship wrecked off Cape Cod. Anglican William and Mary met with the greatest success in England. Its fund-raising efforts, beginning in the 1680s, provided the Virginia college with an endowment that probably surpassed that held by the other eight institutions combined. William and Mary, consequently, became the richest of the colonial colleges by 1776.[39]

Another method of fund raising used during the colonial period was to locate or relocate the college in the town or city which was willing to make the best financial offer. For example, Providence residents contributed more than £4,000 in outbidding Newport, Rhode Island, to obtain Brown. Princeton was nearly a ten-year-old institution when the city whose name it now bears convinced the Presbyterian authorities to relocate it by offering £1,000, ten acres of land for the campus, and 200 additional acres of woodland to heat the college buildings.

Perhaps the most controversial means of raising funds was to conduct a lottery. Princeton officials solicited the services of Benjamin Franklin to print 8,000 tickets, which they sold at a fair profit throughout the colonies in 1750. A few years earlier, the New York State Assembly had authorized a lottery to raise funds for Columbia, and within five years the school received nearly £3,500 from the effort. Thus did the colleges use even unusual means in the effort to remain solvent.[40]

The battle to remain solvent has been an ever-present one in Christian higher education. From the colonial period to the present, college officials have struggled to maintain balanced budgets, but if the struggle usually has been difficult, it also usually has been successful—at least for those colleges that survived the trauma of birth to become firmly established institutions.

Chapter 2

The Old-Time College

The American Revolution marked the end of the first chapter in the history of higher education in the new world. Until then, imperial control had served to limit the founding of colleges, especially in the South. Between the war and the end of the eighteenth century, however, the number of new permanent colleges to appear was approximately twice the nine of the colonial period, and by the Civil War approximately 180 permanent institutions were in operation. Similarly, the college population in the 1800–1860 period grew four times as fast as did the overall population.[1]

Several factors contributed to this great boom in college founding. One major stimulus was the religious zeal stemming from the Second Great Awakening. Another was the growing tendency for local communities to want to have their own colleges. Finally, the growing spirit of democracy, which characterized American society during the administration of Andrew Jackson and beyond, resulted in a much higher percentage of middle-class and even lower-class students enrolling in college. Many of these common-class young people came from the rapidly growing Methodist and Baptist denominations, both of which began to lose their fear of higher education after about 1830 and to establish colleges in each of the southern and midwestern states into which they were spreading. Even the growing number of state universities operated almost without exception as Protestant institutions. This period thus became one of maximum influence for the Christian faith in America's system of higher education.

With the exception of its numerical growth, higher education did not change dramatically between the Revolution and the Civil War. Its dominant intellectual force continued to be the Christian faith, and the curriculum changed only modestly. Especially noteworthy, however, was the rise of the literary society as the primary extracurricular activity.

THE EXPANSION OF CHRISTIAN HIGHER EDUCATION

The Second Great Awakening (approximately 1800–1835) brought the American college from what may have been its lowest point spiritually into its fastest growing era. A surprising number of students on the late-eighteenth-century campuses professed skepticism and even atheism while belittling orthodox Christian beliefs. At Dartmouth in 1798, only one member of the class of 1799 publicly professed the Christian faith; at Yale in 1796, only the senior class could claim more than one such believer. The new Williams College in western Massachusetts (founded by the Congregationalists in 1793) identified as Christians only five of its ninety-three graduates in the 1790s.[2]

Then came the awakening which swept through all of the country and all of the major denominations and their colleges! The state of religion in the eastern colleges changed sufficiently that some referred to the revival as the "Protestant Counter-Reformation."[3] Stimulated by the Second Great Awakening, the eastern denominations sought to convert the West. Accordingly, they sent home missionaries to the new developing regions. In order to guarantee that the changes wrought by the missionaries would become permanent, denominational representatives together with local officials established colleges to train future ministers and to indoctrinate the younger generation with the eternal verities.

Thus colleges sprang up rapidly throughout the frontier regions between 1780 and 1860, with the greatest proliferation occurring after 1830. The traditional authority on college founding in this era identifies only 29 permanent colleges as beginning before 1830, while 133 began in the 1830–1861 period. By the eve of the Civil War, the denominations with the most colleges were the Presbyterians, 49; the Methodists, 34; the Baptists, 25; and the Congregationalists, 21. The total college enrollment in 1860 equaled approximately 30,000.[4]

A major factor in the rapid growth of higher education was that the two denominations that experienced the greatest increases in membership because of the awakening, the Methodists and the Baptists, at the same time came to accept the idea that a trained mind might help rather than hinder a minister's effectiveness in proclaiming the Gospel. Consequently, in the generation after 1830 the Methodists founded such schools as Randolph-Macon (Va.), McKendree (Ill.), Wesleyan (Conn.), Emory (Ga.), Wesleyan (Ga.), DePauw (Ind.), Emory and Henry (Va.), Ohio Wesleyan, Centenary (La.), Baldwin-Wallace (Oh.), Lawrence (Wis.), Taylor (Ind.), Albion (Mich.), Northwestern (Ill.), College of the Pacific (Cal.), Wofford (S.C.), Duke (N.C.), Willamette (Ore.), Illinois Wesleyan, Cornell (Ia.), Hamline (Minn.), Iowa Wesleyan, Birmingham-Southern (Ala.), Mt. Union (Oh.), and Baker (Kan.).[5]

Also during the antebellum generation the Baptists organized Colby (Me.), George Washington (Washington, D.C.), Georgetown (Ky.), Denison (Oh.), Shurtleff (Ill.), Franklin (Ind.), Mercer (Ga.),

Samford (Ala.), Wake Forest (N.C.), Richmond (Va.), Hillsdale (Mich.), Mississippi, Furman (S.C.), Rochester (N.Y.), Carson-Newman (Tenn.), and Kalamazoo (Mich.).[6]

Often graduates of the revived colleges led in the founding and developing of newer institutions in the West. Especially significant in this respect were the alumni of Yale, the stronghold of orthodox Congregationalism; Princeton, the stronghold of orthodox Presbyterianism; and Oberlin (Oh.), the stronghold of an evangelical and aggressive social reform emphasis. Oberlin's students and faculty helped establish a number of institutions including Olivet and Hillsdale in Michigan, Tabor and Iowa in Iowa, Drury in Missouri, Ripon in Wisconsin, and Carleton in Minnesota. Of the American college presidents in office before 1840, thirty-six had graduated from Yale—that "mother of colleges"—and twenty-two from Princeton. Yale and Princeton exerted much greater influence than can be identified by direct connections, however, for it was the largely conservative religious and curricular patterns of these Ivy League schools that set the tone for higher education in general during this period.[7]

As much as the Second Great Awakening influenced college founding in this era, many institutions came into existence because community leaders in the West were anxious to work with the ministers in founding colleges. While religious factors may have loomed large in the motives of the ministers, it was only one of several factors influencing community leaders to seek colleges.

Not unimportant was the element of prestige. A community with a college rated higher on the social and cultural scale than did its less sophisticated neighboring towns. Also important was the economic stimulus which a college could bring to a town. Population growth was a major criterion of success for a community, and the establishment of a successful college insured the influx of a significant number of residents. More residents, of course, meant a greater volume of business for the town merchants.

While the role of denominations in founding colleges has been exaggerated, that of individual ministers has not. Frequently, enthusiastic preachers, working somewhat ahead of their denominations, negotiated with community leaders in several potential areas to see where they could obtain the best local offer. For example, in Michigan, four frontier Methodist preachers cooperated with a local business group known as "The Albion Company" to begin Albion, and three aggressive pioneer farmers doubling as Free Will Baptist missionaries fought to overcome the reluctance of their denomination before opening Hillsdale.[8]

The typical old-time college, then, operated more as a Christian community college than as a denominational institution, and rarely did it reflect narrowly sectarian interests. It gained wide support from the members of the affiliated denomination and other denominations. The town and surrounding area supplied a high percentage of the students, many of whom boarded in the community. The college's public events made it a cultural center for the locality, and the area citizens responded favorably to fund drives (college agents did much of their fund raising within a fifty-mile radius of the college).[9]

One of the reasons the colleges were popular in their communities was that often they provided the only secondary instruction in the area. The great majority of students studied on the secondary level. For example, at Oberlin, whose enrollment surpassed 1,300 during the 1850s, only one-eighth of the students were enrolled in a regular college course, and only one-third were pursuing college work of any type. Similarly, only 10 percent of Wheaton (Ill.) students in 1860 were studying at the college level, and when Colorado College opened shortly after the Civil War, only one-fourth of its enrollees were college-level scholars.[10] The Christian colleges devoted major attention to training secondary students in part to meet local needs, in part to generate sufficient total tuition to justify offering instruction to a limited number of college students, and in part to assure a supply of students with adequate training and interest to enroll in their college programs.

While most of the western colleges were local in nature, one can find examples of institutions which reflected the regional nature of the colonial colleges. For example, Transylvania (Ky.) became one of the leading colleges in America by instructing many of the future leaders of the Old South. By 1860 its medical school had taught with distinction over 6,000 students and had graduated nearly 2,000 doctors. Perhaps the majority of trained physicians practicing in the South and Southwest in the antebellum period had studied at Transylvania. The graduates of the Transylvania Law School were fewer in number but more widely known. Among the alumni from this period are Stephen Austin, Albert Sidney Johnston, Cassius Clay, Jefferson Davis, John Breckenridge, John Marshall Harlan, and John Crittenden.[11]

The wide distribution of many new colleges meant that higher education was becoming increasingly accessible to the middle and lower classes. Many students of modest means lived at home while studying, and in a day when room and board charges rather than tuition comprised the principal part of college expenses, this was especially significant. The growing democratization of higher education did not characterize only the West, for even New England after 1800 witnessed a sharp increase in the number of students from poor families. Some of these went to Harvard and Yale; however, they enrolled primarily at Brown, Dartmouth, and six new colleges: Williams, Middlebury (Vt.), Vermont, Bowdoin (Me.), Colby (Me.), and Amherst (Mass.).[12]

The overall increase in college enrollment over the colonial period occurred less from sharp growth in individual colleges than from the greater number of institutions which came into existence to serve modest numbers of students. In the mid-nineteenth century, a large eastern institution like Yale would enroll about 500 students. As a typical school in the West, Beloit (Wis.) in 1860 enrolled only 60 college and 108 normal and preparatory students. Some institutions operated with even as small a student body as that of Franklin in 1847 with its 25 college and 25 preparatory students.[13]

THE CONTINUING MISSION

The old-time college leaders sought to create an environment in which the Christian faith and Christian morality influenced every aspect of the collegiate experience. Often founders located their institutions in remote, rural places in an effort to protect the students from undesirable recreational centers. For example, James McBride, an Ohio legislator who was influential in the founding of Presbyterian-oriented Miami, argued for a rural location for the school by stating, "I had rather send my son to a seminary of learning provided there were able professors even though it should be immersed in the gloom of the deep woods than to send him to an urban setting like Cincinnati where he would be exposed to the temptations and vices which are always prevalent in large cities."[14]

College officials made certain that students properly observed the Sabbath. Most required their students to attend Sunday worship in one of the neighborhood churches, and some added a second service on campus later in the day. Some colleges held classes on Tuesday through Saturday, using Monday as the second weekend holiday and thus reducing the need to spend Sunday preparing for classes. Other institutions which did hold Monday classes found means of discouraging study on the Sabbath. For example, Amherst professors arranged their assignments so that the students did not need to make specific preparation for Monday classes.[15]

The faculty members were often ministers and almost invariably dedicated Christians; therefore, they sought to promote the spiritual development as well as the intellectual growth of their students. The instructors watched for natural opportunities both inside and outside the classroom to lead an unconverted student to receive

Christ as Savior. Many parents expected the college to serve as an evangelistic agent for their youths. The parents of one Wofford student sent the faculty a letter expressing great appreciation for the recent conversion of their son: "We felt that if we could obtain the means of sending him to Wofford, God would convert him."[16]

The old-time colleges played a larger role in evangelizing their students than do contemporary Christian colleges with equally strong evangelistic goals, because then a much smaller percentage of Protestant college students were professing Christians. The explanation is simple. In a day when nearly every college was a Christian college, the non-Christian student who aspired to a higher education had little choice but to enroll in a religious institution. The colleges, in turn, rarely imposed a religious test as a basis for admission.[17]

Probably fewer than one-half of the antebellum students were professing Christians. One comprehensive study by the American Education Society in 1831 considered it very encouraging to note that following the Second Great Awakening, 683 of 3,582 students in fifty-nine colleges were "hopefully pious." An 1856 study by the Amherst College Society of Inquiry showed litttle more than one-third of the students in eleven New England colleges as claiming to be Christian. The highest percentages were at Wesleyan (75 percent) and Amherst and Middlebury (60 percent each), while the lowest percentage was at Harvard (10 percent).[18]

The most effective method for bringing a large number of unsaved students into the fold was the periodic revival. College after college almost annually reported sweeping revivals which not only converted many students but led Christian youths to consider seriously careers as ministers and missionaries. Many students changed their manners of living, and often the changes were permanent. For example, Princeton witnessed an unusual awakening in the winter of 1814–1815 when "in many a chamber where formerly mischievous youths plotted to burn an outhouse or to set off firecrackers in the lecture rooms, there was earnest prayer or anxious discussions over religious matters." Sometimes a revival upset the regular college routine, as at Randolph-Macon in 1852 where a student reported: "Lessons and text books are fast being supplanted by prayers and hymn books and Bibles. Study seems today as if it were entirely a secondary matter." Sometimes such enthusiasm combined with the natural adolescent desire to seek temporary escape from the academic routine. In the midst of a revival season at DePauw in 1842, a student burst into a classroom with an announcement to the scholars that "President Simpson preaches at the Campground at 1:00." The result was immediate confusion, and the students "without dismissal or leave gathered up their books and hastened away."[19]

Insightful revivalist leaders warned that emotional awakenings were not the ideal religious activity. President Jonathan Blanchard of Knox (Ill.) and Wheaton (Ill.) preferred no revivals at all if the work of the church could be realized without them. "When they are successful," he said, "they tend to make us vain and conceited because we do so much. Then they beget disrelish for ordinary labors in the church and make them seem tedious, and they also exalt religious activity above the grace of God. If unsuccessful, they produce discouragement, faintness of heart, and fretfulness in the church."[20]

While evangelism was one aim of the old-time colleges, it was not their primary purpose. After all, churches could evangelize, but they could not provide the necessary education for aspiring ministers; among clergymen and denominational officials, at least, the ministerial training function was cited regularly as the most important reason for founding a college. Contrary to popular opinion, very few colleges enrolled only or even mostly ministerial candidates (this was the case briefly at Mercer and Geneva in Pennsylvania). It is true, however, that colleges sometimes placed undue pressure on students to consider ministerial careers. For example, one Denison student just after the Civil War stated that "it would be probably impossible to exaggerate the prominence given to the duty of devoting one's life to the ministry or missions." He especially remembered how "old Professor John Stevens speaking in chapel on the Day of Prayer for Colleges would cast his eyes solemnly over the assembly and remark 'Let those who must study law.' "[21]

While the colleges eagerly welcomed ministerial candidates, they also were pleased to train students for a variety of other professions, especially including law, medicine, and teaching. Usually no more than 25 percent of the graduates of a college were preparing for the ministry, but a great majority of them were planning to enter some profession. On the eve of the Civil War, approximately 16 percent of the students in eleven New England colleges were ministerial candidates. During the whole of the antebellum period, approximately 20 percent of the graduates of Randolph-Macon and between 20 and 25 percent of the graduates of the Michigan church colleges entered the ministry. By comparison 80 percent of the graduates of Randolph-Macon and 90 percent of the graduates of Amherst prepared to enter one of the four major professions.[22]

Of the campus activities officially designed to promote the Christian faith, the one most regularly scheduled—although probably

not most popular—was the chapel. As had been the case in the colonial period, most colleges held a chapel service immediately following an early rising bell and again late in the afternoon. Frequently,
these services took the name "prayers" because of their brevity—
usually not longer than fifteen minutes—and because they often
seemed less like worship services than family devotions. A typical
service included singing, Scripture reading, prayer, and perhaps a
brief homily. At some institutions, such as Episcopal Columbia
about 1800, the service might be very formal. There, at a typical
service, President Johnson alone or with the students recited or
chanted the Ten Commandments, thirty verses of Psalms, the
Gloria Patri, a collect, the One-Hundredth Psalm, the Nicene
Creed, the Lord's Prayer, and other prayers.[23]

There is evidence that most colleges did not make their chapel
services as attractive as they could have. A student at Amherst in
the 1840s, William Hammond, probably expressed the sentiments
of many students in other colleges when he noted, "I really think
that these public prayers do more harm than good to the religious
feeling of the majority of the students; they are regarded as an idle
bore." Students did not seem to object to the required Sunday services as much as to the chapel services, perhaps because home habits
had accustomed them to attend Sunday worship—but not religious
exercises every morning and every afternoon. The students especially objected to the early morning services. At Yale, where morning prayers in the winter began at 5:30 in an unheated chapel, one
student observed that it was "cold, cold, cold work to get up and
march to chapel by moonlight in the early dawn of winter morn-
ings." The timing of the afternoon chapel was scarcely better
planned, for it was held at a time of day when the physiology of
the body is more conducive to physical activity than to mental
concentration.[24]

Some colleges, however, succeeded in planning effective chapels.
The students seemed to accept more readily a service that included
a dynamic sermon than one which did not. When a college had
an especially eloquent president as a regular chapel speaker, the
effect upon the students could be electric. This was the case, for
example, at Yale under Timothy Dwight, Princeton under John
McLean, Brown under Francis Wayland, and Oberlin under
Charles Finney.[25]

Student religious societies began at least as early as 1719 when
a group of pious students at Harvard organized the "Society of
Young Students." They organized partly to promote their own
spiritual welfare but also as a reaction to the significant number
of irreligious students then in attendance. Student religious societies,

however, became much more prominent in the first half of the nine-teenth century, and most of these organizations took the name of "Theological Society," "Society of Inquiry," or "Society of Missionary Inquiry." One of the earliest theological societies was organized at Harvard. There, in the late eighteenth century, students debated questions such as "Whether the prevailing spirit of tolera-tion proceeds more from an enlarged and liberal way of thinking than from an indifference to matters of religion?" and "Whether poverty be more injurious to religion than ignorance?" The societies of inquiry promoted academic discussion, debate on the problems of religion, and they also sought to stimulate the devotional and moral lives of their members. Usually the societies limited their membership to professing Christians, and some of them required additional commitments. To become a member of the "Yale Moral Society," for example, a student promised to regulate his conduct by the rules of morality contained in the Bible and to refrain from profane language, playing cards, and the intemperate use of alcoholic beverages.[26]

By far the most important type of college religious society in this period was the society of missionary inquiry, which was designed to study and promote foreign missionary activity. On college cam-puses and in churches alike, a sharp increase in foreign missionary interest developed from the Second Great Awakening. American historians usually date the beginning of the modern missionary movement from a group which met under a haystack at Williams in 1806. The group, led by Samuel J. Mills, retreated to the haystack for shelter during a thunderstorm and proceeded collectively to pledge to volunteer for foreign service wherever God called. The young men met regularly for the next two years and influenced others, including Luther Rice and Gordon Hall, also to dedicate their lives to foreign service. At almost exactly the same time, Andover Theological Seminary (Mass.) came into existence as an expression of protest by the evangelicals of New England against the increasing influence of Unitarianism, particularly at Harvard. When in 1810 one of the members of the Williams group transferred to Andover, he took with him the handwritten records of the mis-sionary group and continued the organization on that campus. At Andover, the society quickly recruited new members including Adoniram Judson of Brown, Samuel Nott Jr. of Union (N.Y.), and Samuel Newell of Harvard. Consequently, Andover became not only a bastion of defense for evangelical Christianity but also a center for the stimulation of interest in missionary activity abroad. In 1812 Hall, Rice, Judson, Nott, and Newell sailed for India as the first five modern American missionaries.[27]

Because Christian college leaders believed deeply in the importance of providing Christian higher education for as many qualified young people as possible, they charged very low tuition rates—so low, in fact, that they subsidized the cost of a student's education to a greater extent than do most contemporary colleges. In 1830, comprehensive annual costs to attend college totaled $180–200 at Pennsylvania, $170 at Harvard, $140 at Yale, and $120 at both Brown and Williams. On the eve of the Civil War, yearly costs were $100–120 at Richmond, $176 at Hampden-Sydney (Va.), and $340 at the College of the Pacific. Unlike today, tuition charges comprised only a small part of the total yearly costs. Yale students in 1860 paid $39 annual tuition, while charges at western colleges usually ranged from $20 to $30.[28]

Many western and southern colleges in the 1830s and 1840s sought to reduce their already low tuition rates by providing work in "manual labor" programs for many or even all of their students. The plan was that many students would meet most of their expenses while improving their health and the overall college discipline at the same time. The colleges quickly lost enthusiasm for these programs, however, when they saw that they were running out of work and the students were having too little time to concentrate on their studies.[29] Only rarely (e.g., at Berea in Kentucky) did such a program survive longer than a few years.[30]

Some colleges, denominations, and other religious agencies provided financial aid, especially to ministerial candidates. Most of the scholarships at nineteenth-century Hobart (N.Y.), for example, went to students preparing for the Episcopalian ministry. No agency aided students more generously than did the Congregationalist American Education Society. By the eve of the Civil War, that organization was granting an average of more than $60 per year to nearly 400 ministerial students. Most of these were enrolled in orthodox Congregational colleges and seminaries like Amherst, where 500 of the first 1,300 students received such aid. Elsewhere in New England, about 25 percent of the students in the early nineteenth century obtained funds from sources other than their families or colleges. College-based student loan funds were uncommon, perhaps nonexistent, in this period. Wake Forest claims that one of its students initiated the first such fund in America in the 1870s.[31]

Many of the same groups which aided students also gave support directly to the colleges. Again the Congregationalists provided the most generous support; through their Society for the Promotion of Collegiate and Theological Education of the West, they raised over $500,000 during the generation following 1843 to promote education and evangelism in the western states. Most of the society's aid went to Congregational schools such as Knox, Illinois, Heidelberg (Oh.), Western Reserve (Oh.), Marietta (Oh.), Wabash (Ind.), Beloit, and Ripon. By the time of the Civil War, Theron Baldwin, Yale graduate and long-time society leader, could boast that more than 10,000 students had experienced religious conversion in the thirteen colleges regularly supported by the society since 1844.[32]

One unfortunately widespread fund-raising method introduced in this period was the long-range tuition scholarship. A typical scholarship entitled an individual who paid a given amount, say $100 or $250, to send one student to school tuition-free each year for a long period—frequently twenty years—but sometimes for an unlimited period. These scholarship sales did succeed in bringing immediate revenue to college treasuries, but the long-term results were not good. Gradually, rejoicing over the scholarship sales faded to disillusionment. Often the scholarships had not been completely paid but rather given as promissory notes which were difficult to collect. The major problem, however, was that the institutional leaders had borrowed future tuition income to pay current expenses. When the scholarship funds were spent, many non-paying students remained, and the administrators found themselves in the embarrassed position of having to refuse to honor the perpetual scholarships or else having to buy them back.

Much more successful were the beginning efforts at raising endowment funds and using the interest from them to award scholarships to able students. For example, President McLean of Princeton raised $60,000 for this purpose just before the Civil War.[33]

A COLLEGE EDUCATION

The 1864 Ripon catalog stated: "Instruction will be conducted on Christian principles, and it will be the aim of the instructors to pervade it with a strong and healthful moral and religious influence."[34] Most antebellum colleges shared this goal and regularly employed instructors who applied biblical principles to their disciplines.

At most colleges, students attended classes in the same large building in which they roomed and took their meals. They enrolled according to class, usually in three prescribed recitation or lecture sessions. The classes, interspersed with meals, study sessions, free periods, chapel exercises, and other special college activities, comprised a typical college day.

The curriculum during the first half of the nineteenth century remained much the same as that of the late colonial period except that science instruction became increasingly important—particularly in the eastern colleges—and some institutions broadened the range of their course offerings. Latin and Greek served as the primary subjects for freshmen and sophomores and even continued into the junior year with major emphasis being given to such authors as Livy, Herodotus, Horace, Cicero, Euripedes, and Homer. Also important in the lower-division curriculum were such mathematical studies as algebra, geometry, trigonometry, and conic sections. During the junior and senior years, language and mathematical studies gave way to emphasis upon science, philosophy, religion, social science, and, in some cases, literature.[35]

American educators in general continued to believe that a classical curriculum provided the best intellectual framework for an educated person. Latin and Greek classics were studied because they contained eternal truths and values which every student should know. They were translated because the translation process was an excellent way of shaping the mind. Sometimes this emphasis upon disciplining the mind became so strong, however, that it prevented the students from giving serious consideration to the ideas of the writers. Mathematics also served to "train the mind"; therefore, it ranked next to the ancient languages in importance.

Frequently the most engaging courses were those in philosophy and religion. They were taught almost invariably by the president to the senior class. The most common names for these courses included mental, moral, and intellectual philosophy (described by some as "the science of what ought to be"); evidences of Christianity; logic; and ethics. The exact content of the courses varied according to presidential discretion, but they usually gave emphasis to the social sciences as well as to philosophy and religion. As discussed in detail by Mark Noll in his introduction to this book, these courses almost always sought to combine Enlightenment rationalism with the Christian faith, using the former to support the latter.[36]

Many senior class instructors, particularly in the early years of this period, used textbooks by English or Scottish authors such as William Paley, the Anglican scholar. Yale students, for example, read the Paley texts for over sixty years. His *Natural Philosophy* argued for the existence and goodness of God from nature; his *Evidences of Christianity* offered the data supporting Christianity as the true and supreme revelation of God; and his *Moral and Political Philosophy* presented the personal and social obligations of man that resulted from natural and revealed religion.

Not all students found Paley's prose to be exciting. For example, at Haverford (Pa.) the sophomore class traditionally ended

the school year by burning in effigy the author of the most unpopular textbook. For years the choice was Paley—because of his
Evidences—until a school official decided it was bad publicity for
a Christian college to "burn at the stake the author of the book
that was supposed to safeguard their faith," and he encouraged
the students to redirect their aggressions to the author of the
trigonometry book then in use. After 1835 the Paley texts began
to be replaced by those of such American moral philosophers as
Francis Wayland of Brown; Mark Hopkins of Williams; Joseph
Haven of Amherst; John Dagg of Mercer; Charles Finney, Asa
Mahan, and James Fairchild of Oberlin; Archibald Alexander and
James McCosh of Princeton; and Noah Porter of Yale.[37]

After 1815 the northeastern colleges significantly improved their
science programs. The schools in this region—which as late as 1830
still provided the majority of college graduates—broadened their
science curricula, purchased expensive laboratory equipment (or
philosophical apparatus, as it was called), and hired well-trained
and permanent professors to replace the transitory tutors. Consequently, the number of science professors in America grew from
25 in 1800 to 60 in 1828 to over 300 by 1850. Unfortunately the
status of science instruction did not improve nearly as rapidly in
the South and West, where most schools offered no more than a
smattering of introductory work taught by a single science instructor
who often doubled as the mathematics professor.[38]

Although the quantity and quality of science instruction varied
widely, the approach of the scientists toward the Christian religion
did not. Representative of nearly all colleges and scientists were
the views of Benjamin Silliman of Yale, Walter Minto of Princeton,
and James Dwight Dana of Yale. Silliman, probably the leading
scientist in the country, saw no difficulty in accepting both the find-
ings of science and the record of Scripture, and viewed himself as
"the honored interpreter of a portion of . . . [God's] works."
Minto, a distinguished astronomer, believed deeply that

> The study of natural philosophy leads us in a satisfactory manner to
> the knowledge of one almighty, all wise, and all good Being who
> created, preserves, and governs the universe. . . . Indeed I consider
> a student of [natural philosophy] . . . as engaged in a continued act
> of devotion. . . . This immense, beautiful, and varied universe is a
> book written by the finger of omnipotence and raises the admiration
> of every attentive beholder.

Dana told the American Association for the Advancement of
Science in 1856 that "we but study the method in which boundless
wisdom has chosen to act in creation," and then he observed that

"almost all works on science in our language endeavor to uphold the Sacred Word." Not only were American scientists in this period deeply religious; they also viewed their Christian beliefs as directly related to their scientific investigations, indeed, as providing the ultimate meaning for them.[39]

In the days before the elective system, students sometimes could supplement their required studies with work in other areas by giving extra money and time to such pursuits. For example, in the early nineteenth century Samuel Morse, the future artist and inventor, studied French privately with two recitations per day in addition to his regular work at Yale. Also, when the Yale tutors in the late eighteenth century wished to supplement the regular curriculum with English language and literature, the university approved only on the condition that the courses be taught to interested students outside the regular classroom schedule.[40] Only a few colleges officially introduced the teaching of written composition and literature before the Civil War, while many schools suspected that moral evil resulted from reading novels. Reflecting the concern of his college, one Oberlin student explained in verse what tends to happen when girls become addicted to novel reading:

> *The live, long day does Laura read,*
> *In a cushioned easy chair,*
> *In slip shod shoes and dirty gown,*
> *And tangled, uncombed hair,*
> *For o the meals I'm very sure*
> *You ner' did see such feeding*
> *For the beef is burnt and the veal is raw,*
> *And all from novel reading.*[41]

Only rarely did a literature course in the English Bible appear in the official curriculum. President Alexander Campbell of Bethany (in present-day West Virginia) claimed that his school opened in 1840 as the only literary college in America to maintain a Department of Sacred History and Biblical Literature as an integral part of the curriculum. Also, Geneva, from its start in 1848, offered a Bible curriculum as well as the proscribed classical curriculum. The religion courses at Geneva included Psalms, Bible history, and church history as well as the more traditional Greek New Testament and evidences of Christianity. Bethany and Geneva were exceptional, however. Biblical literature courses did not become common until the late nineteenth century, and then more because of the introduction of the elective system than because of a decision that Bible courses per se ought to be offered in the curriculum of a Christian college.[42]

While study of the Bible rarely appeared as part of the official course offerings, the colleges almost always offered it as a vital part of their unofficial curricula. In the early nineteenth century, Princeton students studied Bible lessons on Sunday after morning prayers and before breakfast. After morning church and dinner, they recited to the president on five chapters of the Bible. Oberlin in the 1860s required student participation in extracurricular Bible study courses which met one hour per week. During the typical four college years, an Oberlin student studied nearly the entire Scriptures. At Lafayette (Penn.) in the 1860s, faculty minutes note that the college "designed to make the Bible the central object of study in the whole college course." The Sunday requirements at Wake Forest included not only a Sunday morning worship service but also a Sunday evening Bible class for which all students prepared recitations. These nearly universal extracurricular Bible studies, when added to the regular senior-level religion courses and the frequent injection of biblical values into the entire curriculum, meant that students studied the Bible and the Christian faith nearly as much as do students in the seriously Christian liberal arts colleges today.[43]

Heretofore this discussion of curriculum has included only the college-level programs. As noted earlier, however, outside of the Northeast most colleges enrolled fewer—sometimes far fewer—college students than preparatory pupils. They had to operate their own preparatory departments in many cases because of the absence of public secondary institutions during most of the period. Ideally, secondary students were preparing for entrance into college, but often they never achieved this goal. The preparatory course included both advanced common school subjects and college preparatory courses, and many of the students were taking courses to aid them in their work as common school teachers. Some of the common-school subjects taught were reading, grammar, geography, and arithmetic, while elementary courses in Latin, Greek, and higher mathematics prepared students for college entrance.[44]

A limited number of colleges offered graduate instruction before the Civil War. Andover Seminary, which opened in 1808, was probably the first autonomous graduate school. Also a few established institutions introduced programs in medicine, law, and theology. Harvard began schools in all three of these areas before 1829, and Yale achieved the same by 1843.[45]

With the increase in the number of middle-class students who brought to college their interest in agriculture and business, there gradually developed a demand for a less traditional curriculum. President Wayland of Brown led the movement for a program of study that would better meet the needs of the new type of student. He argued:

> That such a people should be satisfied with the teaching of Greek, Latin, and the elements of mathematics was plainly impossible. Lands were to be surveyed, roads to be constructed, ships to be built and navigated, soils of every kind under every variety of climate were to be cultivated, manufactures were to be established . . . all the means which science has provided to aid the progress of civilization must be employed if this youthful republic would place itself abreast of the empires of Europe.

In essence, Wayland was calling for the abandonment of the fixed, four-year course and the introduction of an elective system in which colleges would establish courses to meet newly developing societal needs, and students would choose from a variety of offerings those which would best meet their intellectual needs and educational goals.[46]

The response of the American colleges before the Civil War was not to discard the old curriculum but rather to create an alternate "scientific" or "literary" degree program. This alternate curriculum either reduced or replaced the classical studies and gave greater emphasis to modern languages, physical and biological sciences, history, literature, and the application of science to commerce. Students studying this alternate curriculum earned a Bachelor of Science degree.[47]

In one way or another, the American colleges have always offered master's degrees. The earliest of these followed the medieval tradition in which a student needed to study seven years to earn such a degree. Consequently, during the early period at Harvard when most students were studying for the ministry, they were encouraged to spend part or all of the three years following the receipt of the baccalaurate continuing their studies on campus "reading divinity" with the president and perhaps serving as tutors for the undergraduates as well. For example, during the 1649–56 period, fifty-three Harvard men earned an A.B. degree and thirty-five an M.A. degree; of the thirty-five earning graduate degrees, nearly all continued their studies in residence, although not all stayed the full three years.[48]

By the eighteenth century, one could earn a master's degree with less effort. Often a student needed to complete no assignment other than to deliver a thesis in public assembly and to serve usefully in some vocation for three years following his undergraduate studies. By the early nineteenth century, however, even this minimal requirement disappeared, and a common joke among undergraduates was that all that it took to earn a master's degree was to "keep out of jail for three years and pay the five dollar fee." The modern type of master's degree involving significant graduate work began to appear in the 1850s, and by the 1870s it had largely replaced the essentially honorary degree of the early part of the century.[49]

By twentieth-century standards, most pre–Civil War professors possessed an inadequate academic background. In the best eastern schools the typical professor had completed nothing more than the classical course of undergraduate studies and some theological training. Only a few instructors held Ph.D. degrees before 1860, and they earned these in European universities. Most of the frontier colleges employed a mixture of professors with and without degrees; presumably the students on degree programs did most of their work with professors who held degrees.

An effective college program required a minimum of four instructors. This allowed for professors in moral philosophy (usually the president), the classics, mathematics, and one—frequently a person with some science training—for the rest of the curriculum. While many frontier colleges felt fortunate to have four such professors, the larger eastern institutions employed much larger staffs. For example, twenty-four professors taught at Harvard in 1860, and seventeen at Princeton in 1868. Few professors were specialists, at least by the modern definition of that word; yet, the early schools thought that many of their instructors were very learned. One early Olivet professor described even a retired minister who served as a substitute teacher as being very competent in every area: "It did not matter what the lesson was to be, for in every department he was a proficient scholar."[50]

Faculty salaries varied widely from reasonable levels in the better eastern colleges to bare subsistence wages in new struggling institutions in the West. At Brown in 1827 the president earned $1,500 and professors $1,000 per year. Princeton in 1868 paid a professor $2,100 and the occupancy of a rent-free house. Bucknell in 1873 provided the president with $2,000 and the professors with $1,200 to $1,800. By contrast, on the Michigan frontier of the 1840s, Professor Oramal Hosford of Olivet received $36 for teaching six hours daily during the college's first year, and James Stone, president of Kalamazoo, earned approximately $200 per year at the same time. By the 1860s the Michigan salaries were better; Kalamazoo and Olivet paid their professors $600 to $700 per year, while the Kalamazoo president earned $1,500.[51]

Historically, college professors have been willing to work for moderate or low pay because of the deep sense of satisfaction inherent in their work. They are free to use their creative skills in dealing with the great issues of life, and they have opportunities to influence young people in a life-changing manner. Christian college instructors frequently view their vocation as a calling from God equally sacred as that of a call to the ministry; some even have seen the teaching profession as providing greater opportunities than the ministry. For example, Jonathan Blanchard resigned from his very satisfying pastorate at the Sixth Presbyterian Church in Cincinnati because "he saw in teaching the possibility of multiplying his efforts at the source through the inculcation of Christian . . . principles among young men who would go forth to spread them abroad."[52]

THE EXTRACURRICULUM

The literary society was by far the most influential activity in American student life before the Civil War. The literary society movement began during the late colonial period and in some places continued well into the twentieth century; however, it reached its peak during the first two generations of the nineteenth century. Nearly every college maintained at least two societies which competed intensely against each other in a variety of activities. Each sought to recruit the most capable members of the freshman class, each sought to have a larger and better library collection than the other, each sought to outfit its society hall more lavishly than did the other, and each sought to win the intersociety contests in oration, debate, and written composition.[53]

In each college the societies worked to enroll both the best and also the largest number of freshmen each fall with a vigor equal to that with which modern-day athletic coaches recruit athletes for their teams. Society scouts traveled to neighboring towns to board the trains bringing new students to the college town. They also visited preparatory schools and delivered highly passionate speeches extolling the virtues of their societies while denouncing the demerits of the opposition. At Wake Forest the Euzelian Society so desired to enlist the son of a Chinese missionary that it promised to pay his tuition if he would join.[54]

One is amazed that the students were willing to pay large sums of money, which in some cases equaled their tuition charges, to decorate their societies' lavish halls and to build their impressive library collections. At DePauw the students of one society spent over $8,000 on portraits to hang in their hall.[55]

The societies disciplined their members as rigorously—and more effectively—than did the colleges themselves. The Philomathesian Literary Society at Middlebury fined absent members twelve cents and tardy members eight cents. At Oberlin, where students also fined one another for irregular attendance, one society boasted in 1877 that not one member had missed a performance in eleven years. At Princeton the official society censor carefully watched the behavior of members even when away from society meetings and activities; any member who neglected his work, wasted his time at a tavern, or displayed other than exemplary behavior might be admonished or even suspended. On one occasion the society moderator himself received punishment when he became irritated at the levity of a member whom he was swearing into office and hit him over the head with a copy of the organization's constitution.[56]

The most important society activities occurred at the regular meetings, where students competed in debates, oratory, and oral criticism. This emphasis on developing articulate and persuasive speaking skills served a functional purpose, as the great majority of students were preparing for public careers in the ministry, politics, law, or teaching. Often students exerted greater intellectual effort in preparing for literary society activities than in studying for their regular classes. In the days before the rise of athletics, the debate hero was the college hero. To be recognized as such was more highly prized than to be acclaimed the classroom valedictorian. The most popular debate topics involved current events (e.g., "Have the United States justly acquired Texas?"), but the students also enjoyed debating historical issues (e.g., "Was the Reformation the Result of Natural Causes or the Special . . . [Intervention] of Divine Agency?"). Philosophical and religious topics received less attention from student debaters than they were given in the classroom. Probably the most popular debate topic during the decades before 1860 was that of slavery.[57]

The highlight of the year for student orators occurred during commencement week when the seniors or the star orators from each of the societies performed before large audiences. At Randolph-Macon, the faculty dismissed the seniors from all classes for four weeks prior to commencement to allow them to write, memorize, and polish their orations with one of the instructors. At Oberlin, as commencement week approached, "Strange sounds might have been heard at any time of day, and sometimes far into the evening, issuing from any of the groves in the vicinity. Every available stump was pre-empted, and the attention of quietly grazing herds was arrested by the scores of orators in training for those grand occasions." The student narrations served not only as the climax of the literary society activities for the year, but also as major public relations events for the colleges. The college presidents anxiously desired that the students perform ably and, above all, that they avoid any controversy that might embarrass college officials. Consequently, at Bucknell the president carefully monitored the orators during their preparation period. He required the students to submit their orations to him well in advance so that he might strike any objectional passages. If the student chose to use forbidden material on the day of graduation, he forfeited his degree.

The students enjoyed the excitement of the oratory performances, but they displayed much less enthusiasm for another commencement week activity, namely the public examinations, when not only the faculty but also trustees and other educated gentlemen might quiz them on their recently completed courses. Sometimes the students resented the trustees for pretending to know more than they actually did. One such indignant Princeton student noted that "trustees are monstrous humbugs as well as arrant bores."[58]

The literary societies maintained significant libraries to provide resource material for students preparing for their public performances. In some cases, the society libraries exceeded in size the college library. For example, in 1839 the Yale society libraries numbered 15,000 books while the college library had only 10,500 volumes. In the same year at Union, the society libraries had 8,450 books, 300 more than the regular library collection. The two literary society libraries at Trinity (Duke) in 1866 contained 2,200 volumes each, while the college library had only 650 books. The societies developed such extensive library collections only because the college libraries were inadequate[59] and inaccessible. The typical college library held a disproportionately large number of old theological, legal, and medical books. The Dickinson library of 3,100 volumes in 1837 contained 700 works in theology, 600 in law and politics, and 400 in medicine and chemistry. Even worse, many of these studies were long outdated. For example, of the 400 volumes in medicine and chemistry, 35 had been printed in the sixteenth century, 244 in the seventeenth century, 53 in the eighteenth century, and only 4 in the nineteenth century. Furthermore, only 11 of the 400 volumes were in English.[60]

Even when a student demonstrated a special interest in an area where his library was strong, he faced considerable difficulty in gaining access to the collection because few college libraries held regular hours for students. For example, at Columbia, "Freshmen and sophomores were allowed to visit the library only once a month to gaze at the back of books; the juniors were taken there once a week by a tutor who gave verbal information about the contents of the books, but only seniors were permitted to open the precious volumes which they could draw from the library during one hour on Wednesday afternoons." The society libraries, then, invariably exceeded the college libraries in the breadth of their collections and in the extent of their usefulness and availability to the students.[61]

It is difficult to exaggerate the extent to which the literary societies exerted a positive influence upon student life. They provided some of the best intellectual activities—often better than those found in the classroom—and served as the only major organized social activity at the schools. They broadened the students' scope of information by emphasizing areas of knowledge that complemented more than duplicated the classroom work. They forced the students to analyze current events and to develop skill in precise reasoning and oral persuasion. Also, as the one aspect of campus life that was not dominated by the faculty, they provided students with a sense of participation in campus government and the opportunity to develop leadership skills. Many if not most colleges in this period could have echoed the experience of Hillsdale, whose historian wrote of the societies that "nothing else ever exerted so profound an influence upon Hillsdale students." Many students could have identified with the comment of William Seward, secretary of state under Abraham Lincoln, who stated about his years at Union (N.Y.) in the early nineteenth century: "If I were required now to say from what part of my college education I derived the greatest advantage, I should say the exercises of the Adelphic Society."[62]

After the Civil War, the literary societies in colleges in the Northeast and Southeast began to decline, while those in the newer schools in the West reached their peak in the period before 1900. The eastern societies declined in part because many of the newer middle-class students began to prepare for vocations in which oral persuasion was not of major importance; in part because other types of competitive extracurricular activities (musical organizations, athletic teams, and fraternities) began to appear; and in part because the new courses added in the late nineteenth century absorbed many of the areas of inquiry that the society students had found most exciting.[63]

After the Civil War, intercollegiate athletics were to offer the greatest challenge to the monopoly of the extracurriculum by the literary societies, but almost no such organized athletic activity existed before the war. Faculties generally frowned upon most sports contests as unbecoming of gentlemen and scholars and perhaps even dangerous to their health. At best the games were tolerated. One of the earliest athletic games was a very rough form of football known as "rushing," which was as much fighting as sport. After 1840, handball and cricket appeared at Princeton, and a few colleges began to construct gymnasiums. Boating was the first organized sport, with Yale forming the first club in 1843. Nine years

later Yale and Harvard rowing crews competed on Lake Winnipe-
saukee (N.H.) in the first intercollegiate sports event in America.[64]

In the days before organized sports, many of the institutions
which introduced manual labor systems also placed great emphasis
upon the value of regular programs of physical labor. Dartmouth
was an early leader in promoting the idea that manual labor should
be part of the students' education. President John Shipherd of
Oberlin viewed the manual labor system as part of his department
of physiology. President George Junkin of Lafayette argued that
"the healthful pursuits of mechanical and agricultural labor
preserve the youthful constitution from the wasting effects of mental exertion and at the same time give to the mind that strength
and independence which always results from the proud consciousness of self support."[65]

Few colleges encouraged or even allowed the existence of student government organizations until after the Civil War. Perhaps
the first experiment with student government in America appeared
at Amherst in 1888 when the president, Julius Seelye, established
a college senate comprised of students and himself; he presided and
also held veto power. The "Amherst system" gained wide recognition; however, Amherst students viewed it with mixed feelings, not
being certain that the college was much different than it would have
been without the system.[66]

A limited number of colleges and their students participated in
social reform activity. Oberlin and several midwestern colleges
influenced by it were noteworthy centers for the promotion of a
variety of causes, including temperance and especially abolitionism.
When in 1833 Lane Seminary trustee Asa Mahan and his abolitionist students transferred from the Cincinnati school to Oberlin,
the northern Ohio institution quickly organized the 7,000 member
Oberlin Anti-Slavery Society. The southern students were less likely
than their northern counterparts to establish organizations to
promote their views on slavery; nevertheless, the southern church
colleges, primarily through their faculty spokesmen, served as
important centers of proslavery promotion. Presidents A. B.
Longstreet of Emory, William A. Smith of Randolph-Macon, and
Thomas R. Dew of William and Mary were influential writers of
proslavery literature.[67]

If a college leader promoted one reform, he very likely might
crusade for other causes as well. For example, when Knox president Blanchard—who once led the entire student body to a
neighboring town to support him in a four-hour debate with Senator
Stephen Douglas—saw his emancipation goals realized, he immediately transferred his energy into opposing secret societies. In the

latter cause he found considerable support from other college leaders, probably because of their concern about the secret activities of many of the newly developing college fraternities.[68]

Discipline in the old-time college continued to be nearly as severe as that practiced during the colonial period. The colleges still specified the students' daily schedule for rising, studying, attending classes, playing, and retiring as well as the rules for them to follow. The rule books were usually explicit and often very detailed. For example, the laws of Union in 1802 consisted of eleven chapters, each of which contained from seven to twenty-three sections. Wheaton had a similarly long list including the usual forbidden activities of Sabbath breaking, foul language, games of chance, alcohol, tobacco, and disorderly conduct. Then, as if to make sure it had forgotten nothing, the catalog concluded with the comment that "everything is forbidden which will hinder and everything is required which we think will help students in the great object for which they assemble here which is the improvement of mind, morals, and heart." Sometimes the presidents assisted the tutors and residence hall supervisors in enforcing the rules. President McLean of Princeton frequently took evening walks to catch offenders and sometimes chased them to their rooms or up trees.[69]

The discipline enforced in the pre–Civil War colleges appears severe to the twentieth-century observer, but for several reasons it is not fair to judge these schools by modern standards. The students were younger; more than half were of high-school age and thus needed closer attention than do today's older college students. Furthermore, as mental discipline was one of the basic goals of the prevailing curriculum, it should not be surprising that social discipline was also strongly emphasized. Society in general approved of this type of control at the colleges. For example, in 1867 the Michigan legislature passed a law forbidding the sale of alcohol to students in public or private schools and prohibiting the students from playing cards, dice, billiards, or games of chance in buildings where liquor was sold.[70]

It is difficult to know the extent to which students violated the rules of their schools. College histories frequently describe the most celebrated student pranks, and many alumni delighted in recalling their youthful escapades (e.g., J. Sterling Morton, who became President Cleveland's secretary of agriculture and the founder of Arbor Day, recalled his student days at Albion: "I achieved the unenviable reputation of being so full of the devil that the very pores of my skin were said to exude the essence of diabolism"). People have generalized too much from these stories. The behavior of the students was probably no worse than that of similarly aged young people in other social settings then. Some student actions were harmless or merely annoying—such as scraping feet on the floor under the dining hall or classroom tables to express disapproval of food preparation or teaching performance, making frequent loud noises such as the inappropriate use of college bells and horns, and placing animals in unexpected places (such as the ram which appeared suddenly in the Davidson chapel and then proceeded to butt a professor out of the hall). College authorities worried more about the periodic smashing of doors and windows, the rolling of canon balls down the dormitory halls, the greeting of patrolling tutors with showers of sticks and stones, and the relocation of outhouses from neighboring properties to the college lawns. The Princeton lads thought it delightful to awake in the middle of the night to the cry of "heads out, heads out" and then to look out the windows to the back campus where a privy had been set on fire. On some campuses a limited number of students would engage in "hazing" practices two or three times a year. On such occasions they might victimize other (usually younger) students by cutting off their hair, branding their bodies with indelible ink, smearing them with paint, or leaving them bound and gagged in a cemetery all night. Still more rare were reports of students seriously wounding or even killing faculty members.[71]

While the targets of aggression usually were other students or instructors, students sometimes engaged in small wars with town residents. Most college communities witnessed at least some tension between the students and the local citizenry. The townspeople often resented the social and educational privileges of the college students and the real or imagined arrogance that resulted. The likelihood of "town-versus-gown" riots was greatest in those college communities where there resided unusually large numbers of non-college young men, such as the lumberjacks near Bowdoin or the sailors near Yale. Even instructors were not free from attack by town bullies. Such a mob once sent an arsenal of clubs and stones through the windows of the house of Professor Silliman of Yale, an incident which led him to carry two loaded pistols for the remainder of the summer. Fortunately, however, most town-and-gown conflicts were not physical battles.[72]

THE STATE UNIVERSITY AS A PROTESTANT COLLEGE

At least since 1754, when William Livingston, a New York state assemblyman, unsuccessfully sought to convince his legislative colleagues to establish a state college, interest has existed in the idea of publicly controlled universities. It was not until after the Revolution, however, that such institutions began to appear, the first of these being the University of Georgia in 1785. By 1849 state governments had founded thirty-six colleges of all types, and by the time of the Civil War there were twenty-two major state universities in operation.[73]

Almost without exception, these institutions were Protestant in nature and emphasis even though theoretically under public control. The University of Michigan, for example, operated as a Christian college by virtually all standards of measurement. The faculty professed belief in the Christian faith, and most of them were members—and frequently clergymen—of the Methodist, Baptist, Presbyterian, or Episcopal denominations. The president and faculty frequently sought to instill Christian teachings in the minds of the students. President Henry Tappan delivered lectures entitled "Evidences of the Christian Religion," and Erastus Haven preached 600 sermons during his six-year tenure as president. Despite the fact that the university admitted very few preparatory students, it still watched over the students' morals with rules as rigid as those in the denominational schools (the prohibited list included gambling, playing cards, intoxicating liquors, profanity, and violence and vice of all types). The University of Michigan regents also acted from a sense of religious duty. After 1860 they frequently opened their meetings with prayer, and when they discharged a professor in 1851 for expressing unacceptable views, the justification was that he "openly advocated a doctrine which is unauthorized by the Bible."[74]

By contrast, when Thomas Jefferson founded the University of Virginia in 1819, he intentionally avoided official religious influences, explaining his purpose as follows: "By bringing the rival sects together and mixing them with the mass of other students we shall soften their asperities, liberalize and neutralize their prejudices, and make the general religion the religion of peace, reason, and morality." Accordingly, there was no chapel at all at the University of Virginia until 1846, at which time both chapel and Sunday church attendance were voluntary.[75]

The University of Virginia's neutral approach toward religion did not, of course, characterize higher education in this period; its significance lies in its exceptionality. It was, rather, the University of Michigan's approach which typified the manner in which state institutions as well as private ones sought to promote both the Christian faith and learning in general.[76]

Almost invariably the leaders of early state institutions obtained their posts in part because of records of spiritual leadership. In 1840, 67 percent of the state universities—as well as 85 percent of the denominational colleges—had ministers as presidents. For a century after 1811, the University of Georgia hired only preachers as presidents. An admirer praised an early leader of a state agricultural college because "he could run a Methodist revival, an educational campaign, a domestic science class, or an agricultural and fine stock meeting with equal success." Colleges considered themselves very fortunate to have professors like James Thornwell of the University of South Carolina, who experienced notable success in leading students to Christian conversion.[77]

Like the church colleges, state universities almost invariably required students to attend chapel services and Sunday religious exercises. In many cases these requirements continued through the end of the century. As late as 1885, the faculty of the University of Illinois expelled a student for willfully missing compulsory chapel. Also, the faculty at Miami and the trustees at Ohio State voted against presidents whom they considered negligent in maintaining attendance at the daily compulsory chapel exercise.[78]

The state institutions also required study of religious courses and encouraged student participation in voluntary religious organizations. In the years before the introduction of the elective system, the state schools offered the same religion courses taught in the church colleges, namely moral philosophy, natural theology, and evidences of Christianity. Religious organizations at the University of Michigan included a missionary society, a Christian library association, weekly prayer meeting groups, and a student Christian association. At nearby Michigan State shortly after the Civil War, the college Christian union was the most active campus organization, with a majority of the student body participating in it.[79]

The state university rules governing behavior and amusements varied little from those found in church colleges. Some state institutions (such as Ohio University) simply adopted the regulations in effect at one of the church colleges. Despite the similarity of rules, however, there is some evidence, especially in the South, that students in the church colleges behaved better than did those in state universities. For example, in the southern institutions there was no record of dueling in the church colleges as there was in the state universities, and the student riots in the church colleges were not as severe as those in the universities where, on occasion, the militia was called in to bring order.[80]

If one cannot distinguish the state universities from the church colleges on the basis of their approach to the Christian religion, so also one cannot sharply distinguish the two on the amount of public financing which they received or on the basis of how they were controlled. State governments provided very little in the way of financial resources. Furthermore, a number of states gave aid to church colleges.[81] Since the Christian religion and higher education had been directly associated in America throughout its history, and since Protestantism commanded very wide respect in the generation between the Second Great Awakening and the Civil War, it was natural that the denominations would seek to exert the maximum possible influence in the new state universities. In many cases the denominations exercised greater administrative authority over the universities than did the state governments. For example, during at least part of the time before the Civil War, one or more denominations directly controlled the universities of Tennessee, North Carolina, Vermont, Kentucky, Miami, Indiana, and Alabama. In a number of other cases, the denominations largely influenced the environment of the state universities.[82]

Probably no denomination exceeded the Presbyterian in the amount of control it exerted over a large number of state institutions. At Miami, for example, most of the faculty were Presbyterian ministers, many of the trustees were Presbyterian ministers or laymen, and until 1885 every president was a Presbyterian minister. As the Miami historian noted, "Though Miami University was created by the federal congress and established by the State of Ohio, it could not have been more Presbyterian if founded by John Knox."[83]

Although antebellum state universities operated as Protestant institutions, many denominational leaders opposed them because they believed them to be insufficiently religious or feared that they would become so. The church colleges doubted that state universities would emphasize Christian values sufficiently in teaching and in upholding moral standards to assure that students would not lose their religion. Professors at Emory and Davidson (N.C.) had the state universities in mind when they argued that education without religion "may illumine but it cannot heat; it may shine, but it cannot burn; nor can it infuse the warmth of moral life and religious hope into the world," and that ". . . the great sin of the mother of mankind was a thirst for intellectual knowledge without a corresponding desire for holiness." Similarly, Michigan Methodist leaders in 1857 expressed great concern that their young people might enroll in the state university: "We are compelled to fear . . . that it [the university] is so defective in those moral and religious restraints and influences which ought always to be thrown around students of literary institutions that it cannot be patronized by our citizens without imminent peril to . . . those youths who may be sent there." President Haven, who faced similar expressions of concern by certain church leaders during his presidency of the Ann Arbor school in the 1860s, expressed with insight the real nature of this concern when he suggested that "it is not a Godless education that they fear, but a Christian education not communicated through the forms and channels over which they preside."[84]

While the denominations often opposed the state universities, the universities in turn sometimes sought to limit the effectiveness of the church colleges or to eliminate them altogether. In Georgia, North Carolina, and South Carolina, the state universities for many years were able to influence their legislatures to prevent the founding of any denominational schools. Also, in Michigan the state university interests before 1855 convinced the legislature to give the university a monopoly of the degree-granting power and to place maximum valuation and income allotments upon the already established church colleges.[85]

The key to sound higher education in the antebellum period— as well as in later periods—was free competition between rival institutions and dialogue between prominent points of view. American higher education soon came to accept the former but only rarely has realized the latter. The public university, in particular, has an obligation to serve as a sounding board for all prominent points of view. On such controversial issues as religion, unfortunately, the free exchange of views has not regularly occurred. During the antebellum period when orthodox Christian belief was prominent, most state institutions would not have tolerated an honest hearing for unorthodox views—those of agnostics or even of Unitarians, for example. Today the problem is reversed, for as Andrew TenBrook, a University of Michigan professor, realized as early as the 1870s, the likelihood that the university would fall under the control of some parochial religious group was much smaller than the likelihood that evangelical Christianity would be forced out of the university. TenBrook's fair view on the role of religion in the state university was that "in the state universities the question of religion may always be embarrassing. . . . If nothing is taught upon which men do not think alike, then teaching may be suspended for no subject can be traced far in any direction without ramifying into disputed territory."[86]

While scholars agree that the Christian religion dominated higher education before the Civil War, they disagree on whether the colleges of this period served the country well. During the 1950s and 1960s, the most influential educational historians expressed mostly critical comments about the antebellum colleges. A summary of their judgments would run something like this: The first half of the nineteenth century represents the low point in the history of American higher education, for this era witnessed the unfortunate proliferation of countless numbers of poor, weak colleges by competing Protestant denominations. These religious groups established institutions that were intellectually inferior and morbidly moralistic in their emphasis on evangelical piety and paternalistic discipline. Consequently, the students often rioted, the colleges became very unpopular with their larger constituencies, the enrollments declined, and many schools went out of existence. The salvation of higher education came only with the reforms of the late nineteenth century, when many institutions gradually began to discard the anachronistic religious requirements and classical curriculum and to replace them with a broader range of relevant courses, more highly trained professors, and an intellectually open environment. The result was a popular and democratic system of higher education which for the first time began to serve the real needs of the American public.[87]

Historians writing in the 1970s, by contrast, sharply challenged the validity of the above view. They argued that the older historians viewed the antebellum Christian liberal arts college from the perspective of the later secular university with which they identified, and that they too easily based their conclusions on a limited number and variety of sources. The most telling point of the younger scholars is that an increasing number of recent monographic studies provide data which show that many of the previously accepted views were inaccurate.

The results of this historiographical revolution present the old-time college in a favorable light. They show that the pre–Civil War college was less dominated by narrow, sectarian purposes than by broad, Christian ones; that the college served local needs as much as denominational ones; that in most respects it was very popular with its constituent groups; and that the supposed proliferation of needless colleges is explained more by the high number of "paper" institutions that never developed into legitimate colleges (80 percent of identifiable colleges failed either to open at all or to survive beyond a very brief period) than by an excessive number of fully operating institutions (most colleges that survived long enough to develop a full four-year program and actually to award degrees became permanent institutions).[88]

Chapter 3

New Colleges and New Programs

The pre–Civil War period witnessed (1) very limited collegiate opportunities for blacks and white women, (2) only beginning efforts at significant curricular reform and expansion, (3) very few specially trained professors, and (4) only a slight hint of the extent to which athletics later would emerge as a major extracurricular activity. After the war, however, there began to appear an increasing number of colleges not only for blacks and women but also for groups outside the Protestant mainstream, many of whom had recently come from Europe. Of course the denominations which had been most active in college-founding before the war—the Congregationalists, the Presbyterians, the Methodists, and Baptists—continued to found colleges in the newly developing regions in the West. Gradually most colleges, following the lead of Harvard, began to allow students to choose from an increasingly broad range of courses which were taught by professors whose training had become increasingly specialized. Intercollegiate athletics, especially football, not only began to surpass the literary society as the dominant extracurricular activity but also—for better or worse—captured the fancy of the general public to a degree never previously realized by a college program.

HIGHER EDUCATION FOR BLACKS

Very few black students pursued college work before the Civil War. Of those who did advance beyond the elementary curriculum, most studied in apprenticeship, teacher training, or nondegree programs. It is doubtful whether even fifteen blacks enrolled in American colleges before 1840. The first recorded black college students were two Gold Coast seamen, Bristol Yamma and John Quamine, who, with the encouragement of Newport, Rhode Island, clergymen Samuel Hopkins and Ezra Stiles, enrolled at Princeton in the mid-1770s with the idea of preparing for missionary service in their African homeland.[1] With some notable exceptions (e.g., Oberlin, Western Reserve, and Berea), few colleges routinely admitted qualified blacks. Representative of the reluctance of the northern colleges was an incident at Union in which officials agreed to admit a black student, but only on the curious condition that he swear that he had no Negro blood in his veins. One major philanthropist, Gerrit Smith, after 1835 granted aid to colleges that freely admitted eligible blacks. He gave Oneida Institute over $3,000 and 3,000 acres of land in Vermont, and he contributed to Oberlin large amounts of money and 20,000 acres of land in Virginia.[2] Of the black students that gained admittance to college, fewer than thirty graduated in the period before the Civil War. The first two blacks to earn baccalaureate degrees—both in 1826—were John Russworm at Bowdoin and Edward Jones at Amherst.[3]

Most of the early black students gained admittance to college with the sponsorship of either the colonizationists or the abolitionists. The goal of the colonizationists was to train black leaders who then would migrate to Liberia and other parts of Africa to practice their skills. The colonizationists, however, directed most of their efforts toward educating American blacks after they had moved to Liberia. They established no college in this country. The abolitionists, by contrast, founded several antebellum educational institutions in the North and one in Kentucky. The most notable of these were Lincoln (Penn.), Wilberforce (Oh.), and Berea. The Presbyterians founded Lincoln, and the Methodist Episcopal Church began Wilberforce, but Berea opened apart from denominational affiliation under the leadership of two southern abolitionists.[4]

Wilberforce and Berea were exceptional schools. Most of the original students at Wilberforce were mulatto children of southern planters; legally they could not obtain an education in the South. After the Civil War, the African Methodist Episcopal Church assumed control of the institution, thus making it the first black-controlled campus in the country. Berea was the first college in slave-holding territory to invite blacks to enroll; even more dramatic was its identification as an antislavery institution in a slave state.[5]

Berea began through the efforts of John Fee, a native of Kentucky and the son of a slaveholder. Fee became thoroughly converted to the antislavery cause while enrolled at Lane Seminary in Cincinnati. Subsequently he served as an agent of the Congregationalist-sponsored American Missionary Association. Later, with a fellow abolitionist, Cassius M. Clay, he purchased a large tract of land in the Kentucky mountains where he began his school in the hope that it would be "to Kentucky what Oberlin is to Ohio, an antislavery, anticaste, antitobacco, antisectarian school—a school under Christian influence; a school that will furnish the best possible facilities for those of small means who have energy of character that would lead them to work their way through this world."[6]

The college operated as an integrated institution until 1904, when the Supreme Court upheld the controversial Kentucky school segregation law—although not without a famous dissent from Justice John Marshall Harlan of Kentucky. Harlan argued:

> I am of the opinion that in its essential parts the statute is an arbitrary invasion of the rights of liberty and property guaranteed by the Fourteenth Amendment against hostile state action and is, therefore, void. . . . The capacity to impart instruction to others is given by the Almighty for beneficent purposes and its use may not be forbidden or interfered with by government.

The outraged white students at Berea sent a letter to their former schoolmates expressing their dismay: "Our sense of justice shows us that others have the same rights as ourselves, and the teachings of Christ teach us to 'remember them in bonds as bound with them.' " Berea remained segregated until the Kentucky legislature in 1950 revoked the earlier law.[7]

When during the Civil War flocks of freedmen began following the Union armies, northern generals appealed to the public to help meet the needs—including the educational needs—of the former slaves. Consequently, for four years northern missionaries literally followed the trail of the Union army, establishing Sunday schools and elementary schools for the largely illiterate freedmen. At the end of the war, the federal government's Freedmen's Bureau, led by the humanitarian general Oliver Howard, cooperated closely with the missionary groups. The bureau gradually assumed responsibility for providing elementary education for the blacks by opening 4,000 schools; this freed the missionary groups to concentrate on establishing secondary and collegiate institutions.[8]

The church groups worked diligently. They opened more black Protestant colleges during the next twenty-five years than have been founded in all other periods. A dozen began by 1868, and forty of the fifty-four private Negro colleges in existence in the 1970s first admitted students during the quarter century following the Civil War. The most effective of these church groups was the American Missionary Association of the Congregational Church. The association combined dedication with skill in raising money; immediately after the war it raised $250,000 to found some of the best black colleges including Atlanta, Fisk (Tenn.), Hampton (Va.), Howard (Washington D.C.), Talladega (Ala.), and Tougaloo (Miss.). The Methodist Episcopal Church North founded New

Orleans (which later merged with the Congregationalist's Straight to form Dillard), Clark (Ga.), and Claflin (S.C.). Schools begun by the northern Baptists included Shaw (N.C.), Virginia Union (Va.), and Morehouse (Ga.). Later in the century, black denominations began to found their own colleges; in general, they were less affluent than those sponsored by white denominations and thus were considered less prestigious. Because of the large number of denominations and agencies involved in founding colleges, the geographical distribution of these institutions was not always ideal. Certain cities (e.g., Nashville, New Orleans, and Atlanta) acquired more colleges than they needed, while other areas suffered neglect.[9]

Meanwhile, increasing numbers of black students enrolled in northern colleges. During the generation following the war, approximately 200 blacks graduated from northern institutions. Of this total, 75 graduated from Oberlin alone, while the remainder were distributed among approximately 50 other schools.[10]

Although black colleges today include state institutions and private schools that are secular, before 1900 to be a black college meant in almost every case to be a private Protestant institution. During the immediate post–Civil War period, black colleges placed major emphasis upon training ministers and religious leaders. Because the blacks had largely separated from the white churches to form their own, they needed more and better-trained ministers immediately. Even the early technical schools that were less likely to train ministers presented a strong religious orientation. The historian of Hampton, for example, in 1918 described his school as "essentially a spiritual enterprise conceived as a form of missionary service."[11]

The early years of Shaw typify the black colleges in their emphasis on ministerial training. Shaw was founded by Henry Tupper, a graduate of Amherst and Newton Seminary. Following service in the Civil War, Tupper obtained the support of the American Home Baptist Society in New York to train talented freedmen in biblical knowledge so that they might become leaders in the new black Baptist denominations. Accordingly in December, 1861, he formed a class in a room in an old hotel where his first pupils were six deacons and ministers who studied first to read and then to interpret the Scriptures. Similarly, at Morehouse during one of its early years, 150 of 245 enrollees were preparing for the ministry.[12]

Leaders in the early black educational efforts hoped that their students would go forth to spread the Christian faith in Africa as well as among the Afro-Americans. Many believed that God had allowed the blacks to be brought to America to hear the Christian gospel and then to take it back to their ancestral homeland. The

Christian colleges were to be a key instrument in providing the missionary training; thus, well into the twentieth century, schools such as Fisk and Howard listed "African redemption" among their major purposes. The Methodist colleges, black and white, also were very active in promoting African missions. Bishop William Taylor in the 1880s and 1890s inspired hundreds of black and white Methodist students to volunteer for service in Africa. Central Tennessee (Walden) organized in 1887 a "training school for Africa" with a building, staff, and curriculum that included studies in African agriculture and health.[13]

Gradually, the curricula of these schools broadened, and they began to prepare trained Christians for a variety of other vocations. By 1900, the percentage of black college graduates who entered the ministry—11.3 percent—was not significantly different from the percentage of ministerial graduates in other, colleges. By comparison, of the 1,900 students who had graduated from thirty black colleges in the South by the end of the century, 37.2 percent had become teachers in black schools, 4 percent had entered the medical profession, and 3.3 percent had entered the legal profession.[14]

While many white colleges—especially those in the West—enrolled a majority of their students on the preparatory level, the degree to which the southern black "colleges" operated as elementary and secondary schools before 1900 was unmatched. As late as 1920, approximately 80 percent of the pupils in these institutions studied as grade-school and high-school scholars. It should be noted, however, that the schools offered unusually excellent precollegiate training. The colleges sponsored by the northern denominations in particular attracted as teachers highly dedicated graduates of New England colleges.[15] By contrast, the schools run by the black denominations and the local governmental units were greatly inferior.[16]

Most of the early black colleges, then, enrolled very few students who were prepared to study on the college level. For example, the enrollment at Wiley in 1887–88 included only one liberal arts student out of 200 scholars; the others pursued a variety of preparatory, industrial, and other non–college-level programs. While the Wiley situation was extreme, it was not altogether unrepresentative. A thorough study of black education by Thomas Jones for the Federal Bureau of Education in 1916 identified as legitimate colleges only Howard and Fisk. Thus when scores of black institutions used the term "college" or "university" in their titles, they, like many of the white institutions, were proclaiming the ultimate goal of the founders rather than describing current reality. One of the founders of Fisk explained this practice of naming schools ambitiously by describing the thinking of the Fisk founders:

Here was Fisk University . . . with the majority of its classes in the
primary grades. Very well, Moses was Moses as truly in the bulrushes
as when . . . he refused to be called the son of Pharoah's daughter.
. . . The name is in the interests and purpose, in the faith of what
is to be, and in the hope of final achievement. Let us wait two hundred
years and then ask whether or not this child was rightly named
university."[17]

If in the modern period the black colleges more appropriately
wear the college label, they still struggle with the problem of
enrolling quality students.[18] The impact of the Civil Rights Movement led numerous primarily white schools to recruit vigorously
distinguished black students, many of whom otherwise would have
enrolled in black colleges. At the same time, the legacy of segregated
public schools continued to affect negatively the educational
preparation of the average black college enrollees. For example,
the students at Morehouse—one of the better black colleges—in
1965 had an SAT median score of 800; consequently, many of them
needed remedial work, and half of the student body spent five years
to complete the undergraduate course.[19]

Historically, black colleges have attracted much less financial aid
than have white schools. In their beginning years, many of them
operated with almost no resources. For example, Morehouse
originally met in a church basement, and Philander Smith (Ark.)
first held classes in "an open dilapidated church." Until the mid-
twentieth century, the black colleges relied heavily upon northern
whites for philanthropic support. After the Civil War, blacks were
unable and white southerners were unwilling to finance quality
educational programs for blacks. Through the end of the nineteenth
century, the missionary societies of northern denominations provided the major source of outside support.[20]

By the turn of the century, however, several foundations were
making major contributions to black colleges, with the most significant aid coming from the John F. Slater Fund and the General
Education Board Fund. Slater, a Connecticut businessman, in 1882
created a million-dollar fund, the income from which was to be
used to assist students in black colleges, thereby "conferring on
them the blessings of a Christian education." During its first half
century, the fund's administrators distributed approximately $2
million to students in nearly fifty black schools. The Slater Fund
was the first philanthropic organization devoted exclusively to black
education. No foundation, however, contributed more money to
black education than did the General Education Board which John
D. Rockefeller established in 1903. By the 1930s the fund had
allocated over $32 million to the black colleges. After World War

II the General Education Board increasingly concentrated its giving for black education to a limited number of schools, most notably Howard, Fisk, and the Fisk-related Meharry Medical College.[21]

Perhaps the most unique fund-raising method in black schools was designed by George White of Fisk. He combined his interest in university finance and vocal music to organize and lead the Fisk Jubilee Singers, a talented ensemble that, beginning in 1871, toured the North and Europe singing spirituals and making speeches in promotion of the college. The first tour raised $20,000 (including over $4,000 from one concert in the Tremont Temple, Boston), thus allowing the school to pay its debt and purchase its present property site; the tour also produced much public acclaim, an increased demand for concerts, and an enlarged appreciation for the skills of blacks generally.[22]

Financial contributions from the North as well as the presence of northern teachers in the black colleges sometimes aroused suspicion among southern whites. For example, James Vardaman, an early-twentieth-century Mississippi governor and senator, expressed concern that "what the North is sending South is not money but dynamite. This education is ruining our negroes. They're demanding equality."[23]

In the mid-twentieth century, the United Negro College Fund emerged as the most important innovation in fund-raising for black colleges. Black educational leaders organized this agency because of declining support from the old foundations and because of a growing desire to be less dependent financially upon northern whites. Accordingly, both church-related and independent private colleges[24] engaged in annual cooperative fund-raising efforts which by 1960 netted for the institutions a yearly income equal to that which they would have realized from an endowment of $40 million.[25]

COLLEGES FOR WOMEN

As was true with the black institutions, women's colleges founded before 1900 almost invariably operated as aggressively Christian institutions. For example, Mr. and Mrs. Henry Durant combined their wealth and evangelistic fervor to found Wellesley (Mass.) to train missionaries and other Christian workers in the style of Oberlin. They wrote as the original statute of the institution, "The college was founded for the glory of God and the service of the Lord Jesus Christ, in and by the education and culture of women." They required that every trustee, administrator, and instructor be a member of an evangelical church and that the instructors be able to teach the Bible classes in which each student would participate throughout her college course.

Mount Holyoke (Mass.) held to a similar purpose. It developed from one of the most advanced seminaries (i.e., secondary schools) to one of the most effective colleges, and its famous founder, Mary Lyon, described it as "a school for Christ. . . . It is designed to cultivate the missionary spirit among its pupils; —the feeling that they should live for God, and do something—do something as teachers, or in such other ways as providence may direct." In general, such religious foundations characterized the other women's colleges, both in the East and elsewhere in the country. Also, more than American colleges in general, the women's institutions determined to apply Christian ethics to societal problems.[26]

The establishment of colleges for young ladies represented the culmination of a long process of convincing society that women should have educational opportunities equal to those of men. Before the nineteenth century most people did not consider it necessary—or even desirable—for women to receive even the most elementary formal schooling. Only a few young girls joined their brothers in "dame" schools, where they obtained beginning instruction in reading and writing. By the eve of the American Revolution, however, New England girls were attending advanced elementary, or "master's," schools.[27]

While very few separate schools for girls existed before 1820, the number of such private institutions increased sharply after that date. The best of them included Emma Willard's Troy Female Seminary (N.Y.), Catherine Beecher's Hartford Female Seminary (Conn.), and Lyon's Mount Holyoke Seminary. Troy and Mount Holyoke each trained approximately 1,200 students during the middle half of the nineteenth century. Gradually, these and some of the approximately 100 other private secondary schools for women increased the scope and quality of their curricular offerings to the point where their academic programs became part secondary and part collegiate in nature. They convinced those who were willing to examine the data that women as well as men could pursue college-level work.[28]

Other female seminaries operated on a much lower level. In some the curricula were superficial—even frivolous; in some the courses of study were not continuous; and in some the proprietors were more interested in making a profit than in developing the intellectual and spiritual abilities of their pupils. For these reasons and others the academies received wide criticism. Note the following satirical critique of a school run by a Madame Cancan in the late 1850s:

Madame Cancan still lives and still ogles and teaches,
And still her light sermons on fashions she preaches;
Still keeps of smooth phrases the choicest assortments;
Still lectures on dress easy carriage deportment;
And spends all her skill in thus moulding her pets
Into very-genteelly-got-up marionettes.

Yes! Puppet's the word, for there's nothing inside
But a clock-work of vanity, fashion, and pride!
Puppets warranted sound, that without any falter
When wound up will go just as far as the altar;
But when once the cap's donned with the matronly border,
Lo! The quiet machine goes at once out of order.

The average school, of course, was not this bad, just as it was not as good as Beecher's Hartford Seminary or Mount Holyoke. It generally fell below the academic level of the boy's institutions, although it probably exceeded them in teaching cultural appreciation, in its emphasis on practical training, and in developing skills for parental leadership and interpersonal relations.[29]

Both the educational leaders who wished to found colleges for women and the young women who wished to enroll in such institutions—or even in coeducational colleges—met with considerable opposition. Many opponents of higher education for women believed that women were mentally inferior to men and thus could not compete with them in the rigorous collegiate disciplines. Others thought that a woman's physical as well as intellectual constitution would break under such a strain. Many would have agreed with the sentiment of Rev. John Todd who argued, "As for training young ladies through a long intellectual course, as we do young men, it can never be done. They will die in the process." He lamented that, where this was tried:

The poor thing has her brain crowded with history, grammar, arithmetic, geography, natural history, chemistry, physiology, botany, astronomy, rhetoric, natural and moral philosophy, metaphysics, French, often German, Latin, perhaps Greek, reading, spelling, committing poetry, writing compositions, drawing, painting, etc., etc., ad infinitum. Then, out of school hours, from three to six hours of severe toil at the piano. She must be at the strain during school hours, study in the evening till her eyes ache, her brain whirls, her spine yields and gives way, and she comes through the process of education, enervated, feeble, without courage or vigor, elasticity, or strength. Alas! must we crowd education upon our daughters, and, for the sake of having them "intellectual," make them puny, nervous, and their whole earthly existence a struggle between life and death?

Even some who believed women capable of competing with men in colleges thought the practice unwise on the practical grounds that it would lead to a reduction in the number and quality of marriages. As one opponent observed, "Man loves a learned scholar but not a learned wife."[30]

Gradually these arguments received less credence as more people observed women successfully completing college work. Furthermore, even in the nineteenth century it appeared unjust to prevent able women from pursuing their intellectual interests. Perhaps the most convincing argument for the higher education of women was that they gradually began to dominate the elementary teaching profession and thus needed the opportunity to become as well educated as possible.

The most effective of the early advocates of women's colleges was Catherine Beecher. In her *True Remedy for the Wrongs of Women,* she argued vigorously for female institutions that would match the existing men's colleges in curriculum, quality of instruction, and physical resources. She also emphasized the importance of an applied curriculum, particularly in the areas of domestic science and teacher education.[31]

Several institutions claimed to be the earliest female college. Wesleyan (Ga.) cited the earliest date (1836), but some critics doubt that it was operating as a bona fide college as early as were Mary Sharp (Tenn.) and Elmira (N.Y.), which opened in 1851 and 1855 respectively. Actually, during the middle part of the century there were many women's institutions that, like many of their male counterparts, were in the process of developing from primarily secondary to collegiate institutions. They actually operated on both levels for many years. It is difficult, therefore, if not impossible, to try to determine when such institutions actually became "colleges."[32]

Very few institutions for black women developed because there was little need for them. Some black women gained admittance to the white coeducational institutions such as Oberlin, where the first Afro-American woman graduated in 1862. The primary reason for the relative absence of black women's colleges, however, was that most of the black colleges freely admitted women as well as men. Nevertheless, in 1881 Spelman (Ga.) opened as the first institution for black women.[33]

If by the late nineteenth century there were many institutions in which young women could pursue college-level work, there were only a handful of women's institutions operating with levels of funding, quality of faculties, and admissions requirements that could compare with those found in the most prestigious men's institutions. The earliest of these elite colleges was Vassar (N.Y.), which opened in 1865. During the Civil War, Matthew Vassar, a wealthy Quaker, noted that there was not in the world, as far as he knew, a single fully endowed college for women. He determined, therefore, "to be the instrument in the hands of Providence of founding and perpetrating an institution which shall accomplish for young women what our colleges are accomplishing for young men." Accordingly, Vassar opened on a grand scale with an endowment of $400,000 (three times as much as any women's college had held previously), a large new building, a faculty of 8 men and 22 women, and a student body of 353. The fact that Vassar's wealth had come from his brewery investments embarrassed the early college leaders, but not the students who sang his praises:

> *Then there's Matthew Vassar,*
> *Our love shall never fail,*
> *For well we know that all we owe*
> *to Matthew Vassar's ale.*[34]

Other elite eastern women's colleges which opened in the nineteenth century included Wellesley in 1870, Smith (Mass.) in 1871, Radcliffe (Mass.) in 1879, Bryn Mawr (Penn.) in 1885, Barnard (N.Y.) in 1889, and Mount Holyoke in 1893. Collectively these institutions were known as the seven sister colleges, and in prestige they served as the female counterpart to the Ivy League. Academically, the women's colleges exceeded the men's in some areas. For example, Vassar, Wellesley, and Smith all developed excellent departments of fine arts and English literature, and Wellesley became the first college to offer a major in art history.[35]

Most of the alumni of the women's institutions became teachers, missionaries, or homemakers—or some combination of these three vocations. The percentage of graduates entering the teaching profession included nearly 80 percent at Wellesley by 1893, and nearly 70 percent at Mount Holyoke during its first half century. By the late nineteenth century, women held most of the common-school teaching positions in this country; since most teachers were not college graduates, those who did hold college degrees provided as a group the best elementary instruction.[36]

Very few women received formal theological training. The first woman to graduate from a theological school was Antoinette Brown Blackwell, who finished the three-year course at Oberlin in 1851. Women, however, found no difficulty in becoming foreign missionaries. In fact, during the modern period of foreign missions (the nineteenth and twentieth centuries), the clear majority of Protestant missionaries have been women. Missions was probably the first profession in which women achieved status equal to men. When a woman went to a foreign field, she found much more freedom to exercise her leadership and creative skills than if she had remained in America. Even when married to a paternalistic husband, the missionary wife could organize an elementary school for girls; indeed, in many cases she was asked to do this.[37]

Graduates of the early women's colleges found the mission field especially appealing because there they could exercise in a practical way with few limits their zeal in promoting both the Protestant faith and the cause of women's rights. Typical of the experiences of the graduates who pursued missionary careers was that of Isabel Trowbridge Merrill, who graduated from Vassar in 1900. While speaking to the College Girls of America organization later in her life, she advised the young women considering career opportunities:

> The life of a missionary is the happiest, most joyous, most satisfying one I can know. A college girl's whole training is toward activity, and what else can give her so great pleasure and satisfaction as to be in an environment that calls out all her powers and gives her a chance to live such a vital life and a life that tells. Oh girls, it pays so many times over.[38]

The early critics of higher education for women were correct when they predicted that women who went to college would be less likely to marry than their sisters who remained at home. A study of approximately 2,000 college graduates in 1895 found that of those over twenty-five, 33 percent were married, and of those over forty, 55 percent were married; by contrast, 80 percent of all women over twenty were married. It should be noted, however, that these statistics showed a much higher marriage pattern among women who had attended coeducational institutions than among those who had graduated from women's colleges.[39]

In part, the nineteenth-century movement to found women's colleges in the East and South arose as a conservative response to the growing practice of coeducation in the western colleges and, later, the western state universities. After Oberlin admitted four women to its collegiate program in 1837, it became the best-known coeducational institution in the country, with women comprising between 10 and 25 percent of its enrollment in the early years. Many other western Protestant colleges quickly followed Oberlin's example, so that by 1873, of the ninety-seven institutions admitting women, sixty-seven were located in the West.[40]

By contrast, coeducational institutions at this time numbered only five in New England, eight in the Middle-Atlantic states, and seventeen in the South. Before the Civil War, no coeducational college of any type existed in Georgia, the Carolinas, or Virginia. When the institution that ultimately developed into Texas Christian moved in 1873 from Fort Worth to Thorpe Spring, it decided to admit women. This was a sufficiently novel practice in the Southwest that the institution advertised its uniqueness in the school name, "Add Ran Male and Female College."[41]

In the late nineteenth century some institutions, especially in the East, began to think that their earlier insistence upon separation of the sexes for education may have been extreme but they still retained a reluctance to accept fully the idea of coeducation. These institutions adopted a mediating position whereby they located women's colleges adjacent to men's colleges. Thus there arose such "coordinate" institutions as Radcliffe (1879) near Harvard, Barnard (1883) near Columbia, and Pembroke (1891) near Brown. The coordinate college remained a rarity, however, and neither it nor the women's college would in the long run become the primary means of providing collegiate education for the nation's women. It was the coeducational institution that mounted in popularity, with the number of liberal arts colleges admitting women growing from 30 percent in 1870 to over 50 percent in 1880 and 65 percent by 1890.[42]

COLLEGES FOUNDED BY THE NEWLY RICH AND THE NEW IMMIGRANTS

After the Civil War, as America was becoming the leading industrial power in the world, an increasing number of entrepreneurs acquired vast wealth. Some of them chose to give large sums either to transform a small college into a major institution or to launch a new university. Some of the new wealth went to the major women's colleges but most of it went to male or coeducational institutions.

Cornelius Vanderbilt, because of railroad and water transportation investments, possessed much money; his wife and her pastor possessed much interest in Central University of Nashville, which had been founded by the Methodist Episcopal Church in 1872. Consequently, the Vanderbilts contributed $1 million to the college in the 1870s. In appreciation, the school renamed itself after him. Other family members contributed an additional $10 million by 1895.[43]

The Washington Duke family of North Carolina so successfully developed their tobacco business that by 1889 they produced half of the cigarettes sold in America. Duke loved the Methodist church in which he had been converted as a youth, and he wished to express his appreciation by contributing a large sum to the denomination's educational work. He also wished to see a college located in his own town; therefore, when Trinity, the small, struggling Methodist college in Randolph County, North Carolina, needed financial strengthening, Duke and his son Benjamin offered to contribute $85,000 if it would relocate in Durham. The college agreed to move to Durham, and the gifts that Benjamin Duke continued to bestow upon the school reached $2 million by 1925. The family benevolence did not stop there, for a second son, James, created an endowment fund of $100 million, thus establishing what then came to be known as Duke University as a major educational institution.[44]

Like the Duke family, Asa Candler was a devout Methodist millionaire. He had earned his wealth from the manufacture and distribution of Coca-Cola. His gifts and those of his son, Howard, after him transformed small Emory College in Atlanta into the distinguished Emory University.[45]

Southern Baptist institutions benefiting from unusually large gifts included Stetson, Baylor, and Wake Forest. Stetson assumed its present name to honor John Stetson, of the Stetson hat manufacturing family. Stetson's generous gifts to the Baptist academy in his winter home of Deland, Florida, allowed the school to reorganize itself as a collegiate institution. John Hardin gave $1.25 million to Baylor in 1936, and while that institution was already well established by then, the gift represented the largest single contribution in its history. The Wake Forest endowment, which had reached only $100,000 by 1884, sharply increased with the gifts of Jabez Bostwick. Bostwick's contributions began in 1885 and culminated in a $1.5 million stock contribution from his will in 1923.[46]

Few nineteenth-century Americans were as wealthy as John D. Rockefeller, and it was perhaps inevitable that the dedicated Baptist churchman would found a great university. He had long held an interest in higher education, and for years he had offered significant aid to a variety of institutions. His former Cleveland pastor, Augustus Strong, had become president of Rochester Theological Seminary and argued that Rockefeller should found a great Baptist institution in New York. Other Baptist ministers, such as Thomas Goodspeed and Fredrick Gates, pleaded for establishing the university in Chicago. The pro-Chicago leaders won, primarily because they were able to raise $400,000 to supplement Rockefeller's $600,000 gift. Rockefeller wished to establish a Baptist institution and to appoint William Rainey Harper, a Baptist biblical scholar at Yale, to the presidency. He could not have both, however, as Harper was not in favor of making the institution orthodox Baptist. Apparently Rockefeller wanted Harper more than he wanted the college closely tied to the Baptist Church, for the University of Chicago was established as an institution that was neither Baptist nor unequivocally Christian, but whose orientation was broadly religious with a slight preference for the Christian faith. By 1910, Rockefeller had given $35 million to his creation, including $1.5 million for a university chapel that he desired to be the central and dominating physical feature of the campus, just as "the spirit of religion should penetrate and control the university."

While the new Chicago institution chose not to evangelize its students, it did agree to allow evangelical groups to work with the students on terms set by the university. Thus, when YMCA leader John Mott asked Harper for the privilege of organizing a chapter at Chicago similar to those which existed in most other collegiate institutions, Harper declined but invited Mott to participate along with other groups in the university-created Christian Union. The union was a broadly religious organization which started from a Christian framework but was careful to avoid denying the spiritual value of other faiths.[47]

Some other new, well-endowed institutions clearly defined themselves as religious in nature but not Christian. Stanford (Cal.) sought to be as religious as Chicago, while avoiding the latter's modest preference for the Christian faith. While Stanford's founders established voluntary religious services, they expressly forbade the university to offer "sectarian" instruction. They wished to tie the institution to no other religious creed than belief in "the immortality of the soul, the existence of an all-wise benevolent creator, and the idea that obedience to his laws is the highest duty of man."[48]

If Chicago wished to give slight preference to the Christian faith and Stanford only to promote religion in general, Johns Hopkins, founded in Baltimore in 1876 by a Quaker merchant of the same name, sought to avoid all official religious influences. It wanted to avoid the suspicion that it was opposed to religion, however. Accordingly, the leaders of the new institution established a voluntary fifteen-minute chapel service and provided a building site and secretarial salary assistance for the YMCA chapter.[49]

One of the most interesting philanthropists of Christian higher education was Daniel Pearsons, a Chicago financeer. When Pearsons retired in 1890 at the age of seventy, he chose to devote the remainder of his life to giving from his accumulated wealth to small Christian colleges in the West and South. His conviction was that such institutions provided the best training for future leaders. He studied carefully each potential recipient institution to assure himself of its viability. If his assessment was favorable, he offered the college a sizable grant on the condition that it in turn raise significant monies from its constituency and that it broaden the base of that constituency. For example, Pearsons offered Beloit $100,000 on the condition that it raise an additional $400,000 within a prescribed period of time. In this manner he gave approximately $5 million to forty southern and western colleges.[50]

Foundation philanthropy has not been broadly helpful to Protestant higher education. In general, the foundations have given aid to a limited number of already well-endowed colleges. Between 1923 and 1929, for example, of the 1,000 institutions in the United States, 36 received 80 percent of the $100 million given by the five largest foundations. Most of the recipient institutions were ones that were becoming secular. Sometimes this secularization was explicitly rewarded, as in the case of the early-twentieth-century Carnegie Pension Fund. This fund proposed to aid colleges in establishing retirement programs for their instructors, but only when the institutions held no church affiliation. A few foundations, however, such as the Lilly Endowment, which was established in 1937, showed special interest in supporting church-related colleges.[51]

While the industrialization of America during the second half of the nineteenth century produced multimillionaires who could afford to create major centers of learning, the continuing immigration to the New World in the same period brought ethnic and religious groups who chose to found their own colleges. Before the Civil War, most newcomers had emigrated from the British Isles and Germany; however, the post-war pattern became more complex. In addition to the sharply increasing number of Roman Catholics and Jews from southern and eastern Europe and the continuing influx of people who could identify with the older major Protestant denominations and colleges, there began to pour into the Midwest and the north central states Protestant separatist groups such as the Scandinavian Lutherans, the Dutch Reformed, the German and Russian Mennonites, and the German Brethren. Because these groups were more determined than most to retain their unique cultural practices and religious beliefs, they preferred to found their own colleges rather than to allow their young people to attend state institutions or colleges sponsored by other denominations.

Most of the early Mennonite and Brethren leaders in this country distrusted advanced learning under any circumstances. According to a historian of Brethren higher education, most Brethren in the mid-nineteenth century viewed high schools and colleges as "worldly places where the young will at best puff up with proud knowledge and at worst desert the church." When the young people of the German groups became increasingly interested in higher education, church leaders reluctantly and gradually concluded that maybe higher education per se was not evil. Certainly it would be better to fund church colleges to train their young people than to lose them.

Sometimes the churches came to this conclusion belatedly. The eastern Mennonites, for example, were especially slow to change on this issue. The very large and influential Lancaster County, Pennsylvania, Mennonite Conference originally opposed the existence of Goshen (Ind.) which began in 1902; and during the fifteen years preceding the opening of Eastern Mennonite (Va.) in 1917, in the words of one Mennonite bishop, "Much of the best talent was lost to the church because hundreds and even thousands were getting their education in schools where the principles of the Bible were neither encouraged nor recognized."[52]

Consequently, the Brethren founded Juniata (Penn.) in 1876, Ashland (Oh.) in 1878, Bridgewater (Va.) in 1880, McPherson (Kan.) in 1887, Manchester (Ind.) in 1889, LaVerne (Cal.) in 1891, Elizabethtown (Penn.) in 1899, Messiah (Penn.) in 1909, and Upland (Cal.) in 1920. The Mennonites were even slower, opening Bethel (Kan.) in 1893, Bluffton (Oh.) in 1900, and Tabor (Kan.) in 1908, in addition to the aforementioned Goshen and Eastern Mennonite.

The early Scandinavian and Dutch immigrants recognized the need for educated ministers and teachers, but, like the German Anabaptist groups, they were fearful of higher education in institutions not of their faith. Acceptable European universities were too distant and the existing American institutions too untrustworthy. So the Scandinavians and the Dutch began their own colleges to train their own leaders in their own regions; in so doing they were following the example of their spiritual forbearers such as the German Lutherans who founded several eastern colleges before the Civil War and the colonial Dutch who began Rutgers.[53] Sometimes the immigrants established schools as much to train godly teachers as to prepare preachers. The Lutherans remembered the advice of their sixteenth-century founder who had proclaimed, "We can take magistrates and princes as we find them, but not schools, for schools rule the world."[54]

The Swedes and the Norwegians were the most active Scandinavian groups in founding colleges. The Swedish Lutherans began Augustana (Ill.) in 1860, Gustavus Adolphus (Minn.) in 1862, Bethany (Kan.) in 1881, Luther (Neb.) in 1883, and Upsala (N.J.) in 1893. North Park (Ill.) opened in 1891 as the Swedish Covenant school, and Bethel (Minn.) began in 1871 as a Swedish Baptist institution. The Norwegian Lutherans founded Augustana (S.D.) in 1860, Luther (Ia.) in 1861, Augsburg (Minn.) in 1869, Saint Olaf (Minn.) in 1874, Concordia (Minn.) in 1891, Waldorf (Ia.) in 1903, and, with the German Lutherans, Pacific Lutheran (Wash.) in 1894. The Danish Lutherans began Dana (Neb.) in 1884 and Grand View (Ia.) in 1896, and the Finnish Lutherans founded Suomi (Mich.) in 1896.

The schools begun by the Dutch included Hope (Mich.) in 1851 and Northwestern (Ia.) in 1882 by the Reformed Church, and Calvin (Mich.) in 1876 by the Christian Reformed Church.

Slowly but surely the immigrant colleges assimilated American culture. Among the Scandinavians, the Swedish Lutherans led the way. From their beginning years, Augustana of Illinois and Bethany offered instruction in English as well as Swedish. Augustana by the 1890s admitted many "Americans" as commuter students, even though their habits were not controllable by the faculty; also, in 1898 the faculty recommended that morning chapel be conducted in English. The earlier vision of Augustana as an entirely Swedish Lutheran religious institution was changing. Sometimes the colleges made special efforts to retain the old-world culture for the Swedish students. For example, at Bethany as late as the 1920s Swedish-American enrollees were expected to study the Swedish language.[55]

Among the Dutch, the weekly *DeHope*, with many Hope faculty members on its editorial board, served both to preserve the old-world culture and gradually to aid its readers in adapting to their new environment. Its purpose was to help Hollanders become Americans "by assimilation and not absorption."[56]

German and Russian Anabaptists faced a special problem in the acculturation process. Whereas the Scandinavians and the Dutch brought with them a tradition of participating in the culture of the home country, the Anabaptists brought an attitude of separation from and nonconformity toward the prevailing culture of any country in which they resided. For them, the acculturation process was not only a matter of adapting to the American setting but also of adapting to secular culture in general. For many decades after the beginning of the Anabaptist colleges, a sizable portion of the church members greatly distrusted them, partly because the colleges themselves were a part of the suspect ungodly culture and partly because within the denominations the colleges represented the greatest force leading to cultural change. Even such an issue as mode of dress could cause great controversy, as it did at Goshen early in the century when the Mennonite and Amish-Mennonite students began to dress more conventionally than they had in their home communities. Their home churches often criticized them as "dressy" and thus "worldly." Sometimes the students would leave the church, with the membership blaming the college for the desertion.[57]

THE NEW CURRICULUM AND ITS EFFECTS

During the second half of the nineteenth century, America's Industrial Revolution transformed American society. The United States changed from a primarily rural, agricultural country to a primarily urban, technological one. As we have already seen, the wealth resulting from these economic changes helped create a number of well-endowed colleges and universities.

The same societal changes that produced the country's new wealth also demanded that colleges reform their curricula away from traditional classical studies and toward more practical courses that would prepare students for the new roles which many of them must assume. In the new technological society, Harvard paved the way for the Protestant colleges when, beginning in 1869 under President Charles Eliot, it began to discard its required curriculum and to allow its students to choose from a broad variety of curricular options those which best met their vocational and personal goals.

Harvard was not the first to adopt such an elective system. At Union under President Eliphalet Nott, students since early in the nineteenth century had been able to choose widely from classical and other types of courses, and, regardless of their choices, they all received the same degree. The significance of the change at Harvard, however, is that when it introduced the elective system, the practice spread to nearly every other college. By 1886, Harvard retained almost no course requirements, and a student needed only to pass 18 courses—one-quarter of them with a C or better—out of a total curriculum of 153 full and 61 half courses taught by 61 professors.[58]

The Protestant colleges followed the Harvard example with varying degrees of completeness and speed. By 1890, one college out of three still maintained a totally prescribed curriculum, and the average institution offered a curriculum that was 84 percent required. A 1901 survey of approximately ninety-seven colleges showed that forty-six of them operated with at least 50 percent election. By 1940, the curriculum in the average college was only 40 percent prescribed.

Frequently colleges adopted the elective system sooner in theory than they could implement it in practice. It was one thing to agree with the philosophy of election and quite another to locate funds to hire additional professors to teach all of the new courses. Even affluent Harvard had adopted the elective system a full generation before it became a practical reality under President Eliot.[59]

One significant consequence of the elective system was that the Protestant schools and others began to introduce biblical literature courses into their formal curricula. In one sense this was not an innovation. The colleges had always offered Bible study as a part of the extracurricula. Also, the classical studies included—even if indirectly—some instruction in biblical subjects, primarily through the courses in mental and moral philosophy. The difference between religious study in the old curricula and the new courses was something like the difference between a topical sermon that draws upon the Bible to illustrate and give authority to major points and an expository sermon which starts with the biblical text and develops its applications from it. In a few places, such as McPherson, Bible courses appeared as early as the 1880s. More typically, however, colleges added them in the 1890s and 1900s. Such was the case, for example, at Wellesley, Carleton, Franklin, Colorado College, Alabama, Columbia, and Barnard. Some colleges, particularly in the West, introduced Bible courses as late as the second or third decade of this century.[60]

While the more cautious Protestant colleges were gradually accepting larger degrees of election, institutions such as Harvard which had been less inhibited in adopting election began to recognize that students often graduated with courses of study severely lacking in unity and design. Many agreed with Eliot's successor at Harvard, Abbott Lawrence Lowell, that "the best type of liberal education in our complex world aims at producing men who know a little of everything and something well." Consequently, at Harvard and elsewhere in the early twentieth century, colleges began to require their students to choose a course or courses in each of several broad areas (thus the beginning of general education requirements) and also to select a block of courses in one discipline or area (thus the beginning of the requirement to graduate with a "major").[61]

While the elective system contributed to the decline in the integration of learning in the late-nineteenth-century college, the influence of German scholarship upon the increasing number of American professors who obtained their advanced training in that country did also. German universities taught that a trained intellectual should be less a generalist concerned with broad, universal meanings than a specialist concentrating on gaining scientifically accurate mastery of a narrow area of investigation. These German ideals of research and specialization became increasingly accepted in

America as larger numbers of scholars returned from their German training. The number of Americans who had studied in Germany increased from 300 on the eve of the Civil War to 10,000 by World War I. The desire of these professors to pursue more specialized areas of inquiry fitted nicely into the elective system and its encouragement for the instructors to offer more—and, by implication, increasingly specialized—courses.

As professors gained greater expertise in more restricted areas of learning, they relied increasingly upon the lecture rather than the recitation mode of teaching. The growing number of students enrolled in college in the late nineteenth century made lecturing the practical as well as the philosophically preferable method of instruction. Increasingly, the aim of the classroom became discovering new truths rather than discussing traditional ones. To facilitate this new aim, a number of colleges and universities began to introduce laboratories, greatly enlarged libraries, research and seminar courses, and graduate programs. By 1870, Yale and Harvard operated well-developed graduate programs with doctoral students; by 1890, twenty-five universities offered graduate fellowships; and, by 1910 the graduate schools enrolled 6,000 students. In general, the schools adopting these innovations most completely were large, well financed, and, as we shall see in the next chapter, in the process of changing from primarily religious to primarily secular institutions.[62]

While most of the Protestant schools did not introduce graduate programs or actively promote research, most did begin to give an increased emphasis to the library. As new professors came to their teaching positions with increasingly specialized and research-oriented graduate training, and as they began to teach specialized courses, they desired larger libraries for their own use and also for students, whom they now encourgaged to engage in independent and specialized scholarship.

The growth in prominence of the Oberlin library exemplified the general trend. In 1874, the Oberlin collection numbered only 9,400 volumes, a retired minister on a small stipend supervised it, and students and faculty could enter the area housing it for only short periods each day. This began to change in the 1880s, however, and by the end of that decade the library contained 36,000 volumes, which the students were using with much greater frequency.[63]

With the growth of the elective system and the specialized research function, the concept of a uniform college education began to break down. Causing further confusion was the fact that the old admissions procedures were no longer practical. Increasingly, pre-college students obtained their training in public high schools instead of preparatory divisions of the colleges. As the colleges developed individualized curricula, high school officials complained of the difficulty, if not impossibility, of preparing students for widely differing college programs. Also, with the sharply increasing number of students applying for admission, college officials no longer could personally interview all applicants.

The confusion resulting from these changes led the colleges and high schools to cooperate in establishing academic standards and admission requirements. To do this, they formed regional associations. Thus were born the New England Association of Colleges and Secondary Schools in 1885, the Middle States Association of Colleges and Secondary Schools in 1889, the North Central Association of Colleges and Secondary Schools in 1895, the Southern Association of Colleges and Secondary Schools in the 1890s, the Northwest Association of Secondary and Higher Schools in 1917, and the Western College Association in 1924. These associations defined standardized criteria necessary for an institution of acceptable quality. As schools applied for membership in the associations, they were required to meet these standards. The associations gave the high schools guidelines on how to prepare students for college, and they gave the colleges information about the quality of the high schools in which their applicants had studied.[64]

ATHLETICS AND FRATERNITIES

During the late nineteenth century, extracurricular activities on the nation's campuses increased in importance even as they became less directly related to the curricular programs. In the older days when literary societies dominated the extracurricula, debates and orations on important issues effectively complemented the work of the classroom. By 1900, however, college leaders found it difficult to demonstrate that the newer activities were equally appropriate. Many did not even attempt such a justification; Woodrow Wilson, then president of Princeton, found the growth of the new programs very disturbing and complained that "these side shows are so numerous, so diverting, so important if you will—that they have swallowed up the circus. . . ."

Not all college officials objected to the new activities, however. One early and articulate proponent of the idea that colleges should organize well-developed extracurricular programs, particularly in athletics, was Phillip Lindsley, president of the University of Nashville from 1825 to 1850. Lindsley argued that students could not spend all of their time studying. Human bodies needed the invigorating effect of physical exercise. Colleges often faced discipline problems, he thought, because, left to themselves, students devised destructive rather than constructive diversionary activities. It was the responsibility of the colleges, therefore, to provide wholesome activities of several types for all of the students all of the time. "Keep your youth busy," he urged, "and you will keep them out of harm's way."[65]

Gradually, the literary society became merely one of many types of activities in which a student could participate. The decline of the societies occurred most rapidly in those institutions which gave an early and enthusiastic reception to intercollegiate athletics and fraternities. They declined more slowly in the small colleges— particularly those in the West. At Shaw, for example, well into the twentieth century both intramural debating and contests with other members of the Pentagonal Debating League (Morehouse, Knoxville, Talladega, and Johnson. C. Smith) attracted greater student interest than did intercollegiate athletics. Some institutions, like Taylor, not only continued their earlier interests in the literary societies but applied the society emphasis on oratory to reform causes such as those promoting peace and prohibition. Particularly noteworthy were the nationwide student contests of the Intercollegiate Prohibition Association. The general trend, however, was away from debating and oratory, and the most significant activity to replace them was organized athletics. After the Civil War rowing revived, and track and field, lacrosse, archery, polo, and even boxing and wrestling appeared on a limited number of campuses; but it was baseball and especially football that captured the enthusiasm of college students and the general public across the nation.[66]

Baseball became the first organized sport to be played widely on an intercollegiate basis. Although competition in the diamond game began at least as early as the twenty-six-inning Amherst-Williams contest of July 1, 1859, baseball suddenly became very popular during the Civil War; both northern and southern troops enjoyed it immensely. After the war ended in 1865, returning veterans took the new game home—and to college—with them. Consequently, baseball's popularity grew rapidly on campuses and in towns throughout the country—in the West nearly as early as in the East.[67]

The early form of baseball favored the offense. Pitching was slow with no emphasis upon speed or curves, the ball was lively, and defensive players sought to catch the ball without the aid of gloves. Consequently, early scores more closely resembled the results of later basketball contests than of modern baseball games. For example, Wabash defeated DePauw in 1866 by a score of 45 to

32, and a year later the Princeton sophomores triumphed over Yale's second-year men in New Haven by a 58 to 52 count.[68]

Not all colleges accepted the sport immediately. Some opposed it for financial reasons (equipment for the sport was quite inexpensive, although travel costs were a factor). Others thought it might be detrimental to morality and the promotion of Christianity (the non-college teams did tend to attract ruffians as players). Still other colleges thought it dangerous and counterproductive of academic excellence. For example, an 1868 edition of the Albion paper criticized baseball as a "finger destroying" sport which distracted students from higher literary interests.[69]

While baseball was the first big sport to invade the college campus, it did not remain the leading one for long. By the 1870s, college football not only surpassed baseball in prominence, it attracted the interest of the general public to a degree never before realized by any college activity. Beginning with the November, 1869, Rutgers-Princeton game (which resembled soccer more than modern football), the sport spread quickly throughout the East. By the early 1890s, games between Ivy League schools attracted crowds of over 30,000, and Ivy League players upon graduation were often recruited as coaches for other colleges. In the 1890s, over 100 former Yale, Princeton, and Harvard players were coaching at other schools. Thus, what had begun as primarily an Ivy League sport became a national phenomenon by the early years of this century. In 1914, gridiron teams played on 450 campuses.[70]

The enthusiasm which the early game attracted was matched by its violence. In the era before the development of strict regulations and protective equipment, Ivy League teams of the 1870s "kicked not only the ball, but each other." Also tolerated was the practice of "jumping on an opponent's stomach with both feet. . . ." Without effective protective equipment, players died from the violence almost like soldiers in a war, with fatalities from college games reaching a peak of forty-four in 1903.[71]

Responsible educational leaders cried out in protest. President Eliot of Harvard thought that football was to academics what bullfighting was to agriculture. Professor George Groff, a Bucknell faculty member and physician, in 1894 referred to the "barbarous" game of football as a "travesty of athleticism." President Nicholas Murray Butler of Columbia agreed: "This is madness and slaughter." Dean Shailer Mathews of Chicago described football as a "boy-killing, education-prostituting, gladiatorial sport. It teaches virility and courage, but so does war." A college game, he continued, "should not require the services of a physician, the maintenance of a hospital, and the celebration of funerals." Even

John L. Sullivan, the famous heavyweight boxer, noted after watching an Ivy League contest that "there's murder in that game."[72]

Most college officials and medical doctors agreed that the game should be radically altered, if not abolished. At this point Theodore Roosevelt, Walter Camp, and others led a movement to save the sport by ridding it of its most brutal aspects. President Roosevelt had been a sickly asthmatic as a youth and lamented the fact that he had not been able to participate in football at Harvard. Throughout the rest of his life, he repeatedly sought to develop and demonstrate his physical fitness. Camp, later known as "the father of American football," enrolled at Yale in 1876 and made the varsity team in every sport. He was instrumental in beginning the dynasty of Yale teams that thoroughly dominated the sport for the rest of the century.[73] Roosevelt's warning at a 1905 White House conference on football that the kicking, punching, biting, and scratching must end or he would abolish the sport by executive order did result in some improvement; but more was accomplished by the persistent efforts of Camp over several years to lead in the establishment of strict regulations (e.g., eligibility rules and neutral officials with power to penalize unnecessarily dangerous play). Gradually football changed from a violent form of soccer to a relatively humane game which added running with the ball, passing the ball forward, and retaining possession of the ball by advancing it at least ten yards in four plays.[74]

Although baseball and football appeared earlier, it is basketball which has become the most popular sport at the Christian colleges. Basketball was invented in 1891 by James Naismith, a young theological graduate of McGill (Canada) while he was enrolled in the YMCA training school (now Springfield College) in Springfield, Massachusetts. Professor Luther Gulick, chairman of the physical education department, explained to Naismith how not only his Springfield students but participants in YMCA gymnasium activities throughout the country experienced boredom with the lack of an indoor winter sport that could compete in excitement with football, baseball, and track. When Gulick gave Naismith the responsibility for leading a physical education class, he labored intensely to develop a new game that would challenge the students more than the traditional gymnasium activities, yet be less rough than the outdoor sports. Considerable experimentation led to the development of basketball—the only sport of strictly United States origin.

Basketball was an instant success and spread nationwide through the YMCA gymnasiums and the college coaches who had studied at or lived in Springfield. C. O. Beamis, a native of Springfield,

was probably the first coach to introduce the game on the college
level when he taught the sport to his students at Geneva in 1892.
Two former Springfield educators, H. F. Kallenberg and Amos
Alonzo Stagg, coached (and Kallenberg refereed!) the first men's
intercollegiate game, which was won by Chicago over Iowa, 15-12,
in 1896. Women competed in collegiate basketball nearly as early
as the men, even if they usually played a less strenuous form of
the game.[75]

If the early stages of intercollegiate athletics were full of controversy, such also was the case with the other major new extracurricular activity of this period, the fraternity. Technically, the
Greek fraternity movement began with the Phi Beta Kappa Chapter
at William and Mary in 1776. For a time it featured not only literary
interests but also such characteristics of modern fraternities as
oaths, rituals, secrecy, comradeship, a hand-grip, and a desire to
expand to other campuses (Yale and Harvard added chapters in
1779, Dartmouth in 1787, and Union in 1817). Soon, however, with
the encouragement of faculty members, Phi Beta Kappa evolved
into the scholarly honor society that it is today.[76]

The students' desire for secret fraternal organizations controlled
by themselves continued, and the old fraternity idea revived at
Union in the 1820s with the establishment of the first three fraternities that have continued to the present: Kappa Alpha (1825),
Sigma Phi (1827), and Delta Phi (1827). From the New York college, the movement spread rapidly throughout the East, into the
South beginning with Emory in 1841, and across the Appalachian
Mountains where, in the middle 1830s, the Alpha Delta Phi chapter
at Miami became the first western fraternity. Because the fraternity
movement began at Union and because such a large number of
fraternity chapters (400 by the mid-twentieth century) trace their
origins to Miami, both of these institutions claim the title, "mother
of fraternities."[77]

Almost invariably the faculty of a college fought vigorously
against the students' attempts to introduce fraternity chapters;
frequently, however, the faculty conceded to the students after a
bitter battle. For example, at Union in 1832 President Nott strongly
denounced the budding fraternities and warned that "the first
young man who joins a secret society shall not remain in college
one hour." Union lifted this ban a year later. In the late 1860s,
President McCosh of Princeton viewed the fraternities on his
campus as counterproductive to student democracy, discipline, and
morality. He determined that if he "failed to conquer this evil,"
he would resign. The fraternities continued, and so did McCosh
for the next two decades.[78]

It was not only college authorities who opposed the development of college fraternities. In a number of institutions the non-fraternity men—probably motivated by opposition to the social elitism implied by fraternity membership—formed "anti-secret" societies. Typical of the sentiment of these anti-secret student groups is the following statement from the constitution of the Hamilton (N.Y.) Anti-Secret Organization: "Believing that secret societies are calculated to destroy the harmony of college, to create distinctions not founded on merit, and to produce strife and animosity, we feel called upon to exert ourselves to counteract the evil tendency of such associations. . . ." Hamilton's group joined similar organizations at Williams, Union, and Amherst to form the "Anti-Secret Confederation." At Wittenberg (Oh.), nearly as soon as two fraternities appeared, thirty-seven opposing students prepared a thoroughly researched petition calling for college officials to abolish the new student groups.[79]

Sometimes the differences between students and the administration continued long after the fraternities appeared to be well established. By 1870, Ohio Wesleyan had housed Greek societies for seventeen years, yet the trustees suspended all "secret-college fraternities not purely literary." The trustees at Wofford took similar action in 1906 after a full generation of fraternity activity on its campus, and the struggle continued for a decade. After nine Wofford students went to Columbia in 1913 to accept initiation into one of the previously discredited fraternities, they accepted dismissal by the trustees and transferred to Duke. When approximately fifty more Wofford students organized fraternities two years later, however, the trustees, tired of the battle and probably fearful of losing so many students, relented and again officially allowed the fraternities.[80]

Students displayed cleverness as well as persistence in their battles with faculties. For example, the Quakers as a society had opposed secret organizations, but at Whittier (Cal.) in the 1930s Richard Nixon and other students gradually transformed the traditional literary societies into functional, if not nominal, fraternities.[81] The most effective tactic employed by fraternity leaders in their struggles with faculty members was their widespread practice of affiliating local chapter units with the national collegiate fraternity movement. The intercollegiate nature of the fraternal societies was what gave the local chapters their great negotiating strength. Officials of individual colleges often feared to oppose the student groups alone lest they lose their students by transfer to less hostile colleges.

How does one explain the great attraction of fraternities to students and the equally strong reaction against them by school officials? The students enjoyed the sense of power which the fraternities gave them. It was fun to know something that the faculty and administrators did not; it was also satisfying to see the faculty and other students threatened by what in many ways could be defended as good organizations. The fraternities, after all, often gave their members a sense of security, loyalty, and fellowship; they provided experiences in self-government; they sometimes prodded members to greater studiousness; and through their rituals they often promoted moral integrity and the pursuit of religion. The religion promoted by fraternities, however, was usually of a vague, nonspecific variety, as suggested in the following verse by Ernest Crosby:

> No one could tell me where my soul might be;
> I searched for God but He eluded me;
> I sought my brother out and found all three.[82]

Fraternity leaders often exaggerated the virtues of their organizations. For example, many chapters would have viewed as one of their major purposes the claim of the original Phi Beta Kappa chapter that it provided a haven for the free discussion of all issues: "Now then you may for a while disengage yourself from scholastic laws and communicate without reserve whatever reflection you have made upon various objects; remembering that everything transacted within this room is transacted *sub rosa,* and detested is he that discloses it."[83] College students, of course, had always found ways to discuss their innermost feelings in settings apart from the faculty. A major attraction of the fraternity was that it provided an organization to taunt the faculty officially with this reality.

Faculties opposed the fraternities for several reasons. They realized that the Greek societies would reduce their ability to control the lives of the students. Many of them believed that to acknowledge the fraternities officially would be to abandon their God-ordained responsibility to guide the religious and moral development of the students. College officials also shared the concern of the antifraternity students that the new organizations would lead to an antidemocratic elitism. Furthermore, they worried that the introduction of fraternities would upset the off-campus constituencies. Particularly was this the case when a college was affiliated with a denomination which officially opposed such secret societies as the Masons.[84] In general, throughout the past century, the more conservative the theological orientation of a college and its constituency, the less it has received pressure to introduce fraternities and the easier it has been for it to resist whatever pressure has arisen.

While growing democratization, expanding affluence, and curricular and extracurricular development brought major changes to American higher education in the late nineteenth century, the colleges and universities at the same time began to feel the early blasts of the intellectual winds that would come to full force in the new century, largely bringing down the spiritual underpinnings of the old-time college. This ideological revolution is the subject of the next chapter.

Chapter 4

The Movement Toward Secularization

In his 1967 dedicatory address at the opening of Oral Roberts University, evangelist Billy Graham, sensing the university's potential greatness, warned: "If ORU ever moves away from faith in the Bible and faith in God and putting God first, then let us this day pronounce a curse on it. This institution was built by the prayer and the dedication and the money of women and men who love God, who believe the Gospel, and who believe the Bible is the word of God."[1] Graham's concern came from his knowledge that the best-endowed colleges in America have tended to move from a Christian to a secular orientation. Today, even at most church-related colleges, secular modes of thought dominate over the Christian worldview.[2] Students of the subject now use terms like "non-affirming colleges," "Protestant-change colleges," and "post-Protestant colleges" to describe those previously Christian institutions which either have become or are becoming nonreligious in nature.

Gradually over the last century, American higher education in general has changed its spiritual direction to the point that it now exerts a primarily negative effect upon the spiritual development of its students. Whereas during the nineteenth century the great majority of colleges and universities included religious aims among their institutional goals, they identified such purposes only half as frequently by the second decade of the twentieth century. By the 1960s, widespread agreement existed among scholars that the degree of commitment to religious values by the average college student actually declined during his four years of study. A major study by Kenneth Feldman and Theodore Newcomb in 1969 showed that entering freshmen almost invariably listed religious values as their highest values, but religious faith became significantly less important to them by the time they were seniors. A 1962 study of National Merit Scholars produced similar results. In response to the question, "Do you personally feel the need to believe in some sort of religious faith?" 90 percent of the honor students responded in the affirmative as entering freshmen, whereas only 60 percent did so by the end of their junior year. A 1968 study comparing college students with employed non-college students of the same age found two and one-half times as many collegians as non-collegians valued religion less than they did in high school. Not only have most colleges and universities grown in the degree of their secularization; in recent decades an increasing percentage of young people have chosen to enroll in such institutions rather than the continuing Christian colleges.

The process of secularization has not proceeded at a uniform rate in all institutions, yet one still can chart the general course of the secularization process. The major state universities and a limited number of elite private institutions led the secularization movement in the late nineteenth century. They were followed by the second-line state universities and more of the elite private institutions. After the First World War, most colleges of the major denominations began to follow the trend. By contrast, most of the institutions which remain clearly Christian today are aligned with conservative Protestant denominations (e.g., Assemblies of God, most Baptists, Brethren, Christian Reformed, Church of God, Churches of Christ, Evangelical Friends, Free Methodist, Lutheran, Mennonite, Nazarene, and Wesleyan) or, in some cases, transdenominational evangelical constituencies.

Some scholars have observed that the secularization process in higher education is an outgrowth of the secularization of America in general during the last century. To a certain extent this is true; however, one must note that the colleges secularized more than did society as a whole. Before the Civil War, the colleges, as agents of a church dominated by orthodoxy, were much more Christian in their convictions than was society. By contrast, higher education today is considerably more secular than is the populace in general.[3]

SOURCES OF SECULARIZATION

The changes which took place in American thought beginning in the late nineteenth century were so sweeping that they might properly be called a revolution. Before this intellectual revolution, nearly all of the leading thinkers as well as laymen subscribed to a supernatural worldview. Few argued against the idea that the Divine Creator intervenes directly in human affairs in miraculous as well as natural ways, and that he revealed himself supremely through the incarnation of his Son, Jesus Christ, by whose atoning death he seeks to restore sinful humanity to himself. Like the changes in the economy wrought by the Industrial Revolution, the dramatic changes in this prevailing mode of thought occurred gradually and moved forward on several fronts simultaneously. As the Industrial Revolution witnessed interrelated changes in industrial production, agricultural production, and transportation, the intellectual revolution saw simultaneous challenges to the traditional worldview coming from such fields as biblical interpretation, theology, philosophy, sociology, psychology, economics, and particularly the biological and physical sciences.[4]

Higher criticism as a method of biblical interpretation became especially popular in Germany, where so many American scholars were studying during the late nineteenth century. It gained prominence through the promotion of such thinkers as Friedrich Schleiermacher (1768-1834), Albrecht Ritschl (1822-1889), and Adolf von Harnack (1851-1930). Higher criticism contended that a scholar could best understand the Bible and all other books recording the literature and history of ancient peoples by studying them in the historical context of their societies. The orthodox did not automatically reject this approach to biblical interpretation, for they believed that when one pursued it in an attempt to gain a more precise knowledge of God's purpose, it could be very worthwhile. What they did vigorously protest, however, was the tendency of many of the higher critics to combine their approach with an underlying assumption that the Bible was primarily a human book. This assumption became increasingly common in American colleges and universities as more and more of the American graduate students in Germany returned to assume positions in higher education in this country.

One such returning scholar, Benjamin Baker, became pastor of the university church at Yale; he observed in 1920 that "there is no greater service men like ourselves can do for our age than to sweep away the fogs and obscurities which gather around the figures of Jesus and Paul." Professor William Clarke of Colgate also represented this new trend when he wrote:

> Hitherto I had been using the Bible in the light of its statements, but now I find myself using it in the light of its principles. . . . I am not bound to work all its statements into my system; nay, I am bound not to work them all in; for some of them are not congenial to the spirit of Jesus and some express truth in forms that cannot be of permanent validity.

An increasing number of intellectuals, then, began to look to the Bible more as a source of religious history and general wisdom and inspiration than as the unique source of divinely revealed truth.[5]

At the same time, philosophers and thinkers in other areas also began to develop new conclusions about how best to search for truth. A system of thought known as logical positivism began to gain acceptance. Applied first in the natural sciences, logical positivism accepted as valid only those things which could be verified by the scientific method. The orthodox criticized this epistemological approach and labeled it "scientism," or the worship of the new god of the scientific method.

Another increasingly influential approach to truth, developed in Germany, was relativism. First, scholars had become less concerned about searching for universal meanings and more concerned with discovering new, limited bits of factual knowledge. Then, they developed the concept that one no longer could find universal truths. Belief in absolute eternal verities such as those expressed in the Bible increasingly gave way to a philosophy of relativism that suggested that what is true for one may not necessarily be true for another, and vice-versa.

Those who accepted much of the new thought but did not wish to give up all of their traditional Christian beliefs embraced a form of theology called liberal Protestantism. Such a view allowed its adherents to continue to embrace the moral and ethical teachings of the Judeo-Christian tradition while rejecting the supernatural elements of that faith, including the divinity of Jesus. Those who downgraded the supernatural aspects of Christianity often placed a heavy emphasis upon its sociological dimensions. The result was a revival of the social gospel which had characterized much evangelical effort before the Civil War. In 1903, Timothy Dwight, president of Yale (grandson of the earlier Yale president of the same name), compared the emphasis of preachers at his university during the first half of the nineteenth century with those that appeared at the end of the century: "The thought of the personal soul of the individual man . . . is less prominent than it was in the earlier days." By the turn of the century, he continued, the important question asked at Yale about one's religion was "What are its outgoings in efforts for other men?" Similarly, George Harris, president of Amherst, noted that at his college there now was "preaching on the real human Christ and on the service of man to man. Sermons are ethical and spiritual rather than theological . . . and irrational doctrine is discarded, but faith, hope, love, and character are exalted."[6]

Perhaps no college surpassed Oberlin in its social-gospel emphasis. When Theodore Roosevelt stopped there during his 1912 presidential campaign, he noted, "This is the community of the applied square deal . . . what I preach, you put in practice."

Nationally known social-gospel leaders identified with the Ohio school. Washington Gladden of nearby Columbus made regular lecture appearances there, and Walter Rauschenbusch and Josiah Strong enrolled their children in the college. Also, an impressive number of social science professors and leaders in state universities and colleges actively participated in the social-gospel movement. Many institutions of higher education that are predominantly secular now gave considerable emphasis to liberal Protestant theology and social-gospel activity at some period between their orthodox Christian past and the present.[7]

Of the several factors influencing the transformation in the intellectual orientation of higher education from religious to secular, none caused greater controversy nor effected more sweeping change than did the gradual acceptance of Darwinian biology. Darwinism presented a novel perspective which invited reevaluation of traditional values in all the disciplines. As one measure of its impact, science began to surpass classical studies as the most prestigious intellectual subject.[8]

Following the publication of the *Origin of Species* in 1859 and its companion piece, *The Descent of Man*, in 1861, few American colleges rushed immediately to embrace the new thought. A reporter from the New York *Observer* in 1880 asked the presidents of Yale, Rochester, Princeton, Lafayette, Amherst, Union, Williams, Brown, and Hamilton whether they permitted their professors to teach that "man at least as far as his physical structure is concerned" was evolved from the animal kingdom, and each of the presidents responded negatively. Gradually, however, college presidents began to look the other way while the science professors accepted and taught the evolutionary theory. At Amherst, for example, when President Seelye reluctantly allowed Benjamin Emerson to teach physical science in a naturalistic manner, the instructor expressed appreciation that "the old fellow left us alone." Even in those institutions whose presidents quickly encouraged evolutionary teaching (e.g., Harvard, Johns Hopkins, Cornell, Stanford, Chicago), battles still usually occurred within the faculties over the new theory. The late-nineteenth-century Harvard science faculty, for example, contained both the best-known American proponent (Asa Gray) and the best-known critic (Louis Agassiz) of evolution.[9] Generally, the proponents of evolution won these battles and took the theory into the classroom.

Almost invariably, the first generation of scientists to embrace Darwinism attempted to reconcile it with the Christian faith. Asa Gray insisted that Darwinism was not harmful to religion as long as one accepted the view that the Creator designed the process. Professor Albert Wright of Oberlin argued that nothing in the theory necessarily conflicted with the Christian faith, and Joseph LeConte of the University of California proudly declared the ideal Christian man to be at the apex of the evolutionary process. President McCosh of Princeton, one of the most significant early converts, accepted evolution as "the method by which God works."[10]

Others thought differently. While Louis Aggasiz allowed for evolutionary development within the biblical kinds, he insisted that the differing species resulted from separate acts of creation by God. James Dwight Dana of Yale, one of the most respected geologists of the late nineteenth century, steadfastly rejected Darwinian thought. At the end of his career in 1890, he announced in his last public statement: "Science has made no real progress toward proving that the divine act was not required for the creation of Man. No remains of ancient man have been found to indicate a progenitor of lower grade than the lowest of the existing tribes." President Frederick Barnard of Columbia, himself a scientist, insisted in 1873 that if organic evolution were true, then one could no more confidently proclaim the existence of God or the immortality of the soul. "If the final outcome," Barnard argued, "of all the boasted discoveries of science is to disclose to men that they are more evanescent than the shadow of the swallow's wings upon the lake . . . give me then, I pray, no more science. . . ."[11]

The first generation of evolutionists believed they were helping save Christianity by accepting Darwinism. President McCosh of Princeton announced that he was "happy to report that there is little disposition in this college toward scepticism or scoffing. I do my best to guard against these, but, I do this not by keeping the young men ignorant of prevailing errors. . . . This is the most effective of all means to produce infidelity." Even President Andrew D. White of Cornell, whose book, *A History of the Warfare of Science With Theology in Christendom* (1896), greatly helped defeat orthodoxy in academic circles, held strongly as a liberal Protestant to what he saw as the essence of Christianity. He viewed those who opposed the new theory as joining the long, pathetic tradition of antiintellectual zealots throughout history who have fought the discovery of new truth by wrongly tying the Christian faith to outmoded scientific theories. Later White must have been greatly dismayed to note that his campaign to save Christianity by liberalizing it only helped establish an atmosphere congenial to the secularism and relativism which he hated.[12]

John Fiske and Henry Drummond joined White as the most effective spokesmen in persuading American Protestant leaders to combine evolution with their traditional Christian beliefs. Fiske, a lecturer at Harvard and probably the leading American popularizer of and proselytizer for Darwinism, expressed his view in *The Destiny of Man Viewed in the Light of His Origin* (1884). Drummond's *Natural Law and the Spiritual World* (1883) exerted perhaps even more influence than did the work of Fiske in converting American Protestant theologians to Darwinism. To an unusual degree, Drummond combined evangelical zeal with his argument that evolution was God's way of doing things. Yale undergraduate William Lyon Phelps in 1887 brought Drummond to his campus where the author spoke nightly for two weeks. "I have never seen so deep an impression made on students by any speaker on any subject as that made by Henry Drummond," Phelps recalled.[13]

Not all of the early professors and students who accepted Darwinism sought to make it compatible with the biblical record. One Michigan State freshman wrote home that his professor "is a strong evolutionist" who "succeeds in converting many of his students to this theory and although he reconciles it to the Bible, they, when once set thinking, do not always." Some university leaders attempted no such reconciliation either for themselves or for their students. President Eliot of Harvard, a chemist, held to a rather ambiguous concept of God as a glorious "transcendent intelligence." David Starr Jordan, Stanford president and a biologist, was critical of the atheistic evolutionist, but, like Eliot, Jordan did not subscribe to a personal Christian deity. Rather, he believed in an abstract "power that made for righteousness."

In general, the evolutionary theory was accepted earlier and more completely in the state universities than in the denominational colleges and seminaries, in the church colleges under loose control than in the church colleges under tight control, and in the North and West than in the South. It also gained acceptance more easily at an institution if its first advocates there were known for their Christian piety and dedication (such as William L. Poteat, a biologist and later president at Wake Forest).[14]

Methodist and Baptist colleges in the South voiced some of the strongest criticisms of the theory during the nineteenth century. For example, when in the 1880s the West Virginia Methodists not only lost control of the state university at Morgantown but also discovered that professors there were teaching evolution, they expressed great dismay. The annual conference committee on education declared, "No college which permits its professors to insinuate skepticism into immature and impressionable minds, who antagonize scripture with science falsely so-called, can expect any favor from Christian parents." Given this distrust of the state university, it is not surprising that the Methodists three years later began West Virginia Wesleyan college at Buckhannon. One of the most widely publicized cases of professorial dismissal for teaching the new evolutionary ideas occurred at Vanderbilt, when Alexander Winchell lost his position even though his acceptance of the idea of evolution stopped short of including man. Before the turn of the century, most southern professors who felt strongly about promoting the theory had moved North.[15]

Although evolution suffered many defeats, it gradually gained acceptance in most institutions, including many of those that for years had bitterly resisted it. This happened in large part because year after year increasing numbers of science instructors in more and more colleges had received their training in graduate schools where the predominant professors and textbooks expressed sympathy for the evolutionary hypothesis.

While the decline in the acceptance of Christian orthodoxy by the leaders of thought has been the primary source of secularization in higher education, there have been other, more indirect causative factors. Beginning about 1850, American society became increasingly pluralistic. The immigration of Irish Catholics and German Catholics and Jews at mid-century, followed by the larger influx of eastern European Catholics, Orthodox Christians, and Jews between 1890 and 1915, reduced the Protestant religious consensus. No longer would Protestant denominations so easily dominate public institutions, including the state colleges and universities. This growing religious pluralism combined with the new systems of naturalistic thought to lead to the modern concept of the separation of church and state. In the state universities, this separation meant that the Christian faith ceased to be the integrating center of the educational process.

MARKS OF SECULARIZATION

As the new ideological influences began to gain acceptance on many campuses, the philosophical orientation of those institutions began to change. No longer did they operate from Christian premises and promote Christian purposes. The rate and degree of change has varied from college to college, but the process of change has been remarkably uniform; therefore, the characteristics marking that change have been similar.

The ultimate measure of the extent to which a given college in a given period—past or present—has moved toward secularism is how completely the college personnel still believe that the central act of history (and thus the key to ultimate meaning and truth in the universe) is the supreme revelation of God to humanity through

Christ. When doubt begins to grow on this primary issue, many of the later stages in the secularization process follow quite naturally. For example, as key decision-makers begin to believe that the Christian religion is merely one of the many good systems of thought and that Jesus was only a good man, there remains little reason to hire only Christian scholars rather than good and knowledgeable scholars of all religions; to maintain a Bible requirement for all students instead of a course in religion or values in general; or to commit precious college resources to maintaining a carefully planned program for campus-wide Christian worship. Very few, if any, institutions have moved quickly from being predominantly Christian to being predominantly secular. Almost invariably they have gone through an intermediate step in which they seek to promote religious values in general without giving specific preference to the Christian religion.

Colleges in this transition, regardless of when the change has occurred, usually have displayed the following marks:

1. The public statements about the Christian nature of the institution begin to include equivocal rather than explicit phrases; these statements often describe Christian goals in sociological but not theological terms.

2. The faculty hiring policy begins to place a reduced emphasis upon the importance of the scholar being a committed Christian, and subsequently fewer professors seek to relate their academic disciplines to the Christian faith.

3. The importance of the Bible and the Christian religion in the general education curriculum declines.

4. The previously strong official institutional support given to religious activities in general and the chapel service in particular declines.

5. The institution begins to reduce and then perhaps drop its church affiliation or, if it be an independent institution, it tends to reduce its interest in identifying with interdenominational and parachurch organizations.

6. Budget decisions begin to reflect a reduced emphasis upon the essential nature of Christian programs.

7. An increasing number of students and faculty members join the college community in spite of rather than because of the remaining Christian influences, and the deeply committed Christian students begin to feel lonely.

One can tell much about the religious orientation of a college by carefully examining its catalog. A college with decidedly Christian purposes will usually say so unmistakably. For example, note the following statement at the beginning of the 1980–81 Concordia (Moorhead, Minnesota) catalog: "The integrating element for the curriculum and life in the liberal arts college of the church is the revelation of God in Jesus Christ. . . . This concept of our shared life in Christ . . . involves the entire program of the college . . . for all of life is to be viewed as under the lordship of Jesus Christ." On the other hand, denominational colleges which have begun moving in the direction of secularization often describe themselves as church-related rather than Christian because of a fear that the latter term suggests a narrow or sectarian intellectual orientation. Some colleges proclaim a continuing connection with the Christian religion by identifying with its broad social principles as opposed to its specific theological ones. For example, one college currently notes that it retains a "basic Christian outlook in the values it espouses," and another states that "the focus of . . . its church-relatedness is the enhancement of human dignity in the world." Still other colleges frankly describe their relationship to the Christian faith as a historical but not current one.

Some Protestant college catalogs contain misleading claims about the religious nature of their institutions. In some cases, colleges simply neglect to update their philosophical positions. In other cases, the neglect is intentional and is meant to avoid communicating to the constituencies the precise nature of the institutions. This sometimes occurs when denominational colleges seek to placate church constituencies which subscribe to a greater degree of orthodoxy than do the colleges. The old academic proverb, "Nothing lies like a college catalog," contains some truth, but it is probably less true now than in former years, since colleges have become increasingly sensitive recently about possible legal action or governmental intervention resulting from misleading catalog statements.[16]

In addition to examining college catalogs, another way to trace changes in the religious nature of an institution is to compare the earlier and later written histories of the college. When a college has changed from Christian to secular, almost invariably its later historians, as compared to its earlier writers, show much less enthusiasm for—and sometimes less understanding of—the intensity and pervasiveness of the Christian faith in the beginning years.

As late as the 1880s, most church-related colleges still required religious qualifications for faculty members; this requirement also existed in most state institutions for faculty who taught in con-

troversial fields. By the turn of the century, many colleges began
to discard this employment policy. For example, early in the twentieth century Oberlin hired a Unitarian candidate over a Methodist
one to fill a German instructorship because the Unitarian was
apparently better qualified academically. Such a decision probably
made sense for a liberal Protestant institution such as Oberlin had
become because liberal Protestantism and Unitarianism then
expressed similar theological views. In reaction to this tendency,
other institutions began to reaffirm earlier practices of hiring only
Christians. For example, the trustees at West Virginia Wesleyan
in 1900 resolved that "hereafter, no teachers . . . shall be
employed . . . who are not active Christians," and the school has
abided by this resolution through the time of the writing of its latest
history in 1965.

By the mid-1960s, the Oberlin position had become more typical
than the West Virginia Wesleyan one, for by mid-century even most
church-related colleges no longer formally required evidence of
Christian faith on the part of their new appointees. Today, intense
debate continues on this issue in colleges whose constituency
includes both strong conservative and strong liberal forces. For
example, the college and denominational leaders of the Lutheran
Church in America—the most liberal branch of American
Lutheranism—have been struggling recently with the results of their
hiring practices. During the 1960s, when it was difficult to hire
qualified instructors, their colleges began to employ some non-
Christian faculty members. Today 15 percent of the non-Lutheran
faculty members identify themselves as indifferent or opposed to
religion.[17]

Usually, a secularizing institution chooses no longer to maintain
a meaningful general education requirement in biblical studies.
Some institutions which were secularizing at the time of the growth
of the elective system simply failed to introduce courses in biblical
studies to replace the older courses in mental and moral philosophy,
natural theology, and evidences of Christianity. Others that did
add such courses either did not require them or later broadened
the requirement by choosing between a Bible course and a wide
range of other religious and metaphysical subjects (e.g., "Living
Religions of Asia," "Patterns of Religious Experience," or
"Religion as Story"). Such a curricular arrangement often suggested that the college, while continuing to believe that the study
of religion was important, no longer believed that the Judeo-
Christian tradition was uniquely important in understanding the
meaning of the universe. Some colleges and universities—
particularly the state-owned ones—even adopted the curious posi-

tion that the Christian religion was no longer an appropriate area for intellectual inquiry.

A decrease in the strong institutional support given to religious activities has been one of the more visible symptoms of a decline in the Christian orientation of colleges. It often has followed gradually after the appointment of increasing numbers of noncommitted Christians to the faculties. This mark appears in something as simple as a decrease in the tendency to open faculty meetings with prayer or as basic as the reduction and then elimination of campus community worship services. Repeatedly, the secularization battle has been fought most visibly on the issue of required chapel. Usually the practice of required chapel continued well into the period of secularization, so that required chapel—or even chapel at all—seemed somewhat out of place. Frequently when a secularizing school continued chapel, it did so to provide a sense of institutional unity. Nevertheless, chapel services in secularizing institutions usually became increasingly unpopular with the students because the students saw the requirement as inconsistent with the changing position of the institutions and because this reduced commitment made the colleges reluctant to allocate sufficient resources to guarantee quality programming.[18]

Sometimes, growth in the size of the student body beyond the seating capacity of the chapel provided the occasion for giving up required chapel. If a college's growing secularization was not itself a sufficient force to cause the institution to abandon required chapel, the contemplation of the expense necessary to provide an enlarged facility did. The value of required chapel no longer continued to rank sufficiently high on the list of institutional goals to warrant a major financial investment to continue it. Even the building of a new chapel has not always been an indication that a college was not moving in the secular direction, for sometimes a college has accepted an unsolicited gift of a chapel from a well-meaning philanthropist so as to be able to retain his good will for future gifts. Under such circumstances, the existence of a new chapel building did not assure that it would serve its intended purpose.[19]

When a college has abandoned its chapel program, it usually has done so slowly. First, the frequency and maybe even the length of the chapel services are gradually reduced. Then required chapel is changed to voluntary chapel, often with impressive sounding rationales such as, "We don't want to force religion artificially on anyone anymore"—as though a chapel requirement is more akin to the medieval state-church system than to the other graduation requirements of the college. Usually when a college ends its practice of required chapel, what it is saying is, "We don't think that Christian worship is very important anymore, certainly not as important as other requirements such as English composition or physical education activities." This isn't always the case, however. Calvin in 1971 "decontrolled" chapel attendance because of an abundance rather than a lack of Christian instruction in other parts of the college program. As the college's historian noted: "Intelligent and spiritual members both of the student body and faculty have never been convinced that chapel is a necessary element in a Christian college whose classrooms professedly embody a religious spirit."[20]

Compulsory chapel disappeared first at the newer state universities—led by Wisconsin in 1869—and then at most of the other major state universities by the turn of the century. Harvard moved to a voluntary system in 1886, and many of the other older private schools followed its example by the 1920s. A large majority of the state colleges also abandoned required chapel before 1930. Most of the smaller church colleges continued their regular religious services into the mid-twentieth century. By the eve of World War II, compulsory chapel still existed at 91 percent of church-related colleges, 56 percent of independent colleges and 11 percent of state institutions. By comparison, at the same time chapel services of either the voluntary or the required type continued to operate in 100 percent of church-related colleges, 84 percent of independent institutions, and 27 percent of state institutions.[21]

A close correlation has existed between the attitude of the faculty and students of a college toward the sponsoring denomination and the extent to which that denomination continued to proclaim an orthodox Christian theology. Secularizing denominations have tended not only to produce secularizing colleges but also colleges which wish to be free of denominational control. For example, church-college relations tend to be much more positive in Lutheran, Episcopalian, Southern Baptist, and the small evangelical and fundamentalist groups than they do in the other major Protestant denominations. The colleges of the latter churches usually are more liberal theologically than are their denominations. Frequently, as the ideological gap between college and church widens, the two reduce and then end their relationship. When the official divorce occurs, it is merely the culminating act of a secularizing process that had been taking place for many years. An important related factor in the separation of church and college is the extent to which the denomination operates with a congregational polity. This factor helps to explain why so many of the earliest church colleges to go independent originally had been associated with the Congregational church.[22]

A development related to the disassociation of church and college but one which is not necessarily a mark of secularization in itself has been the reduced role of ministers in the governance of the colleges. Until the late nineteenth century, most colleges regularly selected ministers for presidents. This pattern ended at Harvard in 1869, Denison in 1889, Illinois in 1892, Yale in 1899, Princeton—in the person of Woodrow Wilson—in 1902, Marietta in 1913, Bowdoin in 1918, Wabash in 1926, and Oberlin in 1927. Similarly, clerical influence on boards of trustees has sharply declined over the years. In the early days of Pomona (Cal.), which opened in 1887, clergymen—especially Congregationalist ones—dominated the governing board. Gradually, however, they were replaced by ranchers, lawyers, and businessmen, so that only two preachers continued on the board by 1930. Between 1884 and 1926, the percentage of clergymen on governing boards declined by 50 percent at Amherst, by 60 percent at Yale, and by 67 percent at Princeton. Additionally, a well-known study of fifteen private colleges showed similar results: the clergy representation on the boards of these institutions declined from 39 percent in 1860 to 23 percent in 1900 to only 7 percent by 1930.[23]

THE PROCESS OF SECULARIZATION: THE UNIVERSITIES

Higher education began moving away from a Christian orientation even before the Civil War, when Harvard embraced Unitarianism. Although the roots of Harvard's movement toward the Unitarian faith began as early as the presidency of Edward Holyoke in the eighteenth century (1737–1769), a more decisive turning point came in the early 1800s when, within a two-year period, the university appointed Unitarian Henry Ware as the Hollis professor of divinity and elected Rev. Samuel Webber, a virtual Unitarian, as president. A few years later, Harvard reinforced its earlier decisions by appointing an unquestioned Unitarian, John Kirkland, to succeed Webber. By 1831 the fourteen Harvard faculty members included six Unitarians, only one Calvinist, three other Protestants, three Roman Catholics, and one Sandemanian. President Josiah Quincy, who succeeded Kirkland in 1829, vigorously defended the school against its trinitarian critics. He charged the Calvinists particularly with seeking not only to rid Harvard of Unitarianism but also to put Calvinism back in control of the institution. Later, President Eliot made the curious claim that the best way to keep Harvard nonsectarian was to appoint only Unitarians to professorships and key positions. Harvard Divinity School, which began in 1816, became even more completely Unitarian than did the college. Before 1870, the seminary hired only Unitarians, and most of the students were preparing for the Unitarian ministry.[24]

Frequently it is easier to start a new institution than to change the orientation of one already established. Just as Yale began a century earlier largely in reaction to the loss of Congregational influence at Harvard, so in the early nineteenth century Amherst and Andover Seminary arose in reaction to the growing Unitarianism at the nation's oldest college. Noah Webster wrote that the professed purpose of Amherst was to "change the progress of errors which are propagated from Cambridge." Andover began in 1808, even before the official beginning of Harvard Seminary, as a place to train orthodox ministers. President Timothy Dwight of Yale long had wished to establish a similar seminary at his institution. Yale realized his goal, however, only after his death. In the 1820s, Dwight's prize pupil, Nathaniel W. Taylor, became the first incumbent of the Dwight professorship of theology and thus the first instructor in the Yale Divinity School.[25]

The family of Oliver Wendell Holmes, Sr. exemplifies the transition from trinitarianism to Unitarianism in the New England intellectual tradition. Holmes's father, Abiel, served as the long-time orthodox minister of the First Congregational Church of Cambridge. Throughout his tenure there (1772-1829), he steadfastly refused to allow Unitarian doctrine to be promoted, even though that position contributed to his demise as minister. Oliver was born in 1809 and grew to manhood while the struggle raged. He attended Harvard during the early period of Unitarian success there, graduating in 1829. He became a committed Unitarian, but, unlike others of that faith, he went beyond the mere neglect of orthodoxy to fight it openly and vigorously. One of his most famous literary accomplishments, "The Deacon's Masterpiece, or the Wonderful One-Hoss-Shay," describes in parable form the downfall of Calvinism. Holmes despised the old theology which he thought only had the effect of

Scaring the parson into fits,
frightening people out of their wits.[26]

Antebellum Unitarianism appeared at other colleges but succeeded nowhere else. President Asa Merser of Brown gradually embraced the Unitarian faith and consequently was forced to resign after twenty-four years as president and thirty-nine years of institutional affiliation. While a student at Bowdoin in 1824, Henry Wadsworth Longfellow noted that only a handful of students joined him as members of the college Unitarian Society: "We are as small as a grain of mustard seed."[27]

In general, the major state universities and the best-endowed private institutions were the earliest to break with the Christian conception of higher education. Harold Bolce, a researcher in the early twentieth century, visited and studied American colleges for more than two years. In 1909, after attending classes, interviewing faculties and administrators, and studying written records, Bolce reported with dismay that relativistic philosophies were replacing Christian ones in the classroom:

> There is a scholarly repudiation of all solemn authority. The decalogue is no more sacred than a syllabus. . . . From the college standpoint there are no God-established covenants. What happens at the primaries is more to the point than what took place in Palestine.
>
> They teach young men and women plainly that an immoral act is merely one contrary to the prevailing conceptions of society; and that the daring who defy the code do not offend any Deity, but simply arouse the venom of the majority—the majority that has not yet grasped the new idea.[28]

Despite the general momentum toward secularism, many state institutions remained considerably religious well into the twentieth century. The first set of rules for Arkansas State, which began in 1909, resemble those in vogue at church colleges before the Civil War. Frank Strong, president of Kansas, in his 1902 inaugural address argued that the state university should provide Christian, even though non-sectarian, training. The country, he stated, needed educated Christian men, and the university because of its "very atmosphere, by the purity of life of its Faculty, by the moral and religious wholesomeness of its entire . . . influence, . . ." should promote the "deepest spiritual life and growth."[29]

Even into the mid-twentieth century some state institutions maintained religious claims. For example, promotional literature issued by the University of South Dakota on the eve of the Second World War referred to its faculty as Christian men and women and advertised with approval the fact that sorority and fraternity pledges were required to attend church each Sunday. As late as the 1950s, Mississippi State collected student fees to support the YMCA chapter. In general, the black state colleges maintained required attendance at religious services later than did the predominantly white state institutions. This happened in part because several state legislatures encouraged it as "a good and safe thing" for blacks, but also because Afro-Americans were religiously homogeneous— overwhelmingly they were Baptists and Methodists. In 1945 one researcher found compulsory religious exercises in eleven of the nineteen black state colleges surveyed. Some of them also required attendance at prayer meetings.[30]

Those who wished to retain Christian influences in the universities fought a steadily losing cause. Some within the universities and especially the church college leaders lamented this loss and expressed their protest publicly. President Noah Porter of Yale reacted against the new theories gaining acceptance at his institution. He perceived that "hasty and superficial generalization characterizes . . . the brilliant remancing of the eloquent scientific lecturer, in the flippant theories that characterize our historic and literary criticism, and the confident dogmatism of our one-sided theorists in psychology, ethics, and sociology." Porter's most controversial professor was William Graham Sumner, who used as a textbook the writings of Herbert Spencer, the man considered by many to be the most dangerous anti-Christian of the age.[31] Sometimes the church college complaints came from narrow sectarians who resented the fact that their denominations no longer controlled the state universities. In other cases, the critics simply lamented the fact that the Christian religion in general received less emphasis in the universities.

The criticisms of the church college leaders frequently were very pointed. The Geneva catalog of 1878 stated that "the determined attempts to secularize . . . higher institutions of learning should be met by the most uncompromising action by all truly Christian colleges." Presidents W. D. Goodman of Baldwin (now Baldwin-Wallace) and Blanchard of Wheaton complained that leaders of the new thought, while claiming a growing objectivity in the search for truth, frequently displayed the worst form of intellectual narrowness. Goodman argued that positivists who deny a first cause and rationalists who refuse to acknowledge the legitimacy of truth obtained through spiritual experience limit themselves in an unscientific way: "This exclusion of any kind of knowledge is unscientific though done in the name of science. To refuse to investigate the supernatural is a form of scientific bigotry." Blanchard was no less severe:

> The discussion of what is vaguely called "the modern method" of education . . . means no Bible and no religion of Christ. The study of psychology is the study of dead men's brains to learn how those brains, while living, secreted thought. Yet these brave champions of liberalism and materialism are really the most intolerant, narrow, and bigoted men . . . they cry up "science," "method," "new education," and whatever fine words are used to cover and conceal the intended complete divorce of education from God and His Word. . . . Christianity speaks now in whispers in common school associations and state universities.[32]

If the church colleges were critical of the secularizing tendencies of the larger universities, university spokesmen sometimes responded in kind with criticisms of church schools. Few opposed the church colleges more vigorously than did President White of Cornell. He accused them of being petty in their criticism, mediocre in their teaching, and narrow-minded. Perhaps he reacted so strongly because the church college leaders viewed his institution as one of the most secular universities in the land. White claimed that Cornell was a Christian university, but a nonsectarian one. In fact, the New York school was neither Christian nor godless. The misunderstanding existed because some denominational leaders equated nonsectarianism with atheism, while White confused nonsectarian Christianity with a Christianity that was moving in the direction of Unitarianism. Cornell students viewed the battle between White and the church colleges less seriously than did the president, and they lightheartedly formed such "tongue-in-cheek" organizations as the Young Men's Infidel Association and the Cornell Young Men's Heathen Association. The press publicized this student activity, and many readers became outraged.

Other university leaders joined the attack. President Eliot of Harvard proclaimed in 1891 that it was "impossible to found a university on the basis of a sect," and that great universities taught religious tolerance, in contrast to the many small, narrow church colleges which presumably did not. Even more extreme was the view of Professor John W. Burgess of Columbia, who argued that church colleges should die and that there would be no need for them if the secondary schools in every large town added two or three years to their preparatory programs. Students completing such local courses could then go directly to a university. Church colleges, Burgess added, are merely ridiculous imitations of universities. President Jordan of Stanford—the institution which YMCA leader John R. Mott in 1901 cited as the "most irreligious" university in America—viewed the church school as "a small university, antiquated, belated, arrested, starved. . . ." President Harper of Chicago not only agreed that the church colleges were intellectually inferior, he claimed that they failed in the very area in which they professed to be strong, namely the promotion of sound religion. More typically, he argued, they merely encouraged hypocrisy.[33]

The running battle between the universities and the church colleges was much more than a philosophical debate. The period after the Civil War when the universities were becoming secularized was also the period when it was not yet clear whether the university or the church college would ultimately emerge as the dominant form of American higher education. At the turn of the century, the church colleges still enrolled approximately half of all college students; thus the battle between the two types of institutions was fought in large part over the question of which would win the largest share of public support and student enrollment.

The universities secularized for a variety of reasons. One reason was their quest for a larger worldview than the denominational emphasis of a particular church. Such a concern reflected the growing American sensitivity to the separation of church and state. Another reason universities excluded religious concerns was because such concerns often involved great controversy and were difficult to organize so as to please everybody. Some could not conceive of nonsectarian religion and assumed that the only alternative to sectarian faith was to dismiss religion altogether. Others wished to deemphasize the Christian faith and to replace it with other value and belief systems.

During the early part of the twentieth century, the universities exhibited more opposition than neutrality toward religion. Some institutions viewed religious studies and student religious societies as inappropriate. For example, the University of Oregon voted against creating a chair of religion in the Department of Philosophy because the governing board feared that such a position stood in violation of the state's need for religious neutrality. Furthermore, the west coast university would not let the YMCA and YWCA chapters construct a building on campus and did not favor formal religious exercises of any type on university property.[34]

During the second generation of the twentieth century, university officials began to recognize that their earlier tendency to suspend religious instruction and activity was an undue reaction to the sectarian control of some universities during the nineteenth century. Consequently, after about 1930, these officials significantly increased their interest in religion. Typical of those who apologized for the earlier extreme position was Robert J. Sproul, president of the University of California, who in 1932 stated:

> Is religion itself a legitimate field of learning in the university? Is it a specific experience of the race, a necessity for each growing citizen, and a way of cultural growth for the future, or is it only a vestigial activity, and an antiquated pre-scientific anachronism? For my part I believe that religion (not the sects) is basic to morals, central in our American culture, unique as a dynamic within the individual, able to save us from ourselves and lead us out into nobility. I believe that without religion we are forced to substitute weak conventions for permanent values and abiding standards; that without religion, civiliza-

tion, with no adequate reinforcement for the great strains that come upon it must yield inevitably to disintegration and decay.

Accordingly, religious programs began to appear on the university campus. Some institutions appointed chaplains and religious counselors, and many added courses or even departments of religion. By 1940, 80 percent of the state institutions and nearly all of the independent colleges offered at least one course in religion, and 30 percent of the state institutions and 85 percent of the independent colleges listed departments of religion.[35]

While the universities by the middle period of the twentieth century acknowledged the value of religion more than they had during the first part of the century, they did not necessarily give more support to the Christian religion in particular than had been the case before 1930. They did not view the Christian faith—or even religion in general—as the integrating whole of the educational process as had their intellectual forebears in the old-time college. Although the exclusion of the study of religion in the universities was less pronounced by mid-century than it had been earlier, nevertheless secular values and, in places, even hostility toward religious faith largely characterized the intellectual orientation of the institutions.

One widely publicized study of the religious orientation—or lack of it—of a prominent institution is *God and Man at Yale*, published in 1951 by the brilliant but highly controversial observer William F. Buckley, who attended Yale in the late 1940s. His book discusses more than just religion, but religion figures prominently in it. Buckley observes that, in the intellectual battle between Christianity and agnosticism and atheism, Yale, by mid-century, did not maintain an atmosphere of detached impartiality but rather an antireligious bias. The strongest such bias, he argued, existed in the social science departments; however, even the Religion Department did little to counter the prevalent trend. This profile, even if somewhat exaggerated by Buckley, nevertheless probably represented not only Yale but the situation in the universities in general at mid-century.[36]

In measuring the extent of the success of secularization in higher education, one should note not only the number of institutions which have accepted a secular worldview but also the number of students who are enrolled in these colleges and universities. Those institutions which have secularized most completely have, in the aggregate, enrolled a sharply increasing percentage of the college student market.[37]

THE PROCESS OF SECULARIZATION: THE CHURCH COLLEGES

Nearly all of the church colleges remained essentially orthodox before 1900. In the New England colleges, for example, students talked regularly about religious issues and attended class prayer meetings and daily chapel services. One of the high points of the year in New England and elsewhere was the annual day of prayer for colleges, celebrated since the colonial period on the last Thursday of January. Despite the fact that some student humorists referred to the special day as "the day of whist" for colleges in reference to those who took advantage of the day off from classes to loaf and play cards, most of the students participated in the services of special religious emphasis that day; and across the nation countless churches devoted their mid-week prayer services on that evening to earnest, heavenly petitions on behalf of the college students and their institutions.[38]

If the church colleges did not become more secular in the late nineteenth century, they did become more denominational. Before the Civil War, the colleges had served community needs and drawn upon community resources. In the years following the war, however, they began to attract their students as well as their financial support from denominational constituencies statewide and beyond. As more and more local communities developed public high schools, there became less need to rely upon the community colleges to provide preparatory education for young people. Also, the significant increase in per capita wealth brought by the growth of the economy meant that more families could afford to send their young people to residential colleges away from their home communities. As the young people went away from home to college, they often chose institutions of their own denominations. At the same time, colleges added more denominational representatives to their boards, and they solicited more funds from the wealthy members of their denominations. The peak of denominational influence came in the 1890s and did not sharply subside until about 1930, when the church colleges began to move in a secular direction. The secularization of the church colleges, then, occurred primarily during the second generation of the twentieth century and continues to the present.[39]

Scholars of American higher education have concluded that by the 1960s the traditional church colleges had become more influenced by secular than by Christian thought. Myron Wicke believes that the major period of change began about the end of World War II. Earl McGrath suggests that some colleges consciously broke their religious links while others merely allowed the secular influences to "wear them away." George Buttrick observes that the typical church-related college of the 1960s tended to "dismiss the Bible as a vague and sentimental affair called 'religion,' as an unwarranted intrusion, as 'indoctrination,' or at best as a matter for private conscience." Manning Pattillo and Donald Mackenzie concluded that "the difficulty is that many academic people do not think of religion as concerned primarily with the truth about ultimate reality. Rather it is regarded as a moral code, as a set of ideals, or as a quaint and antiquated body of ideas which educated people are supposed to have outgrown." Robert Pace predicts that, except for the evangelical and fundamentalist colleges, the church-related institutions in this country will no longer be recognizable as Protestant by the turn of the century. Christopher Jenks and David Reisman think that one could almost make such a statement now, for "in most church-related colleges official religious influence is quite dead."[40]

It will surprise some to note that despite the secularizing trend, the great majority of church-related institutions—87 percent according to the Pattillo and Mackenzie survey—continued into the 1960s to require the completion of course work in religion and theology.[41] This fact is not necessarily inconsistent with the secularizing trend, for even state universities in recent decades have discovered that they can offer such courses as a part of a secular curriculum with the instructors usually teaching only from a historical or sociological viewpoint.

While the general trend since the early twentieth century has been for the colleges associated with major denominations to move gradually in a secular direction, some institutions have reversed that pattern. For example, King (Tenn.), a Southern Presbyterian institution, was on the brink of financial collapse in early 1979. It agreed to a proposal presented by a committee of conservative Presbyterians to rescue the college financially on the condition that they be allowed to "make the school unapologetically and enthusiastically an evangelical institution of higher Christian education." Accordingly, the evangelicals hired Wheaton dean Donald Mitchell as president.[42]

One can understand the secularization process better by tracing its development in specific institutions. The cases of Oberlin, Franklin, and Ripon illustrate the general trend. Secularization occurred at Oberlin somewhat earlier than at most church colleges. The steps in the process of change at the Ohio college included (1) a gradual acceptance by professors and students of the theory of evolution and a gradual decline in their confidence that the biblical record was divinely inspired; (2) a gradual acceptance of the liberal Protestant interpretation of the Christian faith; (3) a gradual willingness to hire non-Christians as instructors; (4) the abandonment of the senior Bible requirement; and (5) a gradually increasing desire to upgrade the general academic quality and reputation of the institution without a concurrent and equivalent desire to sustain the previous religious zeal.

Before the Civil War, Oberlin could claim probably the most evangelically intense student body in the country, but by the eve of World War I, it enrolled a student body which was much more motivated by intellectual than religious goals. For example, a 1911 survey of a majority of the Oberlin students on the goals they sought to realize in college showed that they ranked "development of mental powers" as the most important and "development of religious life" as below average. By the latter item the students undoubtedly meant the experience of conversion and the growth of personal piety. They certainly did not mean by it Christian social activism, for this pursuit busily occupied both the students and faculty, led especially by Professor, and later President, Henry Churchill King. More than any other individual, King directed the turn-of-the-century transition of Oberlin into an institution dominated by the liberal Protestant, social-gospel emphasis. Gradually the pursuit of learning and the acquisition of knowledge replaced social-gospel idealism as the dominant purpose of Oberlin. This goal of acquiring knowledge gradually ceased to be associated with liberal Protestantism and increasingly became combined with secular thought.[43]

In 1900, Franklin College operated as a typical northern Baptist college. Its primary institutional purposes included a desire to train "worthy and willing Christian workers." Most of its students— 80 percent—professed the Christian faith, and the college sponsored strong YMCA and YWCA organizations and regular prayer meetings.[44]

In the early 1920s this orthodox pattern at Franklin remained intact. The Biblical Literature Department had expanded its offerings to ten courses. The college desired that the students not only receive a "technical knowledge of the Bible and kindred subjects," but also that they be "offered the opportunity of acquiring a deeper religious conviction and of fostering a religious enthusiasm and zeal." Every student completed a minimum of six hours of study in biblical literature and attended daily chapel services. The catalog described the student religious activities as strong.[45]

By 1950, the six-hour Bible requirement had changed to a three-hour course and the daily chapel requirement to one chapel and two convocation services, both voluntary, per week. The catalog contained no explicit statement of religious purpose.[46]

By the 1970s, the college held voluntary chapel irregularly, and required no Bible or religion course, although all students did enroll in one on the formation of values. The religion courses presented Christianity as a slightly preferable option to other faiths, but the Christianity being presented was a different variety from the one students had studied earlier in the century. The Philosophy and Religion Department announced that the purpose of such courses was to help students understand the contribution of the Judeo-Christian tradition to the formation of the modern world of thought and culture. Today one need not be a Christian to be hired at Franklin, not even in the Philosophy and Religion Department, and a large minority of the faculty is indifferent to religion. Franklin consultants told the institution in the early 1970s that its purpose was unclear and that it should seek to determine it. Subsequently the trustees developed a statement defining Franklin as "a personal college" which seeks the "development on the part of each student of a value system which will enable him to deal effectively with the complexities of modern life."[47]

Ripon College in 1883 described itself as a Congregational and Presbyterian college with "the earnest purpose to conduct the institution on distinctively Christian principles and to have it pervaded with a strongly moral influence." In 1904, the college repeated this statement and announced that each student was expected to attend religious services once daily and would have opportunities to participate in "plenty of other religious services." In 1926, the college described its aim as that of having "the simplicity of the Christian life permeate the institution"; it listed an even broader array of Bible courses than that contained in the 1904 catalog and proclaimed that such courses "are pursued in the spirit of reverent scholarship."[48]

As had been the case at Franklin, by mid-century the religious climate had changed. The formerly sizable Bible Department appeared as only a single course in the new Department of Philosophy and Theology. Also, the four-per-week chapel service of 1926 had been reduced so that "ordinarily two religious chapels and two convocations [were] held each month."[49]

By the late 1970s, Ripon described its primary mission as being "to foster the growth and integration of intellect and character." A recent institutional statement of goals contained no reference to the Christian faith. In the 1978–79 catalog section on affiliation, however, the college did acknowledge its historic ties to the Congregational church and that the college related currently more to the Judeo-Christian tradition in general than to a particular denomination. The tone of the catalog suggested that the college offered opportunities for study in, reflection on, and worship in the Christian religion for anyone who desired them, but that pursuit of truth in this area was not necessarily more important than the pursuit of truth in any other area.[50]

Secularization occurred more slowly in the elite women's institutions than in their male counterparts. Except for Vassar, which abolished compulsory chapel in 1926, the leading eastern women's colleges continued such required religious services into the mid-twentieth century. Perhaps the religious influence continued this long at the women's colleges because of their relatively late founding by individuals who held intensely spiritual goals for their institutions. In the modern period at Vassar, "about the only vestige of religious formalities is the more or less non-denominational—though Protestant—Sunday services at which attendance is voluntary and the congregation may or may not outnumber the choir." The other women's colleges have followed Vassar's example to a considerable degree.

Students at black colleges maintained regular church attendance habits much later than did students in predominantly white colleges. As late as 1945, over 90 percent of the students in black colleges attended church at least twice a month, even though only one-third of the blacks viewed their fellow students as being religious. Apparently, church attendance served a greater social purpose for blacks than for whites, and this may explain the regularity of their attendance. When measured in terms of deep commitment to Christian beliefs, however, little difference apparently exists between the black and the white colleges, for as one student of religion in black colleges noted in 1973: "the remaining doctrinal ties [between the churches and the colleges] have little influence on the ideological stance of students and faculty. Practically no one thinks of these colleges as instruments to perpetuate religious doctrines."[51]

In many ways, the church-related colleges in the modern period resemble the denominations with which they are affiliated. The denominations with the largest membership and influence tend to have the largest number of colleges (see Table 2).[52] The Episcopalian church fits this pattern less well than any other major denomination, for despite its progressive attitude toward education, its affluence, and the contribution of its members to society, it maintains only seven four-year, accredited institutions. In general, the denominations with the most democratic polity maintain the loosest relationships with their colleges. For that reason, college counting becomes especially difficult in a denomination like the United Church of Christ, the current denominational home of the many colleges which identified previously with the Congregational church. While Pattillo and Mackenzie counted twenty-four United Church of Christ colleges, the denomination itself lists thirty without including most of the older, very well known, historically Congregational eastern institutions. Of the schools currently claimed by the United Church of Christ, none dates its origin earlier than 1829 (Illinois College), and none is much larger than 2,000 students (Franklin & Marshall enrolled 2,040 in 1976).

Perhaps no denomination represents a broader variety of theological expression than do the Quakers, and this wide spectrum of opinion is reflected in the Friends colleges, with Swarthmore (Pa.) and Haverford on the left as Protestant-change colleges; Friends (Kan.), George Fox (Ore.), and Malone (Oh.) on the right as evangelical institutions,[53] and Whittier, Guilford (N.C.), Wilmington (Oh.), and Earlham (Ind.) in the center. No denomination has maintained a larger block of primarily orthodox colleges than has the Southern Baptist Convention. The Southern Baptist colleges hire almost no non-Christians as professors and very few non-Baptists as religion instructors or administrators. Perhaps the most liberal Southern Baptist institution is Wake Forest. It maintains a weekly voluntary worship service in its 150-seat chapel rather than its 1,300-seat auditorium. The North Carolina institution requires one course in religion for all students; however, the course need not be on the Christian religion. A recent statement of purpose declared the college's intent to shape the school's policies and practices by Christian ideals and stated that all students should be concerned for spiritual, moral, and physical development.[54]

Almost invariably, church colleges in the modern period have reflected a more liberal orientation than have the church groups affiliated with them. In the major denominations, the colleges have tended to be less orthodox and more secular than the church creedal statements, the church membership, and the church leadership. Frequently churches have complained of the trends in their colleges. For example, a comprehensive study of the Methodist Episcopal colleges in 1932 lamented that many of the institutions failed to give serious thought to their stated purposes and even operated in violation of them. Also, in the 1950s, a formal proposal by the General Conference Commission on Higher Education of the Methodist Church implied a continuing concern with the secular drift in the denominational institutions of higher education when it proclaimed, "Every institution of learning identified with the

Church should rededicate itself openly to its historic mission as a Christian school." The resolutions even called for the colleges to hold public services of rededication for this purpose.[55]

TABLE 2
DENOMINATIONS AFFILIATED WITH
THE PROTESTANT COLLEGES
(1966)

Methodist Church	102
Southern Baptist Convention	52
United Presbyterian Church in U.S.A.	51
United Church of Christ	24
American Baptist Convention	22
Presbyterian Church in U.S.A.	20
Lutheran Church in America	19
Disciples of Christ	18
American Lutheran Church	13
Lutheran Church—Missouri Synod	12
Seventh Day Adventists	12
Episcopal Church	11
Society of Friends	11
Other (50 religious bodies)	111
	478

The movement toward secularization has caused more pain in some institutions than in others. Probably least affected have been those institutions which because of a western location or another reason began late and also affiliated with a relatively liberal and democratic denomination. By contrast, the process of change has created great difficulty in some of the older colleges of the American Baptist Convention. For example, in Maine, where the state Baptist convention has long been more conservative than the denomination and where Colby and Bates had increasingly accepted liberal Protestant thought, the Baptists responded with great vigor. As noted by the Colby historian, "In Baptist churches from Kittery to Caribou, the modernism and secularism of the colleges were being denounced. One Baptist pastor in a rural community told a mother he would rather see her son dead than enrolled in either Colby or Bates." Accordingly the state convention in the 1930s officially broke with the colleges.[56]

VARIETIES OF PROTESTANT HIGHER EDUCATION TODAY

Before discussing the different types of contemporary Protestant colleges, perhaps it would be useful to note the overall size and general character of these institutions. One of the best and most thorough of the modern studies of Protestant—and Catholic—liberal arts colleges, that of Pattillo and Mackenzie in 1966, identified 1,189 private colleges and found 817 of them to be church related. Approximately 475 of these operated in association with a Protestant denomination and perhaps 25 more with an independent Protestant constituency. If one added to them all of the Bible institutes and Bible colleges in operation then, the number would increase to 750; however, if one included only the accredited Bible colleges—in other words those generally recognized undergraduate theological institutions which have general education components—then the result was approximately 550 Protestant colleges. The 1965 enrollment for the individual church-related liberal arts colleges varied from only 19 to over 22,000, with an average of 1,297.[57]

When compared to the enrollment in higher education in general, the percentage of the nation's college students enrolling in church-related institutions in particular and private institutions in general has continually declined. As recently as the 1950s, private institutions enrolled approximately 50 percent of the students in four-year programs. That figure declined from 48 percent in 1954 to 43 percent in 1962 and 30 percent in 1978.

When one includes the junior colleges—whose enrollments grew very rapidly after mid-century—then the private sector by 1965 compared even less favorably, constituting only approximately one-third of American higher education, with enrollment in the church-related higher educational institutions comprising only 17.3 percent of the total enrollment. By 1978 the private institutions could claim only 22 percent of the total higher education enrollment.[58]

In recent years, church-related colleges appear to have achieved more, relatively speaking, with their resources than has higher education in general and the public institutions in particular. Although church-related colleges enrolled only 17.3 percent of the students in 1965, they conferred 25.6 percent of the degrees, employed 22 percent of the full-time faculty members and 32 percent of the general administrative staff, and owned 42 percent of the total library volumes. They received only 15 percent of the current income for education and general expenses, but they held 22 percent of the annual endowment and 35 percent of the scholarship dollars, and they awarded 37 percent of the scholarships. Furthermore, studies in the modern period have shown that church-related colleges produce a disproportionately high percentage of American college professors, researchers, scientists, and doctors.[59]

In general the church-related liberal arts colleges, when compared to the large public institutions, (1) provide more school spirit and unity; (2) experience more personal friendliness between students and faculty; (3) more successfully challenge the students to offer their time and abilities in service to other people and to society in general; (4) offer a more personalized education with the students being treated as individuals and the professors placing greater emphasis upon teaching than research (despite this emphasis, the professors are as active in research and publication as are professors in the small state colleges); and (5) offer their students greater opportunities for participation in a broad variety of cocurricular activities.[60]

In classifying the major types of Protestant colleges, one could, as a careful scholar of Christian higher education recently did, identify institutions by the closeness of the denominational relationship.[61] The most useful approach, however, when dealing with the secularization process, is to identify institutions on the basis of the degree to which they have moved from being orthodox to secular. Within this frame of reference, most institutions can be identified as (1) essentially secular even if nominally Christian, (2) generally religious, (3) liberal Protestant, or (4) conservative Protestant.

The primarily secular college at its best is an objective and tolerant "multi-university" where any and all views on all issues, metaphysical or otherwise, may be presented and respected. At its worst, the secular college indoctrinates the religion of humanism and agnosticism.

While the secular university usually does not provide a planned dialogue to assist its students in developing an overall worldview, the generally religious college at its best intentionally confronts the students with "the ultimate dialogue," namely that between the differing doctrines on the relationship between God and man. At its worst, the generally religious college makes an end of the dialogue and gives the impression that, while it believes religion to be important, specific religious truth is relative.

The liberal and the conservative colleges at their best would agree with the importance of intentionally structuring intellectual dialogue on the differing doctrines of God and man. However, they would do more than the religious college to influence the outcome of that dialogue, because they believe that Christian answers to questions raised by the dialogue are more valid than others as a basis for developing a worldview and making a life commitment.

The liberal and conservative colleges differ from one another in how they explain the Christian voice in the dialogue. Liberals emphasize the ethical and moral teachings of Jesus, believing that they best interpret how God wishes humanity to live and thus provide the context in which all knowledge should be sought. Conservatives agree that Jesus' moral teachings are basic but add to this the foundational belief that the key event of history is the incarnation of God in the person of Jesus Christ, perfect God and perfect man, through whose atoning death each person, estranged from God, may be reconciled to the Creator. Liberals are less certain about the divinity of Jesus and the authority of the Bible—particularly its supernatural elements—than are conservatives. The liberal Protestant colleges at their worst are ideological way stations between orthodoxy and secularism, and while they may insist that in higher education secularism does not necessarily follow a liberalized Christianity, the conservatives with dismay and the secularists with glee remind them that this is what usually has happened. Conservative Protestant colleges at their worst seek to bypass any dialogue over the differing doctrines of the relationship between God and humanity and simply to tell their students what is truth.

The secular institutions include nearly all of the state universities, most of the elite private colleges, and an embarrassingly large number of church-affiliated institutions. Among the private schools, the tendency is for an institution to become increasingly secular as it becomes increasingly independent of denominational financial support, governance, and recruitment of students, and as it achieves higher academic standing. As the major denominations have watched their colleges become less Christian and an increasing percentage of their young people enroll in state universities, they have begun to identify less with their own colleges and more with the more orthodox denominational student centers near the state campuses.

In a very limited number of predominantly secular institutions (e.g., Miami University of Ohio), religious views are given a fair chance to compete with the prevailing secularism.[62] More typically, however, the intellectual balance of power weighs heavily against Christianity. In the state institutions it is often thought that the modern concept of the separation of church and state precludes a serious institutional commitment to explore the religious dimensions of life. Others at state institutions and elsewhere simply think that such explorations are irrelevant for the modern mind. More frequently than secular educationalists would like to admit, a religious emphasis fails to appear in modern higher education primarily because its advocates are outmuscled in the struggle for influence. Whatever the explanation, impressionable young students clearly receive the message that knowledgeable and intelligent people no longer consider serious intellectual inquiry into religion to be a necessary task for the contemporary scholar.

Only a limited number of colleges actively wish to promote serious religious inquiry without favoring the Christian religion. In institutions as well as in individuals, deep religious commitment usually is made to a specific faith rather than to religion in general. When zeal for promoting the Christian faith wanes, institutions become reluctant to commit their limited financial resources to support well-developed programs for serious student inquiry into a broad variety of faiths. The seriously religious although not specifically Christian colleges include Pomona and Wellesley. Pomona, which began as a Congregationalist college, still wishes to be known as a religious institution and attests to that desire by providing (with the other schools of the Claremont Colleges cluster) Jewish, Catholic, and Protestant chaplains who serve the students on a full-time basis and direct the Center for Religious Activities. In addition, Pomona supports a very active religion department with six professors and a wide-ranging curriculum which emphasizes sociological, philosophical, and comparative religious studies.[63]

Wellesley believes that a student's search for personal and spiritual values is sufficiently important that it provides a college chaplain and staff of counselors who have developed a religious program, including corporate worship, that embraces many faiths. The counseling staff itself represents several religious traditions. While participation in all religious programs and services is voluntary, the college does encourage such involvement. Similarly, the college offers the academic study of religion on an optional basis. A student may meet a general education requirement with a course in religion but need not do so. The Department of Religion and Biblical Studies offers a broad range of courses on a variety of religious faiths, with the biblical studies emphasizing the historical and literary critical method.[64]

Sometimes the generally religious college will describe itself as "truly Christian," by which it means that it is supportive of a broad variety of Christian and non-Christian faiths. Rarely, however, do such institutions promote their general religious concerns as vigorously throughout the totality of their program as do the Christian—particularly the conservative Christian—institutions.

A college whose religious orientation probably lies somewhere between that of "generally religious" and liberal Protestant is Texas Christian. It attempts to provide a campus environment "in which religion, especially the Christian religion, functions as the integrating center of learning. Students of all creeds and faiths are welcome, university religious activities are varied in style, celebrating many traditions and honoring them all." The university requires one course in religion and holds "university vespers" each Sunday evening in the chapel. The institution, in other words, desires religion to be the center of the university, for the Christian religion in particular to receive some preference, and for all other religions to be held in respect.[65]

In 1958, even while many church colleges were rapidly secularizing, the Commission of Higher Education of the National Council of Churches issued a classic statement entitled "What Is A Christian College?" which discussed the characteristics that should be found in a liberal Protestant college. The report called attention dramatically to the distance that was developing between mainline denominations and their colleges. It defined a Christian college as one that attempts to develop the whole personality of every student in accordance with the life and teachings of Jesus Christ. It suggested that a college could call itself Christian if the majority of its continuing personnel—and all of those that direct and implement policy—were consciously and actively Christian. The National Council statement also suggested that in a Christian college "the Christian faith is the preeminent discipline, and that the requirement for the study of it should be at least equal to the requirements in any other area . . . , and should as far as possible be sustained throughout the student's four year career." Finally, the report also stated clearly that a church college should present chapel services as part of its total curricular program, with the entire student body in regular attendance.

The statement of faith contained in the report did not differ much from a statement of, say, the National Association of Evangelicals—at least not in what it explicitly said. It was not clear, however, on the issues of the divinity of Christ, the authority of the Bible, and supernaturalism. It was more clear than most conservative Protestant statements on the ethical obligations of Christians and the brotherhood of man.[66] American higher education today would be very different if all, or even most, of the colleges associated with denominations belonging to the National Council of Churches would follow its higher education commission's blueprint for a Christian college.

While conservative colleges criticize the less orthodox ones for not emphasizing sufficiently the traditional Christian worldview in their educational programs, the more liberal institutions charge the conservative colleges with not combining sufficient rigorous intellectual inquiry with their practice of the faith. As one such critic of the conservative schools noted, "Many a 'secular' professor honors an unacknowledged faith better by his honest confrontation of fact than another who advertises his 'little churchinesses' and offers only Mickey Mouse courses." The continuing Christian colleges do not deny that such teaching takes place in their institutions; neither do they usually approve of it. They would argue, however, that instruction of this type is less characteristic of their institutions than their liberal Protestant and secular critics imply. In fact, representatives of the conservative colleges argue that their institutions probably expose students to a broad variety of opinions on controversial religious and philosophical topics more effectively and objectively than do most other colleges and universities. The advantage which they claim is that usually they openly acknowledge their assumptions, whereas many professors in the secular and secularizing institutions mistakenly assume that because they do not have pro-Christian presuppositions, therefore they have none at all. In addition, Christian professors usually know non-Christian views in their disciplines better than non-Christian professors understand Christian interpretations in their areas of study; therefore, Christian professors can present a broader variety of perspectives. This is true in large part because most Christian professors have studied in secular graduate institutions and therefore know secular systems of thought quite well. Non-Christian instructors in secular institutions, by contrast, often have experienced little or no exposure on a sophisticated level to Christian worldviews.[67]

No longer, then, do the avowedly Christian colleges sit at the apex of the country's educational structure. That mid-nineteenth-century reality is now gone. Some of the old colleges continue to operate as unapologetically Christian institutions, and to their ranks have been added many others during the last century; but the Christian colleges today, although growing in program quality and public respect, do not hold the same position of prestige in society that they once did.

Chapter 5

The Response To Secularization

Because American higher education has secularized more than have the churches or society in general, it is not surprising that Christian students, denominations, and parachurch organizations have sought to counter the trend. The methods they have used to promote the Christian faith have varied from period to period. During the quarter century following the Civil War, the denominations responded by concentrating their efforts less upon the state universities—where they were losing their influence, anyway—and more upon the church colleges, with the result that the latter became increasingly denominational in nature. Meanwhile, on the campuses of both public and private colleges, the largely student-led YMCA and YWCA chapters (collectively known as the "Y movement" or the "Y's") became unusually popular organizations.

Between 1890 and 1925, as increasing numbers of students from the major denominations began to enroll in state universities, the denominations decided again to devote major attention to the public centers of learning. While now acknowledging the largely secular nature of the state institutions, the major denominations sought to reduce this influence first by creating "satellite schools" (Bible chairs or Bible schools with dormitory facilities) at the universities and later by establishing the more common denominational foundation centers. Meanwhile, intercollegiate student religious societies, which now included the missionary-oriented Student Volunteer Movement as well as the Y's, reached the peak of their influence. Also in this period the smaller religious groups, in part as a response to the general secularization pattern, began to organize autonomous Bible institutes and Bible colleges, thus creating a largely new form of higher education.

After 1925, the old student societies as well as a large majority of church colleges became increasingly secular; consequently, there sprang up to take their places new student organizations, led by the Inter-Varsity Christian Fellowship and Campus Crusade, and also new fundamentalist liberal arts colleges.

THE YMCA AND OTHER STUDENT
CHRISTIAN ORGANIZATIONS

It probably was coincidental that during the middle of the nineteenth century the universities entered the beginning stages of secularization at the same time that Christian students began to develop the most influential and widespread student religious organization in American history. It was not mere coincidence, however, that the YMCA and the YWCA organizations reached the peak of their influence when the universities became more secular at the turn of the century. College Christian associations grew so rapidly partly because they filled the religious void left on the campuses as the universities withdrew from their former official promotion of the Christian religion. For example, the historian of the University of North Dakota observed that there the Y's became the most efficient agency of moral and religious training only after the state university backed away from its earlier direct support of religion. Also, the Northwestern historians frankly state that for many years the YMCA and YWCA chapters "kept alive the school's religious character." By the turn of the century, then, as stated by Professor Roswell Hitchcock of Union Seminary, the Christian associations were "the great religious fact in the life of the colleges."[1]

The Y movement swept the collegiate world and received widespread public approval. The movement prospered on both the state university and Christian college campuses. Denominational leaders, university and college presidents, and faculty members all highly acclaimed it.[2] Through the famous summer conferences and other means the movement had a great unifying effect among college students nationally. Before the turn of the century, nothing—not even the fraternity and sorority movements or intercollegiate athletics—did more to promote intercollegiate unity and fellowship.

College histories and contemporary catalogs in institution after institution—both public and private—describe the Y's as the largest, most active, and most influential of all student organizations.[3] By 1884, the 181 colleges with Y organizations counted as members nearly 30 percent of their total enrollment. During the peak period at the turn of the century, the membership percentage grew even higher. For example, membership in the Christian organizations included nearly 50 percent of the students at Furman in 1910, 50 percent of the students at Mississippi State in 1909, and two-thirds of the student body at the University of Alabama in 1887. Even as late as 1946, when the influence of the Y's was largely gone at most campuses, two-thirds of the students at Pennsylvania State (which historically had maintained one of the most effective chapters) still attended the programs of the local organization.[4]

The Y's impact in black colleges matched that in the white schools. The Howard chapter began in 1869, two years after the institution opened, and the Christian association quickly became the most influential organization in the lives of the students there and in the many other new black colleges. Furthermore, just as the most able adults assumed roles of leadership in the black denominations, so also the best students accepted positions of leadership in the campus Y organizations.[5]

Originally, the YMCA maintained no direct connection with college students. George Williams and eleven fellow clerks founded it in 1844 in London to meet the practical needs of city youth in a period of rapid urban growth. It began to spread to the college campuses in America in 1858, when students at the Universities of Virginia and Michigan founded chapter units. During the next twenty years, students in approximately forty colleges organized local associations of the interdenominational, student-led organization. A very influential promoter and organizer of local chapters was Robert Weidensall who visited many colleges during the early 1870s, organized YMCA chapters in twenty-four of them, and became known as the "father of the American student YMCA movement." As early as the 1870 Indianapolis YMCA convention, the local campus units had heard a call to organize into a national organization. The series of events leading to national organization, however, began in 1875, when Luther Wishard transferred from Hanover (Ind.) to Princeton. There, he in particular and Princeton in general generated the activity and enthusiasm which led to the formal organization of the nationwide YMCA college movement in 1877.[6]

During the next decade, an increasing number of women in the coeducational institutions found it awkward—even humiliating—that their only opportunity for organized Christian fellowship existed in an organization whose title suggested that it was for men only. As women assumed increasingly active roles in the local units—for example, at Lawrence (Wis.) in 1882–83, both the president and the corresponding secretary were women—they gradually organized local chapters of the Young Women's Christian Association. By 1885, nearly 2,000 female students had enrolled in approximately seventy YWCA units. The next year the women followed the example of the men a decade earlier and officially organized their local chapters into the national YWCA.[7]

The Y movement in America grew from 40 chapters in 1877 to 181 chapters and 10,000 members in 1884, 345 chapters and 22,000 members in 1891, 628 chapters and 32,000 students in 1900, and 731 chapters and 94,000 students in 1920. The peak period coincided with the national leadership of John Mott.[8]

As a leader, Mott was unusually gifted in many ways. Converted as a Cornell undergraduate in 1886 during the visit of Englishman J. K. Studd to America, Mott assumed the leadership of the Cornell YMCA, and, believing that God placed him there "to do a work akin to that of the Wesleys at old Oxford," he built it into the largest and most effective local chapter. After graduation in 1888, the national YMCA recruited him as a field secretary, and he immediately threw his vast reservoir of energy and organizational skill into the movement. As he developed independent financial resources, he was able to commit himself completely to his evangelistic work. He traveled incessantly, bringing intense spiritual enthusiasm to campus after campus, especially through personal interviews with students, for which he allotted large periods of time. Mott probably influenced more young men than did any other person in this turn-of-the-century period. He was the most widely known figure in the academic life of the country—and probably the world. In addition to his extensive Y work, he intensely promoted evangelism, social justice, international peace and goodwill, and ecumenicity through a variety of denominational, missionary, and church federation activities. Unceasing activity during his long life took him to eighty-three countries, where governmental leaders repeatedly honored him. His awards included the Nobel Peace Prize. Kenneth Scott Latourette, the dean of American church historians, described him as the greatest Christian missionary since St. Paul.[9]

The Y movement in the colleges differed from previous student Christian movements in its effort to become a widespread intercollegiate fellowship and in its emphasis upon the practical application of the Christian faith. Before the Civil War, collegiate religious organizations had emphasized primarily personal piety and theological debate on the local campus. The Christian associations, by contrast, expanded their influence through a national organization, dynamic intercollegiate summer conferences, and a core of traveling secretaries who moved from campus to campus.[10]

In this period before the colleges developed student affairs programs, the Y chapters provided a wide range of services. Chapter members met new students as they arrived on the incoming trains, and they helped them adjust to college life. They published student handbooks, provided book-exchange services, operated employment bureaus and loan programs especially for poor students, assisted ill students, and, in some cases, conducted free tutorial services.[11]

The Y members also sought to serve off-campus through "neighborhood work" in which student groups held religious services in poor houses, jails, rescue missions, and Sunday schools in an effort to lead their hearers to Christian commitments. Frequently they achieved success. For example, in 1898, 80 students from the YMCA chapters in Minnesota reported nearly 400 conversions. Similarly, the University of Michigan chapter in the early period was known as "a persistent soul-winner of an organization."[12]

The evangelistic work also succeeded on campus. During its first seven years (1877–84), the national Y office reported that approximately 7,000 students experienced Christian conversion on the 181 campuses where Y chapters existed. Most of these decisions, the report stated, occurred directly as a result of YMCA work.[13]

In addition to student services and off-campus evangelistic programs, the local chapters regularly conducted prayer and Bible study meetings. The Bible studies proved sufficiently popular that by 1908 approximately one-fourth of all students enrolled in colleges with chapters were engaged in Bible studies using texts published by the association.[14]

The best financed local chapters erected their own buildings, sometimes with gymnasiums, and hired adult secretaries (or directors), some of whom served on a full-time basis. By 1896, forty colleges and universities employed full-time secretaries, and four years later twenty-seven college chapters operated their own campus buildings.[15]

One of the most important aspects of the Y program was the promotion that it gave to missionary activity through its foreign missionary arm, the Student Volunteer Movement (SVM); for thirty years after its official founding in 1888, John Mott headed it as well as the total Y operation. The SVM developed from the famous conference for YMCA student leaders held at Mt. Herman, Massachusetts, in the summer of 1886. Luther Wishard, secretary of the Princeton chapter, with the assistance of C. K. Ober, a recent graduate of Williams, organized the conference with unusual skill and enthusiasm. He persuaded Dwight Moody to address the delegates, hoping that the presence of the evangelist would positively affect the registration. It affected Mott, then a Cornell undergraduate, who stated that he "wanted to go [to the conference] so badly that he considered selling his new *Encyclopedia Britannica* if necessary to obtain the money to study under Moody."

In addition to featuring Moody, Wishard wanted to challenge the delegates seriously to consider foreign missionary service. Knowing that a senior student by the name of Robert Wilder had created great interest in missions at Princeton, he enlisted him to attend the conference and seek to generate similar enthusiasm among the 235 students who came as representatives from 96 colleges. The efforts of Wishard to promote the cause of missions at the conference succeeded dramatically, as 100 of the delegates dedicated their lives to foreign missionary service. Ober suggested that a team of the delegates should travel nationwide to campuses during the next school year to share the story of the Mt. Herman meeting and to seek to generate an even broader base of student interest in missionary activity. The team selected included Wilder and a fellow Princetonian, John N. Forman, a son of missionary parents. Their college meetings were as successful as the Mt. Herman conference itself, for during the 1886–87 school year and the subsequent summer, 2,100 additional college students dedicated themselves to foreign missionary service. This dramatic result led to the formal organizing of the Student Volunteer Movement and the adoption of its famous slogan: "The evangelization of the world in this generation." During the next half-century, at least 13,000 SVM members became foreign missionaries. They constituted one of the best-trained groups of foreign evangelists in the history of the Christian church, and, at least until the decline of the movement, they displayed a concern for both the temporary and the eternal needs of the people to whom they ministered.[16]

The SVM did not operate as a missionary sending agency; rather, it sought to generate interest in missions, to challenge students to offer themselves for missionary service, to lend support and encouragement to students once they made such a commitment, and then to work closely with the denominational and independent missionary boards. SVM units on individual campuses regularly offered study classes in missions, and they kept informed of the work of the movement across the country through the periodic visits of traveling secretaries, the monthly publication, the *Student Volunteer,* and other literature. The most dramatic activity, however, in the SVM program was a quadrennial national conference which regularly attracted thousands of students.[17]

The SVM, like its parent organization, reached its peak between the 1890s and the First World War, and then began to decline during the 1920s. After the war, both the SVM and the Christian associations began to concentrate less on evangelism and more upon social concerns such as international peace and goodwill between nations, race relations, international student relief and other forms of economic development, and ecumenicity in church organizations. As the Y's and the SVM decreased their evangelistic thrust, they found that the remaining "social Christianity" by itself could not generate the enthusiasm of the earlier years.[18]

The decline appeared at least as early as the 1920 student missionary conference at Des Moines. Even though the conference was very well attended, the students displayed more cynicism than enthusiasm. They reflected both the nation's general reaction to the World War and the growing distrust of traditional religion. Worldwide evangelist Sherwood Eddy sensed this attitude and spoke sharply to the delegates:

> My friends, I am speaking to you, if you are out on the sidelines. This is my word to you today. Get off the sidelines of criticism and get in the game. . . . Some of you said to me yesterday, "Why do you bring this piffle, these old shibboleths, these old worn-out phrases, why are you talking to us about the living God and the divine Christ?" All right, we will call him a personal God if you like. . . . Perhaps the trouble is that you haven't yet found or don't know very well that living God, that living Father, or that great living Christ.

In July, 1931, William Miller, an extensive traveler for the Student Volunteer Movement, noted his great shock at the lack of missionary interest in the church colleges as well as the state universities.[19]

Accordingly, the number of enrolled missionary volunteers declined from nearly 2,800 in 1920 to 34 in 1937 and 25 in 1938; the number of volunteers who sailed abroad decreased from 637 in 1921 to 38 in 1934; the attendance at the quadrennial convention dropped from the 5,400 students from 950 colleges in 1920 to 1,700 students from 400 colleges in 1932; and the budget fell from $94,000 in 1924 to $14,000 in 1937.[20]

The Y movement also declined. Between the two world wars, the YMCA and the YWCA college chapters decreased in absolute numbers even though college enrollments mounted sharply. In 1920, approximately 1,000 colleges and universities enrolled 600,000 students; by 1940, 1,700 institutions enrolled 1,500,000 students. Meanwhile, the number of Y chapters fell from 731 college chapters in 1920 to only 430 in 1940, and the student membership dropped from 94,000 in 1921 to 51,000 in 1940.[21]

Several factors contributed to the decline of the Y and SVM movements. One was the growth of the university pastorate movement with its denominational fellowship houses. Also, many of the student services provided by the Y's during their most prominent years had become part of the college-administered student services programs. Moreover, the Y's faced growing competition from the rapidly expanding number of extracurricular activities of all types. The primary cause for the decline of the Christian associations, however, was that they were losing their sense of spiritual authority and evangelical mission.

As the Y movement declined, the university pastorate movement assumed an increasingly important role in ministering to the spiritual needs of students on the state and independent campuses. Beginning at about the turn of the century, many of the major denominations started to realize that not only were an increasing percentage of students from their churches enrolling in state universities, but also that these institutions were becoming increasingly secular. For example, the editor of the *Lutheran Witness* warned that "the typical university teaching . . . [was] unsettling to religious convictions [and that] a professor could undo in half an hour what it had taken years to build up." Furthermore, church leaders believed that because of the mounting enrollments, local churches of their denominations near the campuses could no longer satisfactorily meet the needs of the students, even with the help of the Christian associations. Therefore, the denominations began to establish their own student centers, staffed with their own clergymen, on locations immediately adjacent to the university campuses. The Presbyterians, led by Joseph Wilson Cochran, secretary of the Board of Education of the Presbyterian Church U.S.A., introduced the university pastorate movement at the University of Michigan in 1905 and established similar centers at the University of Kansas later in 1905, the University of Illinois in 1906, the University of Wisconsin in 1908, the University of Colorado in 1908, the University of Arkansas in 1909, and the University of Nebraska in 1909. Other denominations quickly followed the Presbyterian example, and by the 1930s denominational student centers operated on the campuses of at least 100 state and independent universities. The purposes of the movement have been to assist students to grow spiritually as much as the professors were helping them grow intellectually; to urge students to continue their loyalty to the denominations in which they had grown up; and to assist in developing future lay and clerical leaders for the denominations. A few denominations, led by the Disciples, have offered academic instruction in biblical literature at their student centers.[22]

In addition to denominational student centers, another movement which has arisen to succeed the YMCA in ministering to students on the secular campuses is the Inter-Varsity Christian Fellowship. It follows the tradition of the old Christian associations more than did the university pastorate movement, for it is interdenominational, international, and largely run by student members of the local, autonomous campus chapters with the assistance and counsel of traveling secretaries. With the assumption by the universities of comprehensive student services programs, however, there has been no need for the Inter-Varsity chapters to duplicate the earlier efforts of the Christian associations in this area. The objectives of Inter-Varsity have included the promotion of Christian maturity in its members by means of Bible study, prayer, and preparation for witnessing; evangelization on the campuses and stimulation of interest in foreign missionary activity; and the promotion of both Christian maturity and evangelism through the organizational periodical, *His,* and a variety of carefully written books and pamphlets published at the organization's press in Downers Grove, Illinois.

If Inter-Varsity is a spiritual descendent of the early Christian associations, in a direct organizational sense it traces its origin to the Cambridge Intercollegiate Christian Union (CICCU), which developed from the English revivals in the late nineteenth century. Between the world wars, the Cambridge Union considered joining the ecumencially oriented national Student Christian Movement (SCM) in England. The climactic decision of the Cambridge students not to join the Student Christian movement came in 1927 when representatives of CICCU asked the SCM: "Does the SCM consider the atoning blood of Jesus as the central point of their message?" The answer was, "No, not as central, although it is given a place in teaching." Subsequently, the CICCU chose not to join but rather to expand its evangelical witness to other campuses, thus marking the beginning of the Inter-Varsity Christian Fellowship. The movement spread to Canada in 1928 and to the United States in 1938. The University of Michigan, which earlier had organized the first YMCA chapter and hosted the first denominational student center, now formed the first Inter-Varsity chapter in the United States. Two years later, in 1940, the Inter-Varsity Christian Fellowship of the United States of America organized, with Stacey Woods serving as general secretary.[23]

Just as the Student Volunteer Movement arose as the missionary arm of the YMCA, so the Student Foreign Missions Fellowship (SFMF) has become the branch of the Inter-Varsity Christian Fellowship which specializes in challenging students with the need for Christian evangelism in other countries. In a manner very similar to the SVM, the Student Foreign Missions Fellowship enlists volunteers for foreign service; provides the recruits with fellowship, direction, and encouragement; and plans widely publicized, triennial missionary conferences. The SFMF maintained a separate existence until 1945, when it merged with Inter-Varsity. The first international missionary convention following the merger was held in 1946 at the University of Toronto, where 575 students from 151 schools in 8 countries attended. Since 1948, the conferences have met at the University of Illinois. While students have flocked to the Inter-Varsity missionary conventions in greater numbers (they regularly fill the 17,300 seat University of Illinois Assembly Hall) than those who earlier attended the SVM conventions, nevertheless a much smaller percentage of the students on today's secular campuses participate in the activities of Inter-Varsity and other evangelical organizations such as Campus Crusade for Christ and the Navigators than were enrolled in the YMCA and YWCA chapters at the turn of the century.[24]

In 1951, William Bright organized at UCLA an organization which spread from that campus to become with Inter-Varsity one of the two most effective evangelical student organizations on the secular campuses. Today Campus Crusade for Christ operates many ministries, but the most important one continues to be its aggressive program of campus evangelism. During the 1976–77 school year, the organization's 1,500 full-time campus staff members explained the gospel message to approximately 150,000 students, 8,600 of whom professed faith in Christ. In addition, the staff members trained college students in witnessing techniques, and the chapter members led an additional 10,000 students to make Christian commitments. The staff members and students employ as their principal witnessing method an explanation of Bright's "Four Spiritual Laws." This technique is very simple—some say too mechanical—and the program achieves its greatest success on the large state university and private campuses that maintain strong athletic, fraternity, and sorority programs. By contrast, Campus Crusade experiences less success in intellectually oriented, elite schools like Harvard, Yale, and Stanford, where Inter-Varsity with its low key and more cerebral approach is more likely to be effective.

The career of a Campus Crusade staff member is intense, somewhat Spartan, and often short. A new recruit enrolls for eleven weeks of detailed training at the organization's attractive headquarters near San Bernardino, California. The typical new staff member is young—usually middle-to-late twenties—has worked previously as a student member of a Campus Crusade chapter, and raises his or her own financial support (during the late 1970s the usual support was $460 per month plus 17 percent for fringe benefits). The training of the worker as well as the specific techniques which he or she employs in the field are highly programmed. This fact plus the limited income make it difficult for the organization to attract many seminary graduates. More typically, a staff member is a college graduate with a major in almost any discipline.

Campus Crusade's most effective staff representative in recent years has been Josh McDowell, a Wheaton graduate. McDowell, more intellectual in his approach than most Crusaders, in a twelve-year period spoke to 5 million people on more than 500 campuses in this country and abroad.

In 1966, Campus Crusade began a sports ministry program called Athletes in Action. Its purpose has been to capitalize on the broad exposure and public acclaim given to athletes in order to present the Christian gospel. It has organized high-quality teams in wrestling, gymnastics, track and field, weight-lifting, and soccer, but its greatest success has been realized in basketball. During the 1976–77 basketball season, over 100,000 people attended Athletes in Action games and listened to the Christian testimonies at halftime.[25]

The idea of athletic evangelism is at least as old as 1952, when Taylor sent a "Venture for Victory" basketball team to Taiwan at the invitation of Oriental Crusades missionaries and with the active encouragement of Madame Chiang Kai Shek. The Venture for Victory program expanded to include Christian athletes from a variety of colleges and now operates under the name of Sports Ambassadors as a division of the Overseas Crusades Mission. Taylor gained even greater recognition as a school which uses athletics as a means of promoting evangelism in 1964 when football coach Robert Davenport—who had worked with Bright in the earliest days of Campus Crusade—developed the Wandering Wheels bicycle program which has been widely imitated elsewhere.[26]

During the 1970s, Bright expanded his campus-based program to include evangelistic efforts in a variety of other areas. He was able to do so because of his mounting success as a fund raiser (e.g., the organization received $42 million in 1977). A close student of the movement suggests that by the late 1970s Bright was raising and spending more money for evangelism than was anyone else in the country.[27]

THE BIBLE COLLEGE MOVEMENT

The Bible college[28] movement arose in the late nineteenth and early twentieth centuries as a response to the widespread revivalism of Dwight Moody and others, as a reflection of the American movement toward popular education, and as a reaction to the growth of liberal thought in American Protestantism in general and its colleges in particular. Moody was the single most significant leader of what might be called "The Third Great Awakening" (approximately 1875–1915) which, like the earlier major awakenings, stimulated a renewed interest in Christian education and missions. The first two Bible schools, Nyack in New York City and Moody in Chicago, sought to provide quick, practical training for the sharply increasing number of young people who wished to become "full-time Christian workers," even if only as laypeople. They received encouragement from Moody and Nyack founder A. B. Simpson, both of whom believed deeply that if the Christian message was to reach all classes in all countries, the efforts of the regularly trained clergy must be suplemented by those of the less well trained but often more zealous Christian lay workers.

In this turn-of-the-century period before the development of universal secondary education, many of the young zealots were unprepared for admittance to a college or seminary. They were reluctant to commit eight or ten years to such study when their leaders advised them that such extensive preparation was not necessary for all workers. Such young people were advised to enroll in a Bible training school for a year or two, during which they would study theology and practical evangelistic methods. Then let them labor among the neglected lower classes in the American urban ghettos, use their training to improve the level of Sunday-school instruction in church schools across America, and travel abroad to evangelize the most ignorant classes in less-developed countries. The earliest Bible institutes, then, came into existence to serve as an auxiliary means of securing Christian workers.[29]

Although neither Nyack nor Moody was founded primarily to counter the growth of liberal theology, many of the Bible schools which followed them were motivated by this purpose. Indeed, one of the leading historians of fundamentalism has suggested that the early Bible institutes served the interdenominational fundamentalist movement like the headquarters of a denomination. As the major denominations and their colleges became less orthodox, the individual churches which separated from them, as well as the small denominations which had never operated educational institutions of any type, looked to Moody and the other early Bible schools as models for their own schools. By 1960, most of the Bible colleges with denominational affiliations represented groups which had withdrawn directly or indirectly from a mainline denomination in reaction to growing liberal tendencies. In that year the independent Disciples branch (formally known as the North American Christian Convention) of the Christian Church/Disciples of Christ tradition, several Baptist groups, and the combined Holiness and Pentecostal denominations each could claim between thirty and thirty-five Bible colleges. About 1900, and again in the 1920s the conservative branches of the Disciples of Christ disassociated from the original group, and, although they did not organize into a formal denomination, the member churches did cooperate for a variety of purposes including higher education.

The Baptist groups with Bible colleges include the General Association of Regular Baptists, the Conservative Baptist Convention, the Baptist Bible Fellowship, and the Freewill Baptist Convention, all of which are branches that developed from the old Northern (now American) Baptist Convention. At mid-century even the Northern Baptist Convention relied upon the Bible colleges for nearly one-fourth of its ministers. The Bible college movement did not become nearly as popular among Southern Baptists, primarily because the Southern Baptist Convention remained largely orthodox. The Southern Baptists, however, did begin a few Bible colleges in remote areas to train practicing ministers who in most cases had not graduated from college, and more recently they opened Criswell Bible College in Dallas.

The Holiness and Pentecostal groups represent a continuation of the nineteenth-century variety of Methodism. Eight of the nineteen United States Pentecostal colleges in 1960 operated as institutions of the Assemblies of God, the largest Pentecostal denomination. The Assemblies of God originally entered the field of higher education with one-to-three-year Bible institutes. By 1975, the denomination numbered thirty Bible colleges and four liberal arts institutions among its thirty-four institutions of higher education in the world.[30]

While there never has been a Bible college with a liberal Protestant theological orientation, the schools have varied widely in the degree to which they have fought the liberal institutions. During the early years, perhaps the most aggressive of the fundamentalist Bible schools was Northwestern, begun in 1902 in Minneapolis by William Bell Riley, pastor of one of the largest churches in the then Northern Baptist Convention, the First Baptist Church of Minneapolis. Riley, who added to the Bible school a seminary program in 1935 and a liberal arts college nine years later, announced that one of the major reasons for founding his schools was the fact that the "eastern seminaries were largely modernistic." It was "probably past dispute," he argued in 1917, "that there are not three English speaking schools in the entire Northland, belonging to any of the greater denominations . . . that are without an infection of that infidelity known as 'Modernism.' "[31]

Although the Bible college movement is primarily a North American innovation (it has been transplanted abroad by missionaries), the leaders of the earliest Bible schools found inspiration in the efforts of nineteenth-century English religious leaders. Perhaps the first Bible institute was the London Pastor's College, supported by Charles Spurgeon and the Baptist church made famous by his preaching, the Metropolitan Tabernacle in the Southwark section of London. Spurgeon began the institute to train poor ministers who could not afford a classical education. Moreover, Spurgeon doubted the desirability of the elite universities as places to train ministers because in such institutions "the fervor of the generality of the students . . . lagged far behind their literary training."

As a teen-ager in Ontario, A. B. Simpson admired the preaching of a visiting London minister, H. G. Guinness. Later, when Guinness began the East London Institute for Home and Foreign Missions in 1872, the young man who later was to found the first American Bible institute carefully observed its work. Its philosophy challenged the traditional idea that only highly cultured and university-trained workers should become foreign missionaries. Guinness admitted the need for the thoroughly trained workers required of most societies, particularly for performing such tasks as Bible translation, teaching, and administration.

> But were they the only men needed? . . . Did the 90% of the population of China who cannot read or the savages of Central Africa or the New Hebrides demand teachers of a higher stamp than did the working classes in these missionary sending countries? Should we not esteem it a great waste of resources to insist that home and city missionaries should be classical scholars? And are not workers of all classes required among the heathen as much as at home?

During its first sixteen years, the institute accepted 800 of the 3,000 young men who applied for admission, and 500 of these eventually completed their training and became lay Christian workers in England or on the mission field.

Both Simpson and Moody highly regarded another unorthodox promoter of foreign missions, J. Hudson Taylor. Taylor was an English Methodist who went to China in 1853 and shortly thereafter began operating a "faith mission" with more than 900 missionaries. Taylor not only recruited and sent abroad workers without college and seminary training, he also sent them without guaranteeing their salaries. By the end of the century, Taylor's China Inland Mission numbered more missionaries than did any of the other thirty-eight societies operating in the Asian country.[32]

When Simpson opened the first American Bible institute in New York City in 1882, he announced that it would be a school similar to the one Guinness operated in London. Simpson gathered forty students that first year to study the Bible and evangelism methodology on the rented back stage of the Twenty-third Street Theater. In many ways Simpson was an unlikely person to lead such a humble institution, for he was an 1865 high honors graduate of Knox College, Toronto, and had successfully served Presbyterian churches in Louisville and New York City. Yet the pastorate of respectable Presbyterian churches did not satisfy him, and he supplemented his New York parish work with preaching in the poor immigrant sections of Manhattan. Increasingly, he became concerned about the inadequacies of Christian programs for lower classes in this country and abroad. Consequently, he desired to open a training school to "prepare people who might not otherwise go to college to minister to people abroad who might not otherwise hear the gospel." He resigned his New York pastorate in 1881 to begin his work of training the "foot soldiers of God's army."

Meanwhile Moody was developing similar thoughts. In a famous January, 1886, address, he called for "gap men" who could fill the void between the frequently neglected lower classes and the formally trained clergymen. Moody, himself a layman, realized that such individuals, when sufficiently motivated and industrious, could be very effective. His own evangelistic career as a Sunday-school recruiter, a YMCA worker, and an urban mass evangelist had always concentrated on the large population centers. Thus he knew intimately the physical and spiritual poverty of the immigrants and other industrial workers in the urban slums of America.[33]

Essentially, Simpson and Moody sought to develop schools to provide minimal training for the type of Christian workers who in earlier eras had pursued their spiritual endeavors with no training at all. These "gap men" streaming forth from Nyack, Moody, and the other early Bible schools were the turn-of-the-century counterparts of the earlier Wesleyan Sunday-school teachers in England, and the Methodist circuit-riders and Baptist farmer-preachers on the American frontier.

If Simpson and Moody shared a similar vision, nevertheless they applied that vision somewhat differently. While both desired to train the common people of America to take the gospel to the common people of this and other countries, Simpson emphasized foreign missionary activity and Moody gave priority to training home workers. Also, Moody was much more successful than Simpson—and all the other early Bible school leaders, as well—in raising funds to support his institution. Before his evangelistic career, the youthful Moody had demonstrated uncommon success as a Chicago businessman, and thereafter he displayed great skill in raising funds from his business friends to promote his religious activities. Moody established his school on a solid financial basis at its beginning with the assistance of such affluent Chicago businessmen as T. W. Harvey, a millionaire lumber dealer; John Farwell, a dry goods merchant; and Cyrus McCormick, the agricultural machinery manufacturing magnate. Fortunately, upon Moody's death the management of the institute's business affairs passed to the able Henry Crowell, a leading executive of the Quaker Oats Company and other business enterprises. Crowell developed a very large network of regular donors whose contributions then and to the present have endowed the institution to such an extent that it has never charged tuition, but only room, board, and fees. Crowell's success was matched by the efforts of Reuben Torrey, who provided academic and spiritual leadership for the school. Moody hired the Yale graduate as superintendent beginning in 1889, and Torrey continued in that position for the next two decades.[34]

Moody's personal fame as an evangelist, the solid financial and academic base established by Crowell and Torrey, and the institute's central location in one of the most rapidly growing cities in the world combined to bring Moody Bible Institute quickly to a position of leadership in the Bible school movement. If Yale, Princeton, and Oberlin each gained reputations in the nineteenth century as mothers of many liberal arts colleges, Moody became known as the mother of numerous Bible institutes and colleges. Shortly after Moody's death, religious leaders from many parts of the country came to Chicago to study the Moody program with the goal of returning to their homes to found "little Moodys" in their regions.[35]

Two examples of the many Bible schools which began because of the Moody influence are Boston (later Gordon College) in 1889 and the Bible Institute of Los Angeles (later Biola) in 1908. The Boston school began when Moody held his Boston revival of 1887 in a tabernacle built immediately adjacent to A. J. Gordon's Clarendon Street Baptist Church, with the church serving as an auxiliary facility. Although Gordon had graduated from the most prestigious institutions of his denomination (Brown and Newton Seminary), he chose to follow Moody's example and founded what became the third permanent Bible school. On the West Coast, the still infant Bible Institute of Los Angeles in 1912 recruited Reuben Torrey for a leadership position. Torrey proceeded to use his skills to help his new institution develop the reputation that it still maintains as the leading Bible college on the West Coast.

In addition to Moody, Nyack, and the Boston school, other Bible colleges that began in the nineteenth century include Western Baptist (Mo.), a black institution, in 1890; School of the Evangelists (later Johnson in Tennessee), the first Christian Church Bible school, in 1893; Friends (later Cleveland Bible College and then Malone College), sponsored by the evangelically oriented Ohio Quakers, in 1894; Northwest Christian (Ore.), founded by the Christian Church (Disciples) in 1895; Berkshire Christian (Mass.) in 1897; Free Church (later Trinity Seminary) in Chicago in 1897; Azusa (Cal.), originally a Friend's institution, in 1899; God's Bible College (Oh.) in 1900; and Bethel (later Providence Barrington Bible College and then Barrington College, Rhode Island) in 1900.[36]

Although the Bible colleges gradually developed entrance requirements comparable to those of the liberal arts colleges (by 1950 the majority required high school graduation for admission as regular students), during their early decades they placed much more emphasis upon Christian character than educational attainment. For example, Boston maintained no age or formal schooling requirement; rather, "if the record [of the applicant] as a Christian was good and he or she showed a real desire to do Christian work, he was accepted."[37]

The early Bible schools offered very limited curricula. A typical school usually listed some courses in the liberal arts and a large amount of work in biblical studies, theology, and practical Christian training. The early curriculum at Nyack was broader than that at most schools. Its liberal arts offerings included English, logic, speech, language and literature, mental and moral philosophy, natural science, ancient and modern history, and geography; these supplemented its curriculum in theology (e.g., Bible, Christian evidences, New Testament Greek, systematic theology, church history, pastoral theology, and history of Christian work) and "practical" subjects (e.g., homiletics, foreign missions work, Sunday-school work, home missions work, vocal music, and personal evangelism). Dwight Moody's advice on the desirable curriculum suggests what probably was offered to the students in most of the early schools, including his own: "Never mind the Greek and Hebrew, give them plain English and good scripture. It is the sword of the Lord and cuts deep." Moody students listened to Bible lectures in the morning and engaged in practical work in Chicago during the afternoons and evenings.[38]

Every Bible college from the beginning of the movement to the present has made the English Bible the heart of its curriculum. The schools have increased their requirements in the liberal arts, as will be noted later, but they have usually done so by increasing the length of their programs rather than by reducing the Bible requirements. Almost invariably, each Bible college student has majored in biblical studies with perhaps a second major. Today those colleges which meet the requirements of the Bible college accrediting association must enroll each of their three- and four-year students in a minimum of thirty hours of biblical studies. Some schools greatly exceed this minimum standard; for example, Big Sky (Mon.) requires fifty semester hours of biblical studies in all of its three- and four-year programs. [39]

Whether or not they have listed it as a formal part of their curricula, the schools invariably have given major attention to developing in their students a pietistic lifestyle. President Joseph Ramseyer of Fort Wayne (Ind.) undoubtedly represented the Bible college leaders in general when he argued that intellectual knowledge should never be valued above spiritual illumination because one can never acquire the most important knowledge apart from instruction by the Spirit of God. The Bible college educational process was designed to produce holy students as well as students who were knowledgeable about holy things. [40]

It is difficult to exaggerate the extent to which the early Bible schools emphasized foreign missionary activity. Many of them included this emphasis in their original titles (e.g., Moody at its inception was called "The Bible Institute for Home and Foreign Missions of the Chicago Evangelism Society"). The Student Mission Band at Fort Wayne began during the school's first year (1904) to study the mission fields of the world and to pray for missionary efforts. It included the entire student body in its membership, thus making it easily the most important extracurricular activity. Forty percent of the 2,500 students who attended Nyack between 1882 and 1902 eventually entered foreign missionary service in forty countries. The intense missionary emphasis of the early Bible schools joined other forces, including the efforts of the Student Volunteer Movement in the liberal arts college and universities, to allow the United States by the early twentieth century to surpass England as the supplier of the majority of both personnel and funds for Protestant foreign missions. [41]

So great was the missionary emphasis at the Bible colleges that they were producing by the mid-twentieth century a probable majority and by 1980 a large majority of the Protestant missionary recruits in this country. Indeed, this large number of missionary trainees has been one of the unique features of the Bible-college movement. While many schools contributed significantly to the production of missionaries (e.g., Columbia of South Carolina sent 750 and Lutheran of Minnesota sent 400 of its graduates to the mission field during the four decades before 1960), the champion missionary producer has been Moody—which continues to be the largest Protestant missionary training school in the world. By 1952, 3,300 Moody graduates had served as missionaries in 94 countries. In that year, 2,300 of them were active, as were 2,700 Moody missionaries in 1960. The Moody historian claims that by mid-century 5 percent of the total Protestant missionary staff in the world and approximately 13 percent of all evangelical missionaries from North America had studied at the school.[42]

While not all Bible college alumni could become missionaries, studies show that a high percentage—perhaps even a majority—have entered full-time Christian service, and probably an even higher percentage originally planned such a career. For example, of the thirty-two graduates of the 1952 class at the Bible institute in Cleveland, sixteen planned to be pastors, eleven missionaries, three pastors' wives, and one a song evangelist. One comprehensive study of the class of 1946 in forty-three representative Bible colleges showed that 29 percent became ministers and an additional 27 percent missionaries. More recently, a 1980 American Association of Bible Colleges survey found 52 percent of the graduates entering a full-time Christian ministry.[43]

"Practical training"—now known as Christian service—has been a part of the curricula of most schools since their beginning years. Most Bible school leaders would have agreed with F. W. Farr of the Nyack Bible Institute when he said in 1887: "It is best to know and to do, but it is better to do without knowing than to know without doing. . . . In order that we may know and do we must be taught and trained. . . . Teaching imparts knowledge and fills the mind. Training imparts skill and shapes habits." Similarly, the 1946 catalog of Grace (Neb.) expressed how vital practical service has been to the realization of its goals: "The only way to train for Christian service is to do it." Accordingly, Bible colleges have usually been located in cities where they can exert a wider influence and find more opportunities for Christian witness than would be possible in rural areas. In Boston in 1914 the Bible institute claimed that its students constituted "the largest body of city missionaries in New England." In Chicago the Moody students were no less busy. Their early record of service, while proportionately higher than that at most schools, probably reflects the general Bible-school pattern; between 1889 and 1916 the Moody students taught approximately 1.5 million Bible classes, conducted 8,000 other public meetings, made over 2 million calls to homes and visits to hospitals, counseled individually 4 million people, distributed 30 million pieces of literature, and led over 500,000 people to an initial or renewed Christian commitment. Even by the mid-twentieth century, nearly one-half of the schools required Christian service activities of all students, and approximately three-fourths of all Bible school students enrolled in such programs.[44]

Bible colleges are not the only institutions that have placed major emphasis upon Christian service. The recently founded Liberty Baptist (Va.) requires each student to complete one Christian service assignment each semester. Many of these assignments can take place in the very large and nearby Thomas Road Baptist Church, the institution from which the college developed. Although most Christian liberal arts colleges have offered Christian service opportunities as voluntary rather than required activities, they often have attracted wide interest. For example, during a recent year at Wheaton a majority of the students participated in one or more of the college's many evangelism and social service activities. Similarly, at Bob Jones (S.C.) during a period in the late 1950s, ministerial candidates held 33,000 public services, counseled personally 137,000 people, recorded nearly 17,000 conversions to Christ, and distributed 3.5 million tracts.[45]

During the century-long history of the Bible-college movement, the educational programs of the institutions have grown in both quality and breadth. Scholars traditionally have viewed Bible colleges as academically inferior to Christian liberal arts institutions. Many of the liberal arts colleges, however, also began with very modest academic programs, and at the time they were being compared to the Bible colleges most had had a longer period of time to develop. Also contributing to the Bible colleges' reputation for inferiority is the fact that an unusually broad range of institutions have called themselves Bible schools. Over the years, the Bible-school spectrum has included everything from churches offering a few night classes as an extension of their Christian education programs to highly sophisticated collegiate institutions with programs of greater quality than those of many liberal arts institutions.

Growth in the quality of instruction has followed growth in the quality of the instructors. In the early years, most instructors possessed Christian service experience, Christian maturity, and a pious lifestyle, but not often academic achievement. By mid-century, however, the great majority of instructors held academic degrees. One comprehensive study of 536 full-time faculty members in 47 Bible colleges in 1946 found 80 percent with undergraduate degrees, 25 percent with masters degrees, and 11 percent with earned doctorates. By 1979, faculty members in the accredited schools had completed an average of nearly eight years of post-high-school study.

During the first generation of the Bible-school movement, most institutions recruited primarily non-high-school graduates who studied in what were frequently "Bible training" schools for brief periods, usually not exceeding two years. During the 1920s and

1930s some schools began to expand their programs from two to three years, thus allowing for greater specialization in pastoral studies, missions, Christian education, and music; however, even as late as 1950, half of the schools still offered only one course of study. The curricular expansion was accompanied by a modification in institutional nomenclature as many schools began to change their names from Bible training schools to Bible institutes. Also, during this period, an increasing number of students became interested in combining their Bible institute work with study in a liberal arts college. The Bible schools responded by assigning credit-hour value to their courses and by offering an increasing number of liberal arts courses. They made these changes both to ease the process of transfer for students going on to complete a liberal arts degree and also to satisfy students more completely with their own curricular offerings.[46]

The most significant recent development in the academic organization of the Bible-college movement has been the tendency for institutions to evolve from Bible institutes to Bible colleges and even, in a few cases, from Bible colleges to Christian liberal arts colleges. The changes have come in large part in response to student requests such as that expressed in the following complaint: "Why should a student have to spend years of his time studying in a Bible institute, only to receive a diploma, whereas the same years if spent in a secular school would lead to the granting of a degree . . . ?" Accordingly, between the 1930s and the 1960s, many Bible schools—led by Cleveland, Columbia, and Boston— enlarged their general education curricula sufficiently to justify calling themselves Bible colleges. By 1960, approximately half of the schools in North America identified themselves as Bible colleges rather than Bible institutes.[47]

As an educational institution, a Bible college occupies an intermediary position between a Bible institute and a Christian liberal arts college. Like a Bible institute, its students all earn majors in religion and all experience in their academic programs significant practical Christian service. Like a Christian liberal arts college, however, the Bible college enrolls all of its students in a series of general education courses. The Christian liberal arts college student can choose from a wider variety of general education courses and major disciplines; however, the academic experience of a Bible college student compares closely to that of a student who majors in religion in a Christian liberal arts college. A Bible college curriculum is generally four years long and results in an A.B. degree, whereas a Bible institute program is shorter—frequently three years—and results in a diploma.[48] Today, among the institutions accredited by the American Association of Bible Colleges, the trend is to replace the traditional three-year diploma programs with two- and four-year degree programs. Almost all of the accredited schools offer a four-year baccalaureate degree, over half offer two-year degrees, and less than one-third continue to offer the old diploma programs.

A very limited number of institutions, including Biola and Northwestern, combine the characteristics of a Bible college with those of a well-developed Christian liberal arts college. At Biola, all students complete thirty hours of Bible as a graduation requirement and participate in Christian-service assignments each term. The college offers a wide variety of liberal arts majors, and students majoring in disciplines other than Bible usually take five years to graduate. Added to the 2,300 undergraduate students are 650 enrollees in Talbot Seminary and 150 students in the affiliated Rosemead School of Psychology. For Biola, the combination of Bible college and liberal arts college is the philosophical ideal, not, as it has been for some institutions, a transition stage from Bible college to liberal arts college.[49]

The effort to organize the Bible-college movement for the purpose of improving and unifying standards began as early as 1918, when James Gray, president of Moody, called a meeting of Bible institute representatives for this purpose. Nothing came of his effort but thirteen years later another Moody official, Clarence Benson, led in the establishment of the Evangelical Teacher Training Association (ETTA), which might be considered the forerunner of the current American Association of Bible Colleges. Benson and other ETTA leaders believed that the Sunday-school movement, while well-intentioned, had failed to realize its goals because of the inadequate preparation of its teachers. As John Vincent, the nineteenth-century leader of the movement, had observed, "The Sunday school is strong at the heart and weak at the head." The American Sunday School Union began in this country in 1825 as an import from England where forty years earlier Robert Raikes, a Gloucester printer, founded the Sunday-school movement. Raikes sought to help the many children in his hometown who were forced to work four to six days a week by opening a school to educate them in secular and biblical subjects during a five-hour session each Sunday. In America, the Sunday-school movement exerted its greatest initial influence on the frontier, where it was taken by home missionaries and where untrained laypeople did most of the teaching.

The purpose of the ETTA, then, was to use the existing structure of the Bible schools to improve the quality of the nation's

Sunday-school instruction, and by the end of its first decade, more than 100 schools had affiliated with the association. The association identified a "standard training course" which ideally the well-trained Sunday-school teacher would complete. This curriculum called for the completion of the equivalent of one academic year of study in biblical and related subjects. Of course, not all Sunday-school teachers could devote a year to full-time study; accordingly, the association encouraged them to complete a "preliminary training course" involving approximately six credit hours of study in a school or under a graduate of the standard training course. The association set standards for institutions as well as individuals. It designated as "gold seal schools" those Bible schools that (1) required high school graduation for admission, (2) required college graduation for faculty status, (3) provided residence dormitories for day students, and (4) owned a library of at least 1,000 books.[50]

The effort to create an organization which would establish standards for the total program of the Bible colleges finally succeeded in the late 1940s under the leadership of presidents Howard Ferrin of Providence Barrington and Safara Witmer of Fort Wayne, and dean Samuel Sutherland of Biola. These men led in the organization of the Accrediting Association of Bible Institutes and Bible Colleges (AABIBC). The organizational meetings took place in Minneapolis during the annual meeting of the National Association of Evangelicals in 1946 and at Winona Lake, Indiana, in 1947. The new organization profited greatly from the help given by John Dale Russell, assistant commissioner of the United States Office of Education, who displayed unusual interest in helping the Bible schools.

Since the quality of the work offered in the many institutions calling themselves Bible schools varied greatly, the leaders of the new association believed that they must establish rigorous standards for those schools seeking initial membership. In 1948 the AABIBC accredited its first twelve schools, and the same year the United States Office of Education acknowledged the organization as the only accrediting body in the field of undergraduate theological education. Thus the Office of Education began to recognize the schools approved by the AABIBC just as it recognized the seminaries approved by the American Association of Theological Schools.

Students from AABIBC member schools began to find it much easier to transfer credits to another institution. Shortly after the establishment of the AABIBC, Carroll Newson, associate commissioner of Higher Education for New York State, declared: "The New York State Department of Education recognizes the AABIBC as maintaining acceptable standards for four year higher institutions and recommends for transfer purposes full credit for courses which are appropriate to the degree requirements of the institutions to which credit is being transferred. . . .'' Among the earliest institutions to accept work completed at Bible institutes and colleges were New York University, Texas Wesleyan, Wheaton, and Taylor.

Not all of the Bible schools accepted the accreditation movement as desirable, however. For example, L. E. Maxwell, whose Prairie Bible Institute in Alberta, Canada, was widely respected among Bible college officials in the United States, frankly stated:

> We are not personally concerned about becoming uniform with others, or in becoming accredited. God has given us a special method of Bible study second to none, and we are content to do what God wants us to do without having to adjust to that which others feel led to do. . . . We are convinced that many of the present trends will ultimately take these very Bible institutes into modernism. . . .[51]

In the late 1950s the Accrediting Association of Bible Institutes and Bible Colleges shortened its name to the Accrediting Association of Bible Colleges (AABC) and hired President Witmer of Fort Wayne as its first full-time executive secretary. In his new position, Witmer traveled widely to visit many of the Bible colleges in North America. He criticized freely major weaknesses he saw in the colleges but also served as their leading spokesman to the "outside world," which he believed too little appreciated the significance of what Bible colleges were achieving. While Witmer acknowledged that the schools were understaffed, undersupported, inadequate in their ability to integrate general education disciplines with biblical values, and lacking in academic respectability and creativity, he also argued with logic and passion that higher education in general should accept the Bible-college philosophy of education as a viable option. He lamented that "while Bible college education ranks first in values . . . it is frequently regarded as inferior and only partially evolved as an acceptable type of college education." Additionally, he argued that since the Bible college offers both a Bible education and a college education, it provides an integrated worldview in contrast to much of modern education. Most modern education, he added, takes a compartmentalized approach which gives no overarching meaning to the sum of its curricular parts. In the late 1950s and early 1960s, Witmer was generally recognized as the leading authority on the Bible colleges; some even referred to him as "Mr. Bible College."[52]

Meanwhile the AABC continued to grow. The number of North American institutions accepted as fully accredited members increased to thirty-six in 1960, forty-seven in 1969, and seventy-seven in 1980. In each case, accredited and candidate members represented approximately 20 percent of the Bible institutes and colleges. In the modern period, the AABC manual lists the following standards for its member schools: (1) a desirable student-faculty ratio of 15:1, with the maximum allowable being 25:1; (2) a minimal academic training for faculty members of the first graduate or professional degree beyond the baccalaureate; and (3) a high school graduation requirement for admission.[53]

Today, a large majority of the schools accredited by the AABC are Bible colleges rather than Bible institutes. A notable exception is Moody Bible Institute which maintains with conviction its traditional identification. Yet, Moody continues to be recognized as the leader of the Bible-college movement because of the breadth of its Bible and applied curriculum, the size of its faculty and staff (over 500 full-time employees in 1969), the number of its alumni and the size of its student body, the size of its annual budget, and its extensive off-campus services to a wide variety of individuals (e.g., the radio broadcast ministry on WMBI in Chicago and elsewhere, the correspondence division which frequently has enrolled as many as 120,000 students, the Moody Institute of Science Films, and the widely read *Moody Monthly* magazine and Moody Press publications).[54]

Since the early 1960s five of the six regional accrediting associations have accepted as members a total of eleven Bible colleges including Bethany (Assemblies of God), Biola, Pacific Christian (Independent Disciples), and Simpson (Christian and Missionary Alliance) in California; Western Baptist (General Association of Regular Baptists) in Oregon; Northwest College of the Assemblies of God in Washington; St. Paul (Christian and Missionary Alliance); Northwestern in New Jersey; Philadelphia; Gulf Coast (Church of God) in Texas; and Johnson.[55]

One of the major reasons that Bible colleges have experienced such a struggle to improve their academic programs is that throughout much of their history they have operated with very limited financial resources. Typically, the schools have recruited their students from the lower to middle socioeconomic classes, and the students have been preparing for careers that offer more spiritual challenge than financial reward. Consequently, the schools charged minimum fees. As late as the 1940s, approximately half of the Bible colleges charged no tuition fee at all, although sometimes they asked the students to contribute labor as well as room and board expenses. In 1978–79, one of the largest Bible colleges, Baptist of Missouri, charged a tuition of only eight dollars per credit hour. The colleges balanced their books by relying on the voluntary services of ministers of nearby churches and by asking their full-time employees to subsidize the educational expenses of the students by accepting substandard salaries. Sometimes the colleges could offer able instruction despite these limitations, but usually the academic environment they produced was less than excellent. This situation has gradually improved since the organization of the AABC.[56]

Like American higher education in general, the Bible college movement has witnessed significant growth during the twentieth century. While many of the leading Bible colleges began before 1920, the great majority of the 430 contemporary institutions came into existence after 1940. The recent Bible college enrollment pattern compares favorably with the enrollment figures of graduate theological schools. For example, by mid-century only one theological seminary—Southwestern Baptist Theological Seminary (Tex.)—could match Moody's overall enrollment of approximately 1,650. The largest accredited Bible colleges, based on their fall, 1980, enrollments, are Biola, 2,345; Baptist of Missouri, 1,721; Moody, 1,341 (plus 1,975 in the evening subcollegiate program); Southeastern College of the Assemblies of God (Fla.), 1,255; Central, an Assemblies of God school (Mo.), 1,094; Northwest College of the Assemblies of God, 825; Baptist of Pennsylvania, 823; Southwestern Assemblies of God College (Tex.), 713; North Central (Minn.), 701; St. Paul, 658; Bethany, 645; Multnomah (Ore.), 633; Toccoa Falls, a Christian and Missionary Alliance school (Ga.), 619; Columbia, 587; Valley Forge Christian, an Assemblies of God school (Pa.), 535; Cincinnati, 522; Free Will Baptist (Tenn.), 513; Nazarene (Col.), 510; Philadelphia, 509; and Washington (Md.), 500. The average enrollment in the accredited schools is approximately 425 (accredited seminaries, by comparison, average 293 students). Most schools, however, are much smaller. While some Bible college leaders claim that the existence of many small institutions allows the movement to serve more geographical regions and to place a larger number of students in meaningful Christian service assignments, the AABC manual suggests that efficiency of operation is not possible with an enrollment of less than several hundred.[57]

In the 1980s enrollment maintenance continues to be a major concern of Bible college leaders. The growth pattern of the early 1970s has not continued in recent years, and many seminars and discussion groups at recent Bible college professional meetings have focused on this problem. While the general spiritual awakening of the last two decades has affected Bible college enrollment positively, its effects are being offset by factors that concern higher education in general, namely the declining supply of college-age students and the downward turn in the economy. Partly as an effort to aid the student recruitment effort, the AABC in the late 1970s conducted a comprehensive study of the demographic characteristics of incoming Bible college students. It showed that many students did not enroll immediately upon high school graduation (only 52 percent of the new students were younger than 19); most came from homes with modest incomes (44 percent reported 1975 family income of less than $10,000 and 67 percent less than $15,000) and non-urban locations (40 percent came from communities of less than 10,000 population, and 64 percent less than 50,000); and almost none (1.5 percent) plan to enroll in seminary following their Bible college study.[58]

FUNDAMENTALISM AND HIGHER EDUCATION

Any discussion of fundamentalism must begin with the issue of definition, for the word suggests very different things to different people. To many who identify with the movement, fundamentalism refers to those spiritually minded Christians who most faithfully practice God's biblical commands. For some Christians who react negatively to the term, it refers to those to the right of them on the theological spectrum, particularly those who are somewhat difficult to get along with or somewhat insensitive and unthinking in their zeal. For example, one Wheaton student defined a "fundy" as "a person who will ask you in the shower at 7:30 a.m. what the Lord has done for you this morning."[59] Many nonevangelicals use the term to characterize all Protestant individuals, churches, and organizations that still maintain an orthodox approach to Christianity. Finally, to a wide variety of observers the term describes those conservative Protestants who are aggressive in fighting liberal Protestantism and who proudly accept the fundamentalist label; this latter definition is the one that I will assume.

During the early decades of the twentieth century, as most of the major denominations became increasingly influenced by liberal Protestant thought and as their colleges gradually became secularized, Wheaton gained a reputation as the leading fundamentalist college. Wheaton earned this reputation because of its dogged determination to resist secular influence and because its nondenominational nature made it attractive to students from orthodox homes in a broad variety of denominations. On the eve of World War I, the still new Christian and Missionary Alliance, which at that time operated only Bible schools, identified Wheaton as "the officially recognized college of the Alliance" for its young people who desired a baccalaureate degree. One Wheaton historian observed that, by the 1920s, the list of Wheaton supporters "read like a Who's Who of Northern Fundamentalism." Lyman and Milton Stewart contributed heavily to the college; they were the wealthy oil men who financed the publication of *The Fundamentals,* the apologetic series which gave the movement its name. Also, serving as trustees or members of the board of reference during the 1920s were Fleming Revell, the leading fundamentalist publisher and a brother-in-law of Dwight Moody; William Blackstone, author of the widely distributed book on the Second Coming, *Jesus is Coming;* and William Bell Riley, the vocal Baptist fundamentalist. When the death of Charles Blanchard in 1925 brought to an end the second of the long-lasting Blanchard presidencies, the trustees clearly demonstrated their orientation by naming as president an unequivocal fundamentalist, J. Oliver Buswell, Jr., a young but aggressive leader of the orthodox wing of the Northern Presbyterians.[60]

While some schools looked to Wheaton as their model, others viewed the Illinois college as a leading example of what they did not want to become. For example, when Elam J. Anderson interviewed for the presidency of Northern Baptist–sponsored Redlands (Cal.) in 1938, he learned that a part of the trustee board had determined that the next president must be a fundamentalist, and the Redlands must become "the Wheaton of the Southwest."[61] He responded that "if that is the purpose of the trustees, then I must withdraw my candidacy. While I am sympathetic with much of Wheaton's program, I have a deep conviction that the method of compulsion both in doctrine and conduct is not only non-Baptist, but also contrary to sound principles of education."[62]

If Wheaton was the best-known fundamentalist college in the 1920s, Williams Jennings Bryan was the best-known fundamentalist spokesman. During Bryan's participation in the widely publicized Scopes evolution trial at Dayton, Tennessee, in the summer of 1925, he expressed the wish that a men's college would be established in the scenic hill country surrounding Dayton. Shortly after the trial he died, and his followers thought that the development of a major fundamentalist university near Dayton would serve as an appropriate memorial. The Depression, however, severely restricted the fund-raising abilities of the project promoters, and the resultant college which opened in 1930 has developed into a modest-sized liberal arts college rather than a university.[63]

It is appropriate that Bryan wanted to establish a clearly orthodox college, for his almost continuous travels throughout the country afforded him the opportunity to learn about and closely identify with the continuing Christian colleges. For example, when he spoke at Taylor in the early 1920s, he began his address with high praise for the school:

> Parents all over this nation are asking me where they can send their sons and daughters to school knowing that their faith in God and in morality will not be destroyed. I find that this is a college where they teach you the Bible instead of apologizing for it, and I shall for this reason recommend Taylor University to inquiring Christian parents.[64]

Although the fundamentalist movement has been especially associated with conservative factions in the Baptist, Presbyterian, and Disciples of Christ denominations, it also existed within the denomination claiming the largest number of Protestant colleges, the Methodist Church. Near the turn of the century and just before the peak of the fundamentalist-modernist battles of the 1920s, the theological division within Methodism was between the holiness advocates, who wished to perpetuate the early nineteenth-century style of Methodism, and those who favored a more restrained form of worship. The latter thought this restraint appropriate since the denomination's constituency had become largely middle rather than lower class in socioeconomic standing. Between 1890 and 1920 the holiness movement was at its peak. Many contemporary holiness and holiness-pentecostal denominations had their origins in this period. The movement thrived on summer camp meetings led by popular preachers like Henry Clay Morrison, who later served as the first president of Asbury (Ky.). Asbury operated, as did Taylor, as one of the few colleges representing the sizable holiness branch of Methodism. Although holiness Methodist families existed throughout the country, holiness Methodist colleges did not; therefore, Asbury attracted many students from great distances. During Morrison's presidency, for example, students came from forty-seven states and eighteen foreign countries. By 1920, Asbury's leaders thought it necessary to preach against modernism as well as for holiness, with the result that they sounded increasingly like the more Calvinist fundamentalists. Morrison, a crusading religious orator in the style of Bryan, attacked the Protestant liberals for proclaiming what their theology was not rather than what they did believe: "The modernists are as yet up in the air. They have some hesitation as to where they shall light and with whom they shall settle down for permanent abode and active service. As yet they have no inspired Bible, no divine atoning Christ able to save from

sin, no system of theology, no fixed creed, no hymnology, no enthusiastic evangelism to win sinners from the ruin of their wickedness
to a Savior. The fact is that there is a question in their minds as
to whether there is any real sin or a need of a Savior."[65]

Because the fundamentalists fought what at the time appeared
to be a losing battle over such critical issues as the divinity of Christ
and the trustworthiness of the biblical record, the struggle was very
tense. Christian grace, rationality, and due attention to issues other
than theology sometimes suffered. With the passage of time and
the appearance of new conservative Protestant leaders, these
undesirable aspects of the battle—particularly when they continued
for several decades—looked increasingly embarrassing. Consequently, many of the new leaders, without discarding their orthodox
theology, choose to disassociate themselves from the emotionally
laden word "fundamentalist" and instead called themselves
"evangelical." This new theological label became the preferred one
of the majority of orthodox Protestants after World War II. (Today
probably no more than 10 to 15 percent of the estimated 40 million
evangelicals would call themselves fundamentalists.)

The major factor distinguishing recent fundamentalists from the
more moderate evangelicals was the degree to which the former
chose to separate from liberal Protestants and, in some cases, from
other orthodox Protestants. The evangelicals did not insist that
orthodox Protestants withdraw from the large, theologically mixed
denominations. Rather, they thought it appropriate to seek to win
the denominations back to their earlier orthodoxy. The fundamentalists, by contrast, thought it a violation of the separation commandment in 2 Corinthians 6:14 for an orthodox Christian to be
associated with a denomination or any other group that was not
completely administered and populated by fellow orthodox
believers.[66] George Dollar, a fundamentalist historian writing in
the 1960s, identified the following colleges as examples of
evangelical institutions: Barrington, Columbia Bible, Houghton
(N.Y.), Kings (N.Y.), LeTourneau (Tex.), Nyack, Oral Roberts,
Taylor, and Wheaton. Clearly fundamentalist schools, according
to Dollar, included Baptist Bible of Pennsylvania, Baptist Bible
of Colorado, Baptist Bible of Missouri, Bob Jones, Maranatha
Bible (Wis.), Midwestern Baptist Bible (Mich.), and Pillsbury Baptist Bible (Minn.). Colleges between these two types who,
presumably, would favor separating from most of the major
denominations but would not wish to make a major issue of the
fact, would, in Dollar's opinion, include the following: Asbury,
Biola, Cedarville (Oh.), Covenant (Tenn.), Detroit Bible, John

Brown (Ark.), Moody, Philadelphia College of the Bible, Tennessee Temple, and Washington (D.C.) Bible.[67]

Among those institutions which accepted the fundamentalist label, the generally acknowledged leaders today include Tennessee Temple, Baptist Bible of Missouri, Liberty Baptist, and Bob Jones. Tennessee Temple was founded in 1946 by Lee Roberson as an extension of his Highland Park Baptist Church in Chattanooga. The Tennessee Temple "schools" include a Bible college and a seminary as well as a liberal arts college, with total enrollment exceeding 2,300 by 1971. The sponsoring Highland Park Baptist Church, in addition to its variety of programs in Chattanooga, has organized the fundamentalist Baptists in the southeastern United States into an organization called the Southwide Baptist Fellowship.[68]

One fundamentalist institution that is more significant than it is well known is Baptist Bible of Missouri. Its 2,500 students in the late 1970s gave it an enrollment rarely matched in Bible college history. The school is the approved institution of the Baptist Bible Fellowship (BBF), a loose confederation of over 3,500 churches that militantly promote the importance and autonomy of the local church. Despite their insistence upon congregationalism, BBF members recognized the value of some cooperation, and they created the Missouri school for the sole purpose of training workers for their many churches.

The college was organized in 1950 by over 100 ministers who previously had been associated with the World Baptist Fellowship empire of J. Frank Norris, the long-time minister of the First Baptist Church of Fort Worth. By mid-century, personality clashes and organizational disputes resulted in the aging Norris losing most of his following among Baptist fundamentalists. Those who dropped away reorganized themselves into the Baptist Bible Fellowship. Principal leaders of the new group included G. B. Vick, minister of Detroit's large Temple Baptist Church, and W. E. Dowell, minister of the High Street Baptist Church of Springfield, Missouri. When the leaders of the reorganized group agreed on the desirability of establishing a Bible college, they chose to locate it in Dowell's home town and to select Vick to commute from his pastorate in Detroit to serve as the school president.

Few colleges have been organized with as close a relationship to the basic purpose of the supporting denomination as was Baptist Bible. The school described itself as "a training center to prepare young men and women to fit into the fellowship's congregation-building thrust." The local churches were multifaceted and heavily growth-oriented; therefore, there have been sufficient positions in the BBF system for all graduates. Furthermore, the fellowship wanted all of its new ministers to have graduated from the school because, according to Vick, "Preachers, even fundamentalists, who have not been trained by us, don't think like we do."[69]

One of those who did think like the BBF ministers and who graduated from the three-year course at Baptist Bible was Jerry Falwell, who by the 1970s had become one of the best-known preachers in America. Consistent with the church-growth emphasis of the BBF, the young Falwell began Thomas Road Baptist Church in Lynchburg, Virginia, and led its growth from 35 church members in 1956 to 17,000 members in 1980. Also consistent with the BBF emphasis which he learned while in college, Falwell developed a comprehensive church program including a day-school academy, a Bible institute, a correspondence school, a seminary, and Liberty Baptist College. Falwell has been able to build his college and other programs in part by soliciting funds from his radio and television ministry, which by 1980 included nearly 700 television and radio stations. Approximately 18 million weekly listeners sent contributions totaling $1 million a week, with much of the income going to pay the cost of the broadcasts. This widespread media exposure brought Falwell not only funds but also students—in numbers totaling 3,000 by 1978. Falwell has never hesitated to set high goals, and his enrollment targets include 10,000 by 1988 and 50,000 by the end of this century. He also boasts that his school will eventually schedule Notre Dame in football.[70]

Liberty Baptist may some day be the largest fundamentalist college, but the present holder of that title is Bob Jones University (BJU). Bob Jones is not only the largest but also the historic leader of the fundamentalist colleges. The school was founded by the evangelist of the same name in 1926. During the first quarter of this century, Bob Jones, Sr., preached 12,000 sermons to over 15 million people. According to his biographer, 300,000 of these "came forward" to make spiritual commitments and 100,000 subsequently joined a Christian church. BJU, then, like Oral Roberts University in a later era, was built upon a broad publicity base of religious crusades conducted over many years in many geographic regions. Jones states that during his evangelistic travels he became increasingly disturbed with the many reports of how students from Christian families left home to study in college—including church colleges in the process of becoming secular—and then returned without their faith and/or their purity. He described listening to the account of an aged couple who had served as home missionaries in the Northwest, where they helped found a college of their denomination and then gave sacrificially of their meager funds to support it. Naturally they sent their son to study there, but to their surprise the institution in the meantime had hired non-Christians as faculty members. These skeptical instructors led their son astray, and he became a "drunken atheistic bum." Their appeal to the evangelist was this: "Brother Bob, my wife and I are old. You are a young man. Go up and down this country, and tell this story, and warn the people that the educational drift of this nation is atheistic." Jones's reaction to this and similar pleas was not merely to go up and down the country uttering jeremiads but to found a Christian college with sufficient "safeguards" surrounding it to assure that it would not, like the church college mentioned above, ever move in a secular direction. Accordingly, when Jones opened his institution in Saint Andrews Bay, Florida, in 1926, he not only provided it with an orthodox creed but added the following proviso at the end of the statement of belief: "This charter shall never be amended, modified, altered, or changed." In 1933 he purchased the property of Centenary College in Cleveland, Tennessee, and moved the school there, where it remained until its relocation in 1947 to its present Greenville, South Carolina, campus.[71]

In several ways BJU represents both the best and the worst in fundamentalist higher education. Its very attractive $50 million campus serves 5,000 students (1974) who come from nearly every state and approximately 25 foreign countries. The physical plant includes a 3,600-seat dining commons and a 7,000-seat amphitorium where the entire student body meets seven mornings a week for chapel and worship services. During the middle decades of this century, the school's record in training large numbers of young men to minister to large numbers of people and to lead large numbers of people to make initial Christian commitments may be unmatched. Also, in some ways its academic program and facilities are superior. Outside critics have observed that the BJU movie and television studios and its art gallery are among the best on any college campus in the country. Only UCLA, USC, and Boston University operate cinema production programs comparable to that at BJU. The technically excellent films produced in its studios include *Wine of Morning, Red Runs the River,* and *Flame in the Wind.* In 1973 an essayist in the *National Review* expressed utter astonishment at the quality of the univeristy art museum which he described as containing "an array of pictures (medieval, renaissance, baroque, and eighteenth century) that is nothing short of incredible. How is it possible in a short space of twenty years to assemble such a collection . . . at a time when old masters, especially with names like Botticelli, Rubens, Rembrandt, Titian,

Tintoretto, have become so scarce and so expensive so as to be almost unavailable?'' The collection of sacred art, just like the university's emphasis upon excellence in the fine arts in general, is due largely to the efforts of Bob Jones, Jr., who presided over the school between 1947 and 1971.[72]

On the other hand, Bob Jones University encourages some of the criticism made against it both by other Christians and those outside the Christian faith. For example, the catalog descriptions of the institution in places are unnecessarily aggressive, defensive, and boastful. The first page of the catalog, carrying the heading, "Important," states that the university holds the privilege of suspending any student at any time who "in the opinion of the University does not fit into the spirit of the institution regardless of whether or not he conforms to the specific rules and regulations of the University." Also, the BJU motto is at best ambitious and at worst unrealistic and vain; it reads, "Bob Jones University is determined that no school shall excel it in the thoroughness of its scholastic work; and, God helping it, it endeavors to excel all other schools in the thoroughness of its Christian training." In some respects the college may match its motto; in others it clearly doesn't, yet because of its sweeping claim it invites others to examine it closely. Many, for example, will doubt whether the quality of the faculty is commensurate with the claims of the institution for academic supremacy. In 1978, only 14 percent (36 of 257 regular faculty appointees) held earned doctoral degrees (this does not include the 60 graduate assistants who teach half-loads). Admittedly this is only one index of academic quality, but it is one which is easily measurable. Another quantifiable standard is the number of library volumes, which presently is 155,000. In both of these areas, Bob Jones ranks low for colleges of its size.[73]

Some of the things for which Bob Jones receives criticism are not necessarily bad, only different. For example, some object to the university practice of paying faculty members only small cash salaries (based upon family need), but then supplementing this income with on-campus room and board accommodations and hospital privileges. Such a remuneration plan may not be orthodox, but it is no more inappropriate than are, say, similar plans for ordained instructors in Roman Catholic institutions.[74]

Historically, a number of traits have characterized fundamentalist higher education and still are apparent in it. Perhaps the most important of these is an emphasis on evangelism. Fundamentalist schools have stressed not only the training of ministers but, more specifically, the training of "soul-saving" ministers. One of the primary purposes for founding Bob Jones was to serve as "a fundamentalist base for future evangelism''; twenty-five years later this base was well in place with 1,200 of the 3,000 Bob Jones students being trained as ministerial evangelists. *Time* magazine duly noted: ''Bob Jones University has demonstrated that it is possible to take the enthusiasm of a religious revival, transfer it to a campus, and sustain it without missing a beat.'' While today a smaller percentage of BJU students enters the ministry, the number of such ministerial students remains at approximately 1,000.

During his lifetime, the founder of the school gave special attention to the younger men, to whom he referred affectionately as his ''preacher boys.'' He gave them weekly instruction in the practical aspects of the ministry, including evangelism. In the weekly sessions, he counseled them to ''have pure minds and hearts, be honest with people, deal fairly and kindly with them, dress neatly and appropriately, preach from the Bible, know the Scriptures, respect womanhood. . . .'' He also warned them severely against the temptations of money and women. According to Jones's biographer,

> He blasts away at young ministers who would go out just to preach for money or who make decisions to serve God on the basis of income. He thunders at them, like a prophet of yesteryear, to be gentlemen in every respect in relation to girls and ladies, and verbally threatens any young preacher who would go out to hold a meeting or to conduct a service and then become sinful with some single ''fancy female'' who flatters his ego and entices him to ruin all the good he has accomplished.[75]

Each time the class met, the hundreds of preacher boys sang their theme song:

> *Souls for Jesus is our battle cry*
> *Souls for Jesus, we'll fight until we die;*
> *We never will give in*
> *While souls are lost in sin,*
> *Souls for Jesus is our battle cry.*[76]

A similar evangelistic emphasis has characterized the other fundamentalist colleges. During the first twenty-six years of Tennessee Temple, one-third of its graduates—nearly 1,000 students—entered the ministry. President Dowell of Baptist Bible of Missouri represented the conviction of the people at his institution when he stated that ''the only hope of America is the establishment of thousands of independent soul-winning churches.'' One cannot even gain admittance to the Missouri college without expressing the desire to become a Christian worker. At Liberty Baptist, soul saving is an integral part of the theoretical and applied curriculum. All first-year students take classes in Christian evangelism, in which they learn the basic techniques and methods of personal soul winning. Many of the students participate in the evangelistic thrust of the Thomas Road Baptist Church, which conducts intensive revival campaigns each fall and spring; they visit, pray, and help conduct "satellite campaigns" under the direction of the evangelist.[77]

During the past two decades the fastest-growing program of the large fundamentalist churches—as well as many other conservative Protestant churches—has been the Christian day-school movement. Consequently, the fastest-growing program in fundamentalist colleges has been that of preparing teachers for the growing number of Christian elementary and secondary schools. For example, Tennessee Temple began such a program in 1964. Within eight years, it had become the largest division in the college. Whereas in 1950 most of the elementary and secondary students enrolled in private schools attended Catholic, Lutheran, and Christian Reformed institutions, most of the private schools established since then have been operated by fundamentalist organizations. The director of the Association of Christian Schools International claims that by the late 1970s over 1 million students were enrolled in more than 5,000 such schools, with additional ones opening at the rate of two per day. Baptist Bible of Missouri considers it so natural for a church to operate a day school that it requires every pastoral candidate for the bachelors degree to take a course in the history and philosophy of the Christian day-school movement. The great growth of Christian schools developed only in part because of governmental decisions calling for the integration of public schools. More significant has been the reaction against the 1962 and 1963 Supreme Court decisions banning group devotional exercises from the public schools, the decreasing quality of public education, the reduced role of ethical instruction, the increasing public school problems with personal and academic discipline, the proliferation of illegal drug usage, and the increasing national affluence which made it possible for middle-income families to afford private school tuition charges.[78]

Another characteristic of fundamentalist colleges is their tendency to use authoritarian leadership styles. Most such schools have been founded in the middle half of the twentieth century by unusually aggressive and dynamic men who then continued to lead the schools they founded. Their followers often have deferred to them more completely than they would to the leaders of a college that had existed for a century or longer. For example, E. C. Haskell, chairman of the deacon board of Highland Park Baptist Church in Chattanooga, the sponsoring church of Tennessee Temple, described why he generally accepted the view of Lee Roberson, the church's pastor and the founder and president of the school: "I know of no man that I consider to live closer to God than Dr. Roberson; and if this is what he thinks should be done then I will not ask questions." Sometimes, however, lesser officials and instructors in the fundamentalist colleges do ask questions, with the result that what might be an engaging debate on other campuses becomes a traumatic crisis in a highly authoritarian institution. At Bob Jones, for example, in 1953, the registrar, three deans, and a dozen teachers resigned, charging the founder-president with demanding that "the tiniest facet of his thought be considered red letter gospel." The response of Bob Jones, Sr., was to preach a sermon on Judas.

One risk of identifying a college very closely with the personality of its leader is that if the leader falls, the college may collapse with him. Billy James Hargis, the well-known right-wing anticommunist crusader, founded American Christian (Okla.). In addition to denouncing loudly the existence of communism in this country and throughout the world, Hargis preached against a variety of other evils including the decline of sexual morality. His organization even published 250,000 copies of his booklet, "Is the School House the Proper Place to Teach Raw Sex?" When, in the middle 1970s, his former colleagues accused him of engaging in sexual relations with students of both sexes, he resigned the college presidency. The school experienced extreme difficulty raising funds without him, and the enrollment dropped sharply.

An authoritarian leader often works with few people able or willing to assist him in developing his thinking, and when he adopts an extreme interpretation of the biblical commandment for separation from the world, he may end up withdrawing from and denouncing the very people and institutions who should be his natural allies in the promotion of Christian higher education. Bob Jones, Jr., for years has criticized evangelical institutions with even greater emotional fervor than that used in fighting the original enemies of his college, the modernists. He once observed that "Satan's three forces in his war against God are modernism, neo-orthodoxy, and the new evangelism. Of these three, the last group is the most dangerous." More recently he has accused fellow fundamentalist Jerry Falwell of being a tool of Satan. In 1980 the newspaper of Falwell's conservative political lobby, Moral Majority, described a letter written by Bob Jones, Jr., to the 1980 BJU graduates calling Falwell "the most dangerous man in America today as far as

Biblical Christianity is concerned,'' and his Moral Majority program ''one of Satan's devices to build the world church of Anti-
Christ.''[79]

Fundamentalist colleges also tend to be associated with Baptist
''super churches.'' A close correlation exists between the fundamentalist church emphasis on growth and bigness in general (e.g.,
church membership, big buildings, bus fleets, Sunday school enrollment, radio and television broadcasts on increasing numbers of stations to increasing numbers of viewers who send in increasing
numbers of dollars) and their establishment of colleges designed
to enroll increasing numbers of students. This growth emphasis is
related to a desire for mass evangelism organizations that multiply
results; it is also a religious form of boosterism. One example of
this phenomenon is the relationship between Temple Baptist Church
of Detroit and Baptist Bible of Missouri. Temple Baptist Church
has been the leading sponsor of Baptist Bible. The pastor of one
was the president of the other. In 1955, *Life* magazine identified
the Temple Baptist Sunday school as the largest in America. The
1973 *Christian Life* listing of the 100 largest Sunday schools in
America found that 23 of them were led by ministerial graduates
of Baptist Bible. A later *Christian Life* poll showed that each of
the three fastest-growing Sunday schools during the 1968–77 decade
have operated fundamentalist colleges. These include the First Baptist Church of Hammond, Indiana, which grew from 3,300 to
14,000 members and sponsored Hyles-Anderson; Highland Park
Baptist Church of Chattanooga, which grew from 2,400 to 8,000
members and directed Tennessee Temple; and Thomas Road Baptist Church of Lynchburg, Virginia, which grew from 2,600 to 6,400
members and administered Liberty Baptist.[80]

Still another characteristic of fundamentalist colleges is their concern to protect the purity of the Christian faith more than—and
sometimes at the expense of—intellectual freedom. Bob Jones III
frankly admits this to be the case at his institution. ''We're unusual
in our objectives to teach the student what he believes. Most schools
would be appalled at this statement, but committed as we are, we
don't throw out a bunch of theories to them about the religion of
the world and philosophy and this sort of thing.'' The official
biographer of Billy Graham suggests that a significant factor in
Graham's decision to leave BJU after one semester in attendance
was the lack of intellectual freedom that he experienced there: ''Dr.
Bob knew exactly what was true and false in faith, ethics, and
academics. He also stated publicly that his institution had never
been wrong. Independent thought was so discouraged that many
alumni say in retrospect that there was almost thought control.''
Bob Jones, Sr., used to tell the students in chapel that ''if you don't

like it here you can pack your dirty duds and hit the four-lane highway." Graham, among others, accepted that option.

Fundamentalist colleges frequently hesitate to allow their students to attend local churches not directly affiliated with the college; to protect them they frequently provide Sunday worship services as well as weekday chapel services on campus. Tennessee Temple has required all of its students to attend the affiliated Highland Park Church because:

> Students are not always wise in their choice of churches while at school nor in their discernment of truth and error. On several occasions students have become involved in Baptist churches which were pentecostal and have been diverted into the error of tongues. With so many heresies about, it seemed advisable that rather than making a "black list" of churches not to attend, it would be a wiser course to require the students to go where there were no such pitfalls for novices in the Christian faith.[81]

The colleges also define very specific belief and behavioral expectations for their faculty members. Tennessee Temple, at least as recently as the 1970s, required its faculty to join the Highland Park Baptist Church unless employed by another church, to fill out a weekly activity report verifying attendance at one week-night and two Sunday services, to believe in eternal security and premillennial eschatology, and not to play cards, go to the movies, participate in mixed bathing, wear shorts, or—for men—grow a beard or wear long hair. Other fundamentalist institutions hold similar faculty requirements. Consequently, the schools are forced to hire faculty heavily from the ranks of their alumni—or from the graduates of a limited number of similar institutions—so as to obtain people who are willing to submit to the severe restrictions on their personal freedoms. For example, at Bob Jones in the mid-1960s, 130 of 150 regular faculty members had taken at least part of their academic training at BJU.

The colleges sometimes find it difficult to recruit people who are both competently trained and willing to comply with school standards. In 1969, President Vick of Baptist Bible of Missouri stated that he probably would not hire an instructor unless he possessed a baccalaureate degree from an accredited institution and was willing to work towards a master's degree; "Nevertheless," he observed, "we know the dangers, we're aware of history; and we are not going to sacrifice our convictions on anybody's academic altar." Bob Jones, Sr., noted another concern about graduate school training: it tends to make people more analytical, more questioning, and less inclined to accept automatically enthusiastic responses and approaches. On one occasion he remarked—probably half seriously, "Everytime we add one of these Ph.D.'s to the faculty we have to pray and work harder to keep the evangelistic fires burning."[82]

In recent decades, at least, fundamentalist colleges have tended to promote conservative political views and candidates. Bob Jones has granted honorary doctoral degrees to Billy James Hargis and George Wallace, governor of Alabama. Senator Strom Thurmond of South Carolina and the school have found each other sufficiently acceptable for Thurmond to serve as a member of the board of trustees. In the late 1970s President Falwell of Liberty Baptist organized Moral Majority, a political lobbying organization which used its vast influence to support conservative political candidates as well as some causes which evangelical Christians generally supported. Moral Majority crusaded not only for conservative political candidates but against liberal ones. For example, senators Birch Bayh, Frank Church, George McGovern, and Gaylord Nelson found Moral Majority campaigning against their 1980 reelection bids. The lobbying effort was sufficiently successful to attract a cover story by *Newsweek* magazine.[83]

During the middle part of the twentieth century, probably no conservative Christian college attracted greater attention for its promotion of conservative politics than did Harding (Ark.), a Churches of Christ institution. Beginning in 1936, when returning China missionary George S. Benson assumed the presidency of Harding, that institution developed a national reputation as an outspoken proponent of the free-enterprise economic system. Benson was appalled at the growth of government involvement in and control of the economy during the early New Deal years. After he appeared before the House Ways and Means Committee in 1941 to call for the government to transfer funds from New Deal relief agencies to defense purposes, he began to attract increasing attention to himself and his institution. By 1954 his weekly newspaper column appeared in more than 3,000 newspapers, and his weekly radio program, "Land of the Free," was heard on 365 stations. Donations began to pour into the college from people across the nation who supported the causes that Benson advocated.[84]

Although most evangelical colleges have been less aggressive than Harding in promoting specific political perspectives, members of their communities in recent years have shown a clear preference for conservative candidates.[85] For example, a poll of Wheaton students in the 1960s on the political preference of their parents showed that 61 percent favored conservative Republicans, 20 percent liberal Republicans, and only 7 percent Democrats.[86]

The quality of the fundamentalist institutions, like that of the Bible colleges, has been limited by the meager financial bases from which most of them operate. Since fundamentalist organizations represent denominations and individuals that withdrew from the mainline denominations in this century, they have had to start anew in developing their own colleges. Consequently, from the standpoint of tradition and financial resources, many of these schools now are operating at a level of development comparable to that reached a century ago by the colleges of the denominations from which they separated. In too many cases, limited resources have caused the institutions to hire inadequately trained professors to direct courses whose quality has been defended because of the Christian character of the teachers. It is hoped that the academic quality of the fundamentalist colleges will continue to increase until it is as noteworthy as the religious zeal of such institutions.

The student Christian associations, the university pastorate movement, the Bible schools, and the fundamentalist colleges have been the most direct and the most novel responses to the secularization of higher education. They have not been the only ones, however; for the twentieth century has witnessed the founding of a number of traditional liberal arts colleges by new conservative, if not clearly fundamentalist, groups (e.g., the Churches of Christ, the Nazarenes, and the Church of God denominations). These new evangelical colleges together with the Bible colleges, the fundamentalist colleges, and the continuing Christian colleges are the subject of the next chapter on the most recent period of Protestant higher education in America.

Chapter 6

The Reconstruction Of Christian Higher Education

Never since the skeptical 1790s had Christian colleges experienced the degree of demoralization that they did during the second quarter of this century. The secularizing pattern first hit the Christian colleges with intensity in the 1920s and the situation worsened during the 1930s, for added to the growing secularization were the effects of the nation's worst economic depression. The continuing Christian colleges were often the less affluent ones, and it is a testimony to their dedication that so many employed highly sacrificial and sometimes creative measures in the largely successful struggle to survive. For example, at Abilene Christian (Tex.), in 1931–32, faculty members voluntarily returned 50 percent of their salaries to allow the school to balance its budget, while Greenville (Ill.) used its chemistry laboratory as an industrial plant to employ impoverished students in the manufacture of a variety of household toiletries, medicines, and flavorings, which additional students then sold at 30 percent commission throughout the country.[1] By the 1940s the Christian colleges were beginning to recover. Although the movement toward secularization continued, the stimulus of war production ended the Great Depression, and the G.I. Bill brought a record number of enrollees to colleges of all types.

The recovery process has continued steadily in the last three decades until today the Christian colleges are stronger than they have been at any time since the secular revolution. The recovery has not come because secularizing institutions have returned to their earlier orientation (very few have) or because many new, well-developed Christian colleges have been founded (except for a limited number of colleges like Oral Roberts and Pepperdine in California, most of the new colleges have begun with very modest resources). Rather, the recovery has come because of factors that have benefited higher education in general (a relatively prosperous economy, the increasing popularity of attending college, and the new and expanding forms of government aid to students and institutions); because of the decline in the number of additional colleges to begin the secularization process; and because cooperative efforts through such organizations as the Christian College Coalition and the American Association of Bible Colleges have allowed Christian colleges to achieve greater influence and an increased public awareness of their growing quality and clearly defined goals.

THE EMERGING LINE-UP
OF THE MODERN CHRISTIAN COLLEGE

Enough time has passed since the peak period of the secularization challenge for most of the historically church-related colleges to decide whether they are generally accepting of or generally resistant to secular influences. Since so many colleges chose to accept these influences, the Christian college line-up of today is considerably different from that of 1920. The modern Christian colleges include those affiliated with the smaller evangelical denominations, a number of independent evangelical colleges, most Southern Baptist and Lutheran institutions, some Presbyterian colleges, and a few colleges affiliated with other major denominations and traditions. There are perhaps 200 such continuing Christian liberal arts colleges plus the Bible colleges.

The Southern Baptists maintain probably the largest denominational network of continuing Christian colleges. Approximately sixty institutions identify with that denomination. Baylor with its 10,000 students is not only the largest of the Southern Baptist colleges but also the largest Protestant college that seriously seeks to integrate the Christian faith with its educational program.[2] Southern Baptist colleges with leading academic reputations include Wake Forest, Richmond, Baylor, Furman, Mercer, Stetson, Mississippi, Louisiana, and Samford.[3]

The number of colleges associated with the several Lutheran denominations nearly equals the Southern Baptist total and includes thirty-eight senior colleges, ten junior colleges, and five Bible colleges. The largest of these, with 1980 enrollments of over 2,000, are Valparaiso (Ind.), Pacific Lutheran, St. Olaf, California Lutheran, Concordia of Moorhead, Minnesota, Wagner (N.Y.), Wittenberg, Gustavus Adolphus, Augustana of Illinois, Augustana of South Dakota, Capital (Oh.), and Luther of Iowa. The most selective in admitting students include Augustana of Illinois, Gettysburg (Penn.), Gustavus Adolphus, Muhlenberg (Penn.), Pacific Lutheran, St. Olaf, and Valparaiso.[4]

In general, the denominations associated with continuing Christian colleges support their institutions much better than do the denominations whose schools are more secular. For example, of the major denominations, none contributes as much to the operating budgets and building programs of its colleges as do the Southern Baptists and Lutherans. In recent years the Missouri Synod Lutheran Church has provided from one-fourth to one-half of the operating expenses for its synodical colleges. Also noteworthy is the practice of the Christian Reformed Church, which requires all of its individual members, by virtue of their membership, to support the denomination's higher education program.[5]

A comparison of the Christian college line-ups of 1920 and 1980 shows great contrast not only because many secularizing institutions have departed but also because new liberal arts colleges have appeared. While Protestant groups have founded far fewer colleges since 1920 than they did between the Civil War and World War I, nearly all of the new institutions have declared a clearly Christian orientation.[6]

Some new colleges have been founded by the major denominations. For example, Valparaiso began in 1925 as the first comprehensive college of the Missouri Synod Lutherans; the Southern Baptists added Grand Canyon (Ariz.) in 1949; the American Baptists opened Eastern (Pa.) in 1952 and Judson (Ill.) in 1963; and the Lutheran Church in America and the American Lutheran Church together founded California Lutheran in 1959. For the most part, however, the new liberal arts colleges, like most of the Bible colleges, were founded by new evangelical denominations or independent groups that separated from the mainline denominations in protest over the latter's growing liberal theological orientation.[7] For example, the General Association of Regular Baptists founded Grand Rapids Baptist in 1941 and acquired Cedarville (Oh.) in 1953; the Reformed Presbyterians (Evangelical Synod) began Covenant (Tenn.) in 1955; and the Churches of Christ established seventeen currently operating institutions including David Lipscomb (Tenn.) in 1891, Abilene Christian in 1906, Harding in 1924, and Pepperdine in 1937. Abilene and Pepperdine, as the leading schools of the 2.5 million-member Churches of Christ confederation, have become two of the largest Christian colleges in the country; in 1980 the Texas school enrolled 4,372 students and the California institution 7,298 students. Pepperdine was named for its original benefactor, George Pepperdine, who developed the chain of Western Auto Supply stores.

The Pentecostals are the latest major American religious group to enter the field of higher education. Like the older Holiness movement (leading denominations include the Wesleyan Church, the Free Methodist Church, the Anderson, Indiana-based Church of God, the Church of the Nazarene, and the Salvation Army), the

Pentecostal movement (major denominations include the Assemblies of God, the Cleveland, Tennessee–based Church of God, the Pentecostal Holiness Church, the United Pentecostal Church, the Church of the Foursquare Gospel, and the Church of God in Christ) has historic connections with Methodist ideas. The Holiness movement—especially the Wesleyan and Free Methodist churches—began founding colleges in the late nineteenth century, with Roberts Wesleyan (N.Y.), Houghton (N.Y.), Spring Arbor (Mich.), Seattle Pacific (Wash.), Greenville, and Asbury appearing at that time. By contrast, the Pentecostal liberal arts colleges have developed only since World War I, with the best known of these being Lee (Tenn.), begun in 1918 by the Cleveland, Tennessee Church of God; Emmanuel (Ga.), begun in 1919 by the Pentecostal Holiness Church; Evangel (Mo.), begun in 1955 by the Assemblies of God; and Oral Roberts, begun independently by the evangelist in 1965.

The reluctance of Pentecostalism to accept liberal arts education is illustrated by comparing the twentieth century record of its largest predominantly white denomination, the Assemblies of God, with that of the largest Holiness denomination, the Church of the Nazarene. During this period, very few denominations have opened more new liberal arts colleges in this country than has the Nazarene church. It founded Bethany (Ok.), Trevecca (Tenn.), Point Loma (Cal.), Olivet (Ill.), Northwest Nazarene (Id.), and Eastern Nazarene (Mass.), before or during World War I; and Mt. Vernon (Oh.) and Mid-America (Kan.) in the 1960s. By contrast, the 1.3 million-member Assemblies of God has relied primarily on Bible college education; at mid-century it was the largest Protestant denomination in the country without a liberal arts college. When the church leaders finally opened Evangel in 1955, they created considerable controversy throughout the denomination.[8]

The founding and development of Oral Roberts University (ORU) represents the culmination of the entry of Pentecostalism into higher education; however, its significance is even greater than this, for never since the late nineteenth century has a Christian college been so well funded at its inception and so quickly become a leading Christian college in this country. Only six years after the school opened in 1965, ORU could claim a student body of 1,000 coming from 49 states and 23 foreign countries, a library of 121,000 volumes, a physical plant valued at over $30 million, and full regional accreditation. The school developed so rapidly because of the financial base and publicity provided by the Oral Roberts Evangelistic Association. In the early 1970s the association was supplying the school with over half of its operating budget and nearly all of its capital funds. Enrollment has grown to 1,800 in 1972,

3,500 in 1975, and 4,000 in 1978. Also, in the late 1970s the university opened graduate programs in business, theology, medicine, dentistry, and law.[9]

Roberts has desired his school to be the university of the entire charismatic movement rather than a narrowly denominational school of one or more of the traditional Pentecostal churches. As some Pentecostals believe that all converts to the charismatic movement must leave their traditional denominations and join one of the historical Pentecostal churches, it was symbolically significant when Roberts in 1968 transferred his membership from the Pentecostal Holiness denomination to the Methodist Church, with which he had identified as a youth. Roberts has succeeded in his desire for a broadly interdenominational university; by 1972 less than 50 percent of the students came from Holiness or Pentecostal churches, and by 1976 over forty denominations were represented in the student body.

Most of the ORU faculty sympathize with the president's emphasis on the ministry of the Holy Spirit. This emphasis helps make the university's general education program unique. For example, every student enrolls in a two-hour course on the Holy Spirit taught by Roberts, and every student participates in a physical education class each semester. Also, if a student is overweight, he or she, like those who perform inadequately in the classroom, must make satisfactory progress toward removing his or her deficiency in order to continue in school. The capstone of the emphasis upon healing is the recently completed $150 million "City of Faith" hospital, research center, and medical school complex, which the university expects will eventually house a staff of 300 physicians, surgeons, and dentists.[10]

The educational feature of ORU which has attracted the broadest attention is its modernistic application of technology to the learning process. The heart of the institution's academic program is the fourteen-acre learning resources center which combines library, laboratories, classrooms, and office space in an interrelated system housed under one roof. This learning system has earned high praise from the Carnegie Commission and the Ford Foundation, the latter referring to it as "one of the most creative facilities on the American campus today." The institution itself claims that it is the first university to install a computerized information retrieval system whereby students, whether in class, the library, dormitory study lounges, or their own dormitory rooms, have direct-dial access to the audiovisual materials prepared for the courses in which they are enrolled. The college uses the system most extensively for its large-enrollment, general-education courses.

Other campus facilities of note include the 11,000-seat basketball arena and the aerobics center, custom designed for the effective application of Kenneth H. Cooper's nationally famous aerobics program. President Roberts early believed that his athletic teams—particularly his basketball team—would zoom to the top nationally just as dramatically as other aspects of the college have progressed. During the school's initial year as an NCAA member in the major college division, the basketball team earned a ranking among the top twenty teams in the nation. Roberts states that he views athletics as an attention-getting means to an end: "Sports are becoming the number one interest to people in America. For us to be relevant, we had to gain the attention of millions in a way that they understood and they would then tune us in on TV to hear us preach the gospel."[11]

Athletic participation at ORU is not just for the talented few. In fact, probably no school in the nation except the military academies combines a high quality, intercollegiate program with emphasis upon the physical fitness of each student. In describing the school's insistence upon regular vigorous activity by all, Roberts explains: "We don't want to turn out 'educated monsters' who . . . house their minds in weak bodies."[12]

The futuristic architecture of the campus buildings has helped make the college a major tourist attraction. By the mid-1970s, ORU had become the most frequently visited site in Tulsa and one of the leading attractions in Oklahoma. Perhaps the most striking structure is the 200-foot, blue and white, space-needle-like prayer tower, which houses the prayer groups that receive 30,000 requests per month.[13]

Much of ORU's success is due to the wide publicity it achieved through the founder's national television broadcasts that began in the 1950s. Since then, other television evangelists also have sought to capitalize upon their media publicity to found Christian colleges. The evangelist with the greatest potential for matching Roberts's success in college founding was Billy Graham, who after due consideration decided against opening his own institution. Early in his career (1947-1951), Graham briefly had succeeded William Bell Riley as president of Northwestern in Minnesota. To date, the most successful of the other "television colleges" has been Liberty Baptist, the school founded by Jerry Falwell (discussed in chapter five). The most obvious failure is Rex Humbard's Mackinac, which operated for only one year on Mackinac Island in northern Michigan, while Jim Bakker's Heritage (S.C.) is still struggling to develop.[14]

In addition to the "television colleges," a few other unusual types of Christian colleges deserve mention. Very few institutions offer engineering curricula, primarily because of the costliness of the necessary laboratory equipment. While such schools as John Brown, Geneva, and Valparaiso operate programs of varying degress of thoroughness, no Christian college has placed such a high percentage of its resources in technical education as has LeTourneau (Tex.). The school was founded by Robert G. LeTourneau, an inventor-industrialist widely known for designing heavy-duty earth moving equipment and off-shore drilling platforms and then donating most of his earnings to missionary and evangelistic organizations. LeTourneau operated his school as a technical institute from its beginning in 1946 to 1961, when it became a liberal arts college. The school now offers baccalaureate programs in electrical engineering technology, industrial management, mechanical engineering technology, welding engineering technology, and flight technology; and two-year programs in automotive technology, aviation technology, and design technology.[15]

Only a limited number of contemporary Christian colleges have concentrated on educating students from the lower socioeconomic classes. Some colleges that serve denominations with a heavy concentration of lower-class membership have in a *de facto* manner achieved this purpose; such, for example, has been the case at Anderson (Ind.), Evangel, and the several Nazarene institutions, at least in their early years. Still fewer institutions have offered their programs at a lower cost than that charged in the public universities, and only a handful have existed primarily to educate youths so poor that they could not pay for their training.

School of the Ozarks (Mo.) is the most recent institution to educate impoverished students in exchange for their commitment to work for the college. Following in the earlier tradition of Berea and Berry (Ga.), School of the Ozarks admits primarily mountain youths who can demonstrate both an ability to do college-level work and an inability to pay for the experience. The income from a sizable endowment base and gifts provides full tuition scholarships for all of the students. Each student agrees to pay for room and board by working 960 hours per year (20 hours per week) in one of a broad variety of college employment opportunities (e.g., meat processing; furniture manufacturing; clerical, instructional, and personnel assistance; campus maintenance; on-campus and off-campus construction; the specialty gift plant; the dairy; the farm; the kitchen and bakery; the food services; the restaurant; the airport; the theater; and the electrical, plumbing, print, sheet metal, machinery, and engineering shops). The students often carry a reduced academic load while working, but still are able to graduate in four years by studying throughout the summers.[16]

In recent years there has developed increasing interest in the idea of "satellite" Christian colleges. John Snyder, Frank Nelsen, Ron Sider, and others have called for the development of private institutions located adjacent to large public universities. These Christian colleges or centers would provide dormitory and dining facilities, spiritual support services, and limited instruction by qualified evangelical instructors, especially in biblical studies, theology, philosophy, and apologetics. The students would register in a regular university program and would pay very little more for the alternate educational experience.

The satellite idea is still largely experimental. One of the best current North American examples of such a school is Conrad Grebel, established by the Mennonites in 1961 at the University of Waterloo, Ontario. The Grebel professors, most of whom are Mennonite by confession, hold joint faculty appointments with the two institutions. They offer a curriculum which complements rather than duplicates the university's offerings (e.g., biblical studies, peace and conflict studies, interdisciplinary values-oriented courses such as "Quest for Meaning in the Twentieth Century"). Many Waterloo students join the 115 students who reside in the Grebel dormitory in taking Grebel courses and/or participating in its chapel and counseling programs. The university pays the college for the instruction of its students.

The idea of a Christian satellite college related to a state university did not develop only in the last two decades. For example, through much of this century the Methodists have operated Wesley College at the University of North Dakota, and the Southern Baptists established Southern Illinois College of the Bible at Southern Illinois University in 1938. In each case, the university granted credit for work offered by the satellite school. Another variation of the satellite model has existed at Northwest Christian at least since the 1930s. Northwest Christian combines its Bible college curriculum with the course offerings of the adjacent University of Oregon to allow their baccalaureate graduates to earn a double major in biblical studies and a liberal arts area.[17]

THE EMERGING IDENTITY OF THE MODERN CHRISTIAN COLLEGE

If in recent years the institutional composition of the modern Christian college community has become increasingly evident, so also has the character of the contemporary Christian college movement.

These emerging character traits include (1) a growing quality; (2) an enlarged intellectual openness within the realm of orthodoxy; (3) an increasing effort to integrate faith, learning, and living; (4) a continuing effort to promote spiritual nurture and character development; and (5) an increasing degree of intercollegiate cooperation.

While the improvement in the quality of Christian higher education has come gradually, public recognition of this improvement has grown sharply in recent years, perhaps in part because of the increasing publicity given to evangelical Protestantism in general since 1975. The intellectual community as well as the general public is showing greater recognition of and appreciation for Christian higher education. Kenneth Briggs, religion editor of the *New York Times*, recently cited the favorable enrollment trend,[18] the financial stability, and the improved academic standing of evangelical schools. Robert Pace, in his 1972 Carnegie Commission study, was even more specific when he described the orthodox colleges as "the fastest growing group presently among Protestant colleges" and stated that in academic quality they now match the mainline Protestant colleges. Carl Henry believes that the campus resources of the evangelical colleges comprising the Christian College Coalition (see Table 3, pp. 205-07) are the best they have been since the secular revolution. Coalition president John Dellenback now sees these schools as "far stronger" than they were in 1970 and as continuing their improvement in the 1980s.

One of the most important measures of success for a college is its ability to inspire students to achieve their maximum potential. David Reisman observed recently that the evangelical colleges send a much higher percentage of their graduates to graduate or professional schools than would be expected based upon their SAT scores. Also, in the alumni data noted in the 1966 Pattillo and Mackenzie study, the only college to rank high in each of the three categories of producing younger scholars, physicians, and seminarians was Calvin, an evangelical institution with only a moderately competitive admissions policy.[19]

In their efforts to improve, many Christian colleges received able assistance from the Council for the Advancement of Small Colleges (recently renamed the Council of Independent Colleges). The council began in 1955 to assist small independent colleges in achieving regional accreditation.[20] More recently it has concentrated on providing small colleges with highly practical and modestly priced training skills and management services. The organization is heavily funded by external support from individuals, the federal government, and foundations, (especially the W. K. Kellogg Foundation), with grants during a recent five-year period (1973–78) totaling $7 million. Many of the member colleges are evangelical Protestant and Catholic institutions with enrollments of less than 2,000.

Many observers continue to look to Wheaton as the intellectual leader of the evangelical colleges affiliated with either a small denomination or no denomination at all. Some consider it the intellectual leader of the continuing Christian colleges of all types. Students find it difficult to gain admittance to Wheaton, and, once accepted, find the academic environment very rigorous. For example, during the late 1960s, new enrollees entered with an average college board (SAT) score of approximately 1,200, and nearly 75 percent of them had graduated in the top 10 percent of their high school classes. One recent Wheaton student suggested that the competition for grades which he experienced as an under-graduate was more intense than that which he faced in his graduate work at the University of Wisconsin Law School. Knowledgeable and keen outside observers have noted that at Wheaton, "The college creates discussion as intense, perhaps, as any to be found on American campuses, and as consistently directed to ultimate issues." *Time* magazine noted that during the 1920–1976 period, Wheaton alumni ranked eleventh among all four-year colleges in earning Ph.D. degrees and that the school's number of National Merit Scholars in 1979–80 placed it with the very best four-year institutions of similar size.[21]

Recently, Wheaton attracted attention—even controversy—when it invited the Billy Graham Evangelistic Association to build the Billy Graham Center on its campus. The center houses documents recording Christian evangelism and missions in the past and plans to promote such efforts in the future by hosting a broad variety of training sessions and conferences. The archival division of the center of course contains the papers of Billy Graham and his evangelistic association, but it also includes those of hundreds of other organizations and individuals. In fact, the center with its archives, library, and museum already has become one of the world's largest resource centers for the study of the history of evangelism and world missions.

The decision to locate the Graham Center at Wheaton involved risk for the college. While the Billy Graham Evangelistic Association paid the $13.5 million to build the five-story, 200,000-square-foot structure, the college accepted the obligation to raise a $15 million endowment to maintain it. Some of the faculty feared that the center would become a financial liability for the college. The administrative staff and trustees, however, remained confident that as a symbol as well as a continuation and expansion of the Billy Graham ministry, the center would be a long-range boon to the outreach and public relations efforts of the institution.[22]

While modern Christian colleges have been able to develop the financial base to support good—sometimes excellent—undergraduate programs, they have not yet acquired the larger resources necessary to achieve financial independence or to develop graduate programs of sufficient quality and quantity, except in theology. One can point to individual programs of note (e.g., the Baylor School of Medicine, the several able law schools affiliated with Christian colleges, the growing emphasis upon psychology and communications in the seminaries, and the potential of the new professional programs at Oral Roberts and CBN University in Virginia); nevertheless, the statement still holds that save for theology, and especially in the liberal arts, Christian graduate education remains largely undeveloped.

Christian educators have long been aware of this deficiency, and at least since the days of William Jennings Bryan and Charles Blanchard of Wheaton in the 1920s, plans to found a Christian university have been considered seriously. In the late 1950s and early 1960s, Billy Graham, Carl Henry, and others discussed the feasibility of developing such an institution at Gordon because of the latter's large campus (800 acres) and location near "the educational capital" of the country, Boston. One of the reasons for the creation of the Christian College Consortium in 1971 was to provide an organizational base for continuing study of the Christian university idea. To date, however, the vision of what Carl Henry has called a "Christian Johns Hopkins" remains in the dream stage.[23]

During the last generation, the continuing Christian colleges have become increasingly willing and able to expose their students to a broad range of perspectives in all areas, including those which directly consider Christian values. For example, instruction in the religion departments, while retaining the earlier commitment and biblical literature emphasis, now follows a more strictly academic approach and includes a broader curriculum. Also, while science professors believe in the divine creation of the earth and of man, they differ widely on the method and the timetable used by the Creator. Some accept theistic evolution (i.e. macroevolution). A larger number believe in progressive creation, thus allowing for microevolutionary activity within—but not across—the several biblical "kinds." Few evangelical scholars would insist that God created the world in six days of twenty-four hours each.

The Christian college professors also disagree widely on the age of the earth and the earliest man. One group places the origin of man somewhere between 6,000 and 15,000 years ago by interpreting geneological passages in the Bible as being without generational gaps. Others, including many members of the evangelically oriented

American Scientific Affiliation, believe it possible that the original man, Adam, was created as early as 100,000 years ago and certainly before the time of the earliest human or humanlike forms found by archaeologists. Regardless of how they interpret the facts, science instructors usually advise their students that there is no single orthodox Christian approach to the broad subject of origins.[24]

Few themes have received greater emphasis in Christian colleges during the last fifteen years than the integration of faith and learning. While there have always been Christian teachers in secular as well as religious institutions who have sought to realize this idea, the unique element of the modern period is the conscious, overt effort of many Christian colleges to stimulate their faculty members better to achieve it.

While Christian colleges are seeking to apply the faith and learning principle to their entire curricula, secular institutions, since they discarded their Christian orientation, have not been able to find another philosophical center. A generation ago, Dean Bernard Loomer of the University of Chicago Divinity School noted that "there is . . . no concerted and sustained effort to make a university out of the pluralistic and atomistic departments within the so-called university. . . . Few if any universities can set forth a meaningful statement of goals and purposes that would withstand careful scrutiny and be relevant to the needs of our culture." That Loomer's observation in 1951 is still applicable is seen from the widespread recognition that the general education programs in American higher education today are generally lacking in unity and values and barren of meaning.[25]

One of the earliest institutional leaders of the integration emphasis was Calvin, the Christian Reformed college which has been influenced greatly by Abraham Kuyper (1837–1920), the influential Netherlands political (he served as prime minister from 1901 to 1905) and religious leader and reformer as well as educational theorist. Kuyper founded the Free University of Amsterdam not just to produce and teach orthodox theology but also to place all learning on a scriptural base. He defended vigorously the sacredness of what often were called secular areas of investigation, believing that the Christian church had as great an obligation to influence these dimensions of life as the theological area. Otherwise, he argued, the church "bears only a partial witness in its society. To have an institute or a seminary in which only ministers are trained and the rest of professional life is untouched, would be like furnishing an army with only one kind of weapon and expecting it to take successfully to the field."[26]

One could cite numerous examples of the gradually increasing impact of the integration principle. The Christian College Coalition currently cites the faith and learning idea as its most important emphasis. Also, in recent years Christian scholars in Christian colleges as well as secular institutions have organized by academic disciplines to help themselves integrate their faith and their particular fields. These organizations, most of whom count a membership of hundreds or thousands, include the American Scientific Affiliation, the Association of Christian Mathematicians, the Christian Association for Psychological Studies, the Conference on Faith and History, the Conference on Christianity and Literature, Christians in the Visual Arts, the Evangelical Philosophical Society, the Evangelical Theological Society, the Society of Christian Philosophers, the Association of Christian Librarians, the Fellowship of Christian Economists, the Christian Sociological Society, the National Association of Christians in Social Work, and the Christian Nurse Educators.

Other noteworthy integration examples include Goshen's study-service trimester requirement and the conferences of Christian professors and other environmentalists at the Au Sable Trails Institute of Environmental Studies in Michigan. Goshen students combine the Christian service ideal with the opportunity to live in and to study a foreign culture, usually in an underdeveloped part of the world. At the Au Sable conferences, Christian environmentalists discuss how to apply the biblical mandate for stewardship of world resources to the contemporary ecological crisis. The most significant results of the integration emphasis, however, probably are taking place in countless classrooms as individual professors alter their teaching methods to reflect their increased determination to "think Christianly" about their disciplines.[27]

The degree of attention given to the integration of faith and learning in the classroom is an innovation of the modern period, but the Christian colleges also have continued many of the older forms of religious emphasis, including chapel services, Christian social service programs, gospel teams, and revivals. Following the example of the largely urban Bible colleges, more rural liberal arts schools began to form gospel teams in the early to middle decades of this century when automotive transportation became available. A typical gospel team consisted of a small group of students with musical and/or speaking ability. The team would participate in or lead services of churches in the geographic area of the college. Frequently the institution employed some of the best musicians— usually male vocalists—to invest their summer vacation traveling, singing, and promoting the Christian gospel and the college. For example, the Crusader Male Quartet of Eastern Nazarene traveled nearly 10,000 miles in 14 states to appear in more than 150 churches besides radio performances and hospital visits during the summer of 1937.[28]

While revivalism is a less regular, less intense, and less characteristic form of religious expression in the Christian college today than in the nineteenth century or the early twentieth century, it still exists—sometimes dramatically exists—especially in colleges associated with churches which emphasize emotional religious experiences. Through the whole of this century, few colleges have matched the emotional fervor which has broken loose periodically at Asbury. One early twentieth century Asbury student later recalled his first impressions: "There was more noise along with their religion than I had been used to. . . . they let a good deal of physical demonstration enter in. Back in those days it was not unusual for a student to jump over a seat in his ecstacy."[29]

One of the most widely publicized periods of college revivalism occurred in 1950, when the national news media flocked to Asbury and Wheaton to interpret the proceedings to the world. At Wheaton they found a nonstop confessional meeting lasting nearly two days and nights during which the majority of the students apologized and/or testified publicly. As observed by a *Time* reporter:

> Singly and in little groups, sweatered and blue-jeaned undergraduate students streamed onto the stage, filling up the choir chairs to await their turns. Hour after hour, they kept coming. All night long, all the next day, all through the following night and half the following day, students poured out confessions of past sins and rededicated themselves to God.

The nature of the confessions varied from cheating and pride to criticism of teachers (a male student stated: "I want to apologize for making the faculty the butt of my corny jokes") and sins committed toward fellow students. One young woman sought forgiveness in this fashion: "I know it's mostly fellows that say they have impure thoughts, but girls have them too. And I want to apologize if I've ever tempted any of the fellows I've had contact with. I know I've tried, and I'm sorry."[30]

More recently, in February, 1970, a widely publicized revival began at Asbury when a witnessing service continued uninterrupted for 185 hours, closing down classes for a week and then continuing nightly for two weeks after the resumption of regular classroom activity. One student explained the effects of the episode on him: "The revival changed my life. I was a stagnant Christian before. Now I like to read the Bible, and my prayer life is revitalized, and

I can really love people. And I'm not ashamed to talk about it.'' Subsequently, the majority of Asbury's 1,000 students traveled on weekends to colleges in other states and Canada to tell what had happened at the Kentucky institution with the hope of inspiring similar movements elsewhere. The effort was effective, as revivals occurred at many other Christian colleges including Wheaton, Trevecca Nazarene, Taylor, Spring Arbor, Houghton, Azusa Pacific, Oral Roberts, Greenville, and Fort Wayne Bible College.[31]

That Asbury has been known as a major center of revivalism is partly explained by the nature of its student body. Historically, it has attracted a disproportionately large share of students preparing for a full-time Christian ministry. During the 1960–61 school year, for example, no college in the nation except Concordia (Ind.), at the time an institution exclusively for preseminary students, had a higher percentage of its graduates attending seminary. When the same 1960–61 poll ranked colleges in terms of the number rather than the percent of graduates enrolled in seminary, Southern Baptist and Lutheran schools headed that list with Baylor having the highest number (496).[32]

It is generally accepted that Christian college students display more friendliness, community spirit, and general decorum than do students on other campuses. What is less clear is whether the Christian college students display such traits because they come to college with them or because of the impact of the college environment; most likely, home and campus influences reinforce each other. Generally positive behavior has characterized Christian college students for a long time, probably since the period when most non-Christian students began enrolling in other types of institutions. One survey conducted in 1930 asked students at Houghton, Asbury, Taylor, Wheaton, Eastern, and John Fletcher (Ia.) the factors in college which most satisfied them. Except for "Christian influence," students ranked "friendliness" far ahead of everything else. More recently, on the basis of freshman responses on the National College and University Environment Scales, Wheaton ranked in the 90th percentile on propriety or orderliness in behavior, and in the 96th percentile on "community." The Wheaton environment reflects the atmosphere which exists at evangelical schools generally.[33]

As noted in chapter two, students in the pre–Civil War Christian colleges frequently did not behave well. It has been common to blame the behavioral problems of this period on the rigid rules. During the most recent period of major student unrest and misconduct, however, the schools with the tightest discipline tended to remain quiet, while those with minimal demands experienced the most trouble. Probably in both periods the tendency toward student misbehavior in a college depended more upon the type of students enrolled than upon the nature of the institutions' regulatory systems.

In analyzing why Christian colleges remained calm during the general upheavals of the 1960s and early 1970s, one must begin with—but not end with—the observation that students on the Christian campuses possessed more of God's grace and Dad's discipline than did those on other campuses. For example, note the response of one Oral Roberts student to the question of why the students on that campus did not protest: "We're too busy seeking answers in the classroom to the world's problems and trying to help the needy people in the community in our spare time to even think about organizing demonstrations. That's a waste of time compared to what can be accomplished on the one-to-one level. I'd rather spend my time helping persons to feel big and important than in trying to make establishments seem small and irrelevant."[34]

Also important in explaining the Christian college decorum is the fact that Christian college students came from the socio-economic classes which are least prone to use violence. The majority of them grew up in families that were Protestant and nonlabor; that resided outside of major cities; and that held conservative political views on domestic issues. The major public issue which stirred the secular university students to dissent and violence was the Vietnam War; one reason that religious college students did not participate in the violent protest against the war was that most of them did not oppose it. With some notable exceptions (primarily at the Mennonite, Quaker, and Brethren colleges), Christian college students' views on the war did not differ significantly from the Vietnam policies of the Johnson and Nixon administrations.

Probably the most important reason for the relatively nonviolent atmosphere of the Christian colleges was the fact that they made it much easier than did the large secular universities for a student to receive personal attention and to develop a satisfactory worldview and life commitment. In general, Christian college faculty members showed greater interest in teaching and guiding their students, in part because their schools placed minimal or no pressure upon them to conduct and publish research. Because they had more time to give to their students, the students acquired fewer of the emotional reactions which develop from a sense of neglect.[35]

While the Christian colleges have been proud of the character of their students and the social environment of their campuses, they sometimes have been disturbed by the excessive expectations of some parents who look for "safe" and even "miracle working" colleges for their young people. Houghton expressed the sentiments of many colleges when it warned parents of undisciplined young people that, while the college will provide a supportive environment, "the school does not offer itself as a reformatory for young people who are too wayward for home restraints."[36]

Still another characteristic of the continuing Christian colleges is the tendency toward broadly-based, interinstitutional cooperation in the promotion and protection of their religious interests. Colleges of the same denomination have always worked together in many ways, but since the secular revolution many institutions have come to realize that their closest allies now are the continuing Christian colleges irrespective of denominational affiliation. This movement toward interdenominational cooperation has come more easily for colleges affiliated with small denominations than for those related to the large, somewhat exclusive church groups (e.g., Churches of Christ and Independent Disciples, Lutherans, and Southern Baptists). Still, the movement toward cooperation among all continuing Christian colleges is gradually attracting an increasing number from these latter groups, as indicated by their growing interest in joining the Christian College Coalition.

Among the organizations recently developed by and/or for the continuing Christian colleges are the Christian College Coordinating Council for Admissions Officers; the Christian College Referral Service; the *Christian Scholars Review*, an interdisciplinary scholarly journal now sponsored by twenty-six colleges; the Christian College Consortium; and the Christian College Coalition.

The Christian College Consortium began in 1971 with the active encouragement of Carl Henry, editor of *Christianity Today;* Earl McGrath, director of the Temple University Higher Education Center; and the Lilly Endowment. The original member schools (Bethel of Minnesota, Eastern Mennonite, Gordon, Greenville, Malone, Messiah, Seattle Pacific, Taylor, Westmont, and Wheaton) sought to cooperate in a number of areas, including the more effective promotion of faith and learning integration, the more widespread promotion and explanation of the mission and record of the continuing Christian colleges, the development of cooperative national and international academic programs, and the continuing study of the feasibility of the Christian university idea.[37]

Probably the single most important contribution of the consortium has been its founding in 1976 of the Christian College Coalition as a satellite organization with the specific task of protecting the religious and educational freedom of the Christian colleges. The coalition has sought to provide a unified voice in the nation's capital for those evangelical Protestant colleges that previously had lacked such representation. The coalition initially identified its objectives as (1) the monitoring of public opinion, legislation, judicial activity, and governmental regulations on matters which could affect the freedom of Christian colleges to function educationally and religiously; (2) the development of unified positions on the critical issues for presentation to governmental agencies, other organizations, and those influential to the formation of public policy; and (3) the development of an offensive position on potential erosions of religious and educational freedom in the Christian college movement. In short, the organization has worked partly as a lobbying group—although it would not choose that term to describe itself—and partly as a unifying and educational forum for Christian colleges.[38]

TABLE 3
CHRISTIAN COLLEGE COALITION
MEMBERSHIP LIST
(January, 1984)

Anderson (Ind.)
Church of God

Asbury (Ky.)
Independent

Azusa Pacific (Cal.)
Independent

Barrington (R.I.)
Independent

Bartlesville Wesleyan (Okla.)
Wesleyan

Belhaven (Miss.)
Presbyterian

Bethany Nazarene (Okla.)
Nazarene

Bethel (Ind.)
Missionary

Bethel (Kan.)
Mennonite General
Conference

Bethel (Minn.)
Baptist General Conference

Biola (Cal.)
Independent

Bryan (Tenn.)
Independent

Calvin (Mich.)
Christian Reformed

Campbell (N.C.)
Southern Baptist

Campbellsville (Ky.)
Southern Baptist

Central Wesleyan (S.C.)
Wesleyan

Covenant (Tenn.)
Presbyterian Church in
America

Dordt (Ia.)
Christian Reformed

Eastern (Pa.)
American Baptist

Eastern Mennonite (Va.)
Mennonite

Eastern Nazarene (Mass.)
Nazarene

Evangel (Mo.)
Assemblies of God

Fresno Pacific (Cal.)
Mennonite Brethren

Geneva (Pa.)
Reformed Presbyterian

George Fox (Ore.)
Society of Friends

Gordon (Mass.)
Independent

Grace (Ind.)
Grace Brethren

Grand Canyon (Ariz.)
Southern Baptist

Greenville (Ill.)
Free Methodist

Grove City (Pa.)
Presbyterian

Houghton (N.Y.)
Wesleyan

Huntington (Ind.)
United Brethren in Christ

John Brown (Ark.)
Independent

Judson (Ill.)
American Baptist

King (Tenn.)
Presbyterian

The King's College (N.Y.)
Independent

Lee (Tenn.)
Church of God

Los Angeles Baptist (Cal.)
Baptist

Malone (Oh.)
Society of Friends

Marion (Ind.)
Wesleyan

Messiah (Pa.)
Brethren in Christ

Mid-America Nazarene (Kan.)
Nazarene

Mississippi (Miss.)
Southern Baptist

Mt. Vernon Nazarene (Oh.)
Nazarene

North Park (Ill.)
Evangelical Covenant

Northwest Christian (Ore.)
Disciples of Christ/
Independent Disciples

Northwest Nazarene (Ida.)
Nazarene

Northwestern (Ia.)
Reformed Church in America

Northwestern (Minn.)
Independent

Nyack (N.Y.)
Christian & Missionary
Alliance

Olivet Nazarene (Ill.)
Nazarene

Oral Roberts (Okla.)
Independent

Palm Beach Atlantic (Fla.)
Baptist

Point Loma Nazarene (Cal.)
Nazarene

Roberts Wesleyan (N.Y.)
Wesleyan

Seattle Pacific (Wash.)
Free Methodist

Simpson (Cal.)
Christian & Missionary
Alliance

Sioux Falls (S.D.)
American Baptist

Southern California (Cal.)
Assemblies of God

Spring Arbor (Mich.)
Free Methodist

Sterling (Kan.)
Presbyterian

Tabor (Kan.)
Mennonite Brethren

Taylor (Ind.)
Independent

Trevecca Nazarene (Tenn.)
Nazarene

Trinity (Ill.)
Evangelical Free

Trinity Christian (Ill.)
Christian Reformed/
Independent

Warner Pacific (Ore.)
Church of God

Warner Southern (Fla.)
Church of God

Westmont (Cal.)
Independent

Wheaton (Ill.)
Independent

Whitworth (Wash.)
Presbyterian

The significance of the Christian College Coalition is growing beyond that of its original purpose of protecting religious freedom. As its membership continues to increase (as of January, 1984, the number of member schools had grown from the original consortium group to 71 colleges), so also does its reputation as the primary interdenominational confederation of continuing Christian liberal arts colleges. Its mere existence and dynamic nature provide the Christian college movement with enhanced unity, influence, and public recognition and appreciation. Increasing numbers of colleges that wish to be recognized as continuing to be clearly Christian institutions are joining the coalition. Some colleges have joined the coalition because of the encouragement which that affiliation gives them in their efforts to resist the secularization process; others have joined because of the hope that the explicit identification as an orthodox Protestant college will assist their admissions efforts in the shrinking student market of the 1980s. While the coalition is the child of the consortium, it is already on the way toward surpassing the parent organization in operation and significance.

IN PARTNERSHIP WITH THE GOVERNMENT

Since the Great Depression, few factors have affected higher education of all types as dramatically as has the major increase in state and especially federal funding. The share of higher education income from public sources grew from only 21 percent in 1929–30 to 79 percent by 1973–74. This growth in public appropriations has come not only because of the unprecedented increase in the number and size of public institutions but also because of the growing public aid to private education. Indeed, these resources help explain the improvement in quality of the contemporary Christian colleges that was described earlier in this chapter.[39]

Traditionally, public funds for higher education have come largely from the state governments for the state-owned institutions. Before the 1930s, the federal government maintained only minimal involvement in higher education. The limited early federal legislation benefiting education included the Northwest Ordinance of 1787, the first federal allocation of land for higher education; the Morrill Act of 1862, the first nationwide distribution of land for education; and the Hatch Act of 1887, the first federal program giving aid directly to institutions. Especially during the early national period, the central government considered founding a national university but established neither it nor any central educational agency—except for the military and naval academies—until creating the Office of Education in 1867.[40]

During the last half century, the federal government has sharply increased its revenue allocation to higher education. Whereas at the outset of the Depression the federal government supplied only 9 percent of the public appropriations for post-secondary education, by the mid 1970s it was furnishing 45 percent of the total. The first of the modern federal programs was the National Youth Administration (NYA), created during the 1930s when New Deal legislation provided assistance to many impoverished groups in American society. Between 1935 and 1943 the NYA distributed approximately $100 million to the majority of private and public colleges to provide work opportunities for needy students. The GI Bill of 1944 expanded upon both the precedent set by the NYA and also the practice during earlier American wars of rewarding faithful veterans with land or cash bonuses. The GI Bill provided each qualified veteran with funds to pay for post-secondary training in an institution of his or her choice, generally for a period equal to the veteran's wartime service plus one year. More than 2 million of the 15 million World War II veterans enrolled in college under the GI Bill, with the result that by 1946 they comprised approximately one-half of all college students and by June, 1949, the Veterans Administration had issued nearly $4 billion in veterans education payments. The federal government realized that tuition payments did not provide for all of the costs of educating students, and, accordingly, it gave war surplus land, buildings, and equipment to nearly 700 colleges. The GI Bill program continued well beyond the World War II period, as did the wartime practice of funding specialized military training and scientific research. Also, the innovative National Defense Education Act of 1958 passed through Congress as much for military reasons as for educational ones.[41]

By the 1960s, however, it was clear that an enlarged philosophy of federal aid was emerging in Washington. The Kennedy and Johnson administrations convinced Congress that it would serve the public interest for the federal government to help finance higher education costs for an increasing number of Americans, irrespective of what they had done or would do directly for the government. Accordingly, the Higher Education Facilities Act of 1963 and the Higher Education Act of 1965 introduced the idea of extensive federal assistance to public and private colleges for physical plant construction and aid to needy students. With the encouragement of these programs, many Christian colleges during the 1960s built instructional facilities and dormitories and expanded their financial aid services.

While in the modern period the federal government has dramatically extended its involvement in higher education, the state governments have added to their traditional appropriations to the state colleges and universities new forms of assistance that have benefited private as well as public institutions. By the mid-1970s only seven states provided no support of any type to the private colleges within their borders, and these states enrolled very few students in private colleges. Almost one-half of the states gave direct support to the independent schools, and approximately two-thirds provided aid to the students attending such institutions. The most common type of state aid to Christian and other independent colleges has come indirectly in the form of scholarships, loans, and grants to students. Also significant in some states is the practice of allocating aid to institutions in proportion to the number of students enrolled or graduated. For example, in 1976–77, independent schools in New York received $300 for each two-year degree and $940 for each four-year degree awarded. Similar institutions in Georgia received $500 per student, and the private schools in Maryland collected 15 percent of the state institution subsidy rate.[42]

Response to the participation of church-related colleges in the federal and state aid programs has varied widely. Among the most alarmed was C. Stanley Lowell, associate director of Americans United for Separation of Church and State, who argued in 1971 that if a religious college accepted public aid it must admit students and hire faculty without considering their religious orientation, and it could no longer require chapel services or religious studies. The American Civil Liberties Union policy statement of 1965 approved sharply limited forms of aid including scholarships, loans, and GI Bill assistance to students in other than theological schools and for research on nonreligious topics. Of the major denominations, the Southern Baptist Convention has exercised the most caution in approving government aid for its colleges. The general pattern of the Southern Baptist schools has been to allow aid to students but not to accept it, except in the form of loans, for the institutions. Some Southern Baptist colleges accept much more public aid than do others, with the exact policy in each case depending upon the philosophy of the state convention and the degree of autonomy which the convention allows the trustees of a given college. Furman and Stetson caused a national stir in the 1960s when their trustees chose to act contrary to the instruction of their state conventions and accept federal grants for science building construction. Furman, however, agreed to return its $611,898 grant when the South Carolina convention promised to provide similar funds.[43]

One of the bolder responses to the concept of public aid for private institutions was to propose tuition equalization grants to students enrolled in private colleges. In recognition of the declining percentage of college-bound youth enrolling in private institutions because of sharply increasing costs (the ratio between private and public college tuition grew from 3.5:1 in 1956–57 to 5:1 in 1974–75), the Carnegie Council in 1975 called for the federal government to provide grants on a matching basis with the states to pay private college enrollees approximately one-half the average subsidy provided per student in a state university (the state university subsidies in 1973–74 averaged approximately $2,000). Similarly, in 1975 the National Conference of Independent Colleges and Universities called for tuition equalization grants ranging from 25 percent to 75 percent of the state subsidy. By contrast, private colleges have not shown enthusiasm for the legislation proposed by senators Daniel Moynihan (N.Y.), Robert Packwood (Ore.), and others whereby parents would receive up to a $500 annual federal income tax credit for tuition paid to enroll a child in an elementary, secondary, or post-secondary institution. The plan as proposed would greatly aid families with children in private, pre-college schools but would provide little, if any, advantage over present forms of assistance to families of private college students.[44]

Some traditionally Christian colleges have sought the newly availble tax funds so eagerly that they have been willing to abrogate their denominational relationships, sharply reduce or eliminate their religious identities, and drop the mandatory nature of their chapel services and religious courses in an effort to guarantee the continuance of such assistance. Probably the most publicized case of this type was that of Methodist-related Western Maryland which in 1975 gave up, perhaps unnecessarily, much of its religious identity in order to qualify for state aid. The college agreed not to describe itself as church-related, to remain totally neutral in the spiritual development of its students, and to remove all religious symbols from the campus.[45]

Despite the broad spectrum of opinion on the use of public aid, nearly universal agreement has existed among the Christian colleges on the following points: aid to individual students is acceptable whether they elect to attend public or private institutions (e.g., even such a staunchly independent school as Baptist Bible of Missouri has distributed Basic Educational Opportunity Grants and GI Bill benefits);[46] aid to individuals clearly is preferable to direct aid to institutions; and as the state and federal governments reevaluate old and develop new programs of aid to private higher education, they must be careful to avoid violating the "free exercise" clause of the First Amendment by discriminating against the church-related institutions.

Often in American history the appearance of a new and controversial type of legislation leads to litigation to test its constitutionality. During the last decade, the federal and state courts have tried a significant number of cases on the issue of public aid to private colleges. Although the Supreme Court has been hearing similar cases involving private elementary and secondary schools since *Everson v. Board of Education* in 1947, challenges to aid for higher education did not appear until after the adoption of the 1963 and 1965 federal higher education acts and the expansion of the state aid programs. The 1971 case of *Tilton v. Richardson* was the first time the Supreme Court ruled on a suit challenging the constitutionality of federal aid to private higher education. The Court decided that federal aid programs (in this case, the Higher Education Facilities Act of 1963) could benefit such church-related colleges as were not "pervasively religious" in nature. Under *Tilton*, church colleges qualifying for aid included those that did not discriminate on religious grounds in faculty hiring and student admissions, did not maintain compulsory religious activities, did not "proselytize" religious doctrine in their courses, and met the generally acceptable standards for academic freedom. Prior to *Tilton*, the widespread assumption was that public funds could go to religious colleges if the aid served a secular (e.g., science building or dormitory construction) purpose. Now *Tilton* introduced the new philosophy, which the subsequent Supreme Court cases of *Hunt v. McNair* (1975) and *Roemer v. Board of Public Works* (1976) generally supported, that the nature of an institution's religious emphasis was also a factor in determining eligibility. A large number of the continuing Christian colleges might very well not meet all of the criteria established by *Tilton*. It is not clear, however, that one should view the *Tilton* criteria for receiving aid as universally applicable. Even if such were the case, there is little reason to believe that Christian colleges which might be barred from receiving direct governmental aid could not continue to accept students who received assistance under one or another of the federal student aid programs.[47]

The question of the constitutionality of state aid programs is even more complex because of the differing nature and philosophy of the fifty state constitutions, aid programs, and courts. Probably the most important cases to date have come from Maryland, Kansas, and Missouri. In the 1976 *Roemer* case from Maryland, the litigants, represented by the Americans United for the Separation of Church and State, challenged the right of one Methodist and four Roman Catholic colleges to participate in the state program which, as mentioned earlier, distributed to the eighteen private colleges annual grants per pupil equal to 15 percent of the state appropriation per student in the four-year state colleges. In essence the Supreme Court approved the earlier ruling of the federal district court that the colleges in question qualified for the aid program because they met the eligibility criteria of the *Tilton* case.

The issue in the Kansas and Missouri cases was the validity of the state scholarship programs which aided students in religious as well as secular institutions. In *Americans United v. Bubb* (1974), the federal district court applied to the Kansas indirect aid program an even more severe set of eligibility criteria than those listed in *Tilton* for a direct assistance program. It ruled that five colleges did not qualify but could do so by taking remedial action. Accordingly, the five colleges dropped the disqualifying features of their programs, with three of them ending the mandatory nature of their chapel services.

By contrast, the related Mid-American Nazarene (Kan.) case met with a different result. In 1979 the Kansas Attorney General reversed the 1972 ruling of a predecessor that the students in the Nazarene school did not qualify for the state grants because the college chose to continue to require attendance at its chapel services. Also, in 1976 the Missouri Supreme Court sustained the state's tuition grant program which aided students in the seventeen church-affiliated colleges as well as the other private and public institutions. This case was significant partly because it was the first major ruling following the *Roemer* case and partly because the Missouri state constitutional provision calling for the separation of church and state is unusually explicit.[48]

Two major recent cases that indirectly affect the issue of aid to church-related schools are those of Grove City (Pa.) and Oral Roberts. Grove City since 1977 has refused to sign the federal form showing compliance with Title IX of the Education Amendments of 1972 which bans discrimination against women. Grove City bases its action on the principle of institutional autonomy rather than on a desire to defend a questionable institutional practice. The Pennsylvania college has never received any direct aid, and since 1979 it has been in court with the government over whether the latter can deny aid to Grove City students because of the school's refusal to sign the compliance form. Grove City's attorneys are continuing to work in cooperation with the Christian College Coalition, Senator Mark Hatfield of Oregon, and federal executive officials to amend the Higher Education Act to acknowledge clearly a distinction between aid to institutions and aid to individuals.

Meanwhile, Oral Roberts has been battling, not with the government but with a professional accrediting agency. In 1981 an American Bar Association (ABA) accreditation committee recommended that accreditation not be granted the new but well-developed Oral Roberts Law School, primarily because it required a Christian commitment of students and faculty. Oral Roberts filed suit, and a federal court preliminary ruling determined that the ABA action violated the university's right to freedom of religion. The ABA reluctantly amended its standards on religion for religious institutions to require only that such schools advertise clearly their admission and employment policies to students, faculty, and others involved. While few Christian colleges operate law schools, all are very interested in the question of whether the government can withhold aid from students who attend a college that requires religious commitments from the faculty it hires and the students it admits.[49]

A summary of the not always consistent results of a decade of litigation over public aid should include the following points: (1) Christian colleges are not automatically excluded from federal and state aid programs; (2) the courts are more sympathetic to aid for religious colleges than for religious secondary and elementary schools and are more willing to approve assistance to individuals than to institutions; (3) aid to religious institutions cannot be for specifically religious programs; (4) direct aid would probably be denied to pervasively sectarian colleges, although it is often dif-

ficult to determine equitably which colleges fit this category;
(5) there has not yet emerged from these cases a clear set of universally applicable and specific principles because of an inherent conflict between the application of the establishment clause and that
of the free exercise clause of the First Amendment (legislation that
is too inclusive violates the former, while acts that are too restric-
tive violate the latter).[50]

While Christian colleges are worried about the possibility of aid
reductions because of court decisions, reduced appropriations, or
both, they are very irritated and even angry about the recent growth
in the government's efforts to regulate them. For example, since
1970 the following legislation has demanded an expensive increase
in record-keeping: (1) the Occupational Safety and Health Act of
1970, (2) the Higher Education Amendments of 1972 and 1976, (3)
the Equal Pay Act of 1973, (4) the Rehabilitation Act of 1973, and
(5) the Buckley Amendment of 1974. While the increasing federal
proclivity toward regulation has affected all of society (e.g., state
universities as well as private colleges, and business as well as education), some institutions feel more threatened than others. For
example, the nonprofit sector more than business and industry in
general finds it difficult to afford the cost of compliance because
of the greater difficulty of passing the costs to the consumers. Also,
private colleges face the special threat of loss of income-tax exemp-
tion if the government does not like their policies in, say, admissions and hiring; and the religious colleges wonder whether the con-
trols will extend from economic and social areas to include the
domain of religious convictions.

Many of the colleges have viewed the regulatory laws as well-
intended measures. They think unfair, however, the lack of governmental willingness to reimburse them for the high administrative
cost of compliance, especially when most of the regulations relate
not to record-keeping for financial aid programs but to implemen-
tation of governmental goals in other social areas. The colleges also
resent the fact that sometimes the regulatory officials have exercised undue liberty in implementing the legislation, have demanded
in an "assumption-of-guilt" spirit that institutions prove their compliance, and have not allowed diverse institutions sufficient flexi-
bility in their record-keeping methods.

The current emphasis of the Reagan administration is to decrease
both regulation of and aid to higher education. If this plan to reduce
the influence of Washington becomes a long-range development,
then the Christian colleges will once again face the challenge of
adapting their programs to the realities of a new environment.[51]

Epilogue

Christian college leaders are worried as they face the 1980s. Many fear the possibility of increasing government control, but for most the greatest concern is financial stability. National economic woes, the energy crisis, the decline in the size of the college-age population, and the uncertainty of the funding level of federal student-aid programs suggest the likelihood of less money and fewer students with which to run their institutions. This period of retrenchment should not cause unremitting pessimism, however, for the downturn of the 1980s is only a downturn when compared to the affluent 1960s and 1970s when American higher education prospered as never before. During the long span of Christian higher education in America, financial struggle rather than affluence has been the norm; despite this fact, the reader will recall, the distinctively Christian college has demonstrated a remarkable ability to survive.[1]

As the Christian college plans for the future, mere economic survival is not a sufficient goal. Rather, it must survive while retaining the primacy of its spiritual commitment.

If an institution wishes to be recognized as a Christian college it should proclaim that fact openly and boldly. A college which becomes timid and apologetic about its traditional Christian orientation is usually moving in the secular direction. Its reticence may represent the uncertainty of its leaders about what it should hold as its primary mission. A college cannot long remain thus divided; usually it becomes increasingly less Christian in its orientation.

The college which wishes to remain Christian must go beyond a mere statement of that fact. It is not enough to publish doctrinal statements, hold chapel services, and require Bible courses; rather, the whole program must radiate the Christian faith. As William Clark has said, "The Christian college does not have a religious program; it is a religious program."[2]

A Christian college is a community of Christian believers, both teachers and students, who are dedicated to the search for an understanding of the divine Creator, the universe which he has created, and the role which each creature should fill in his universe. The titles of the specific courses may not differ from those in a

215

secular college. What does differ dramatically, however, is the attitude with which Christian scholars approach their areas of investigation. To Christian learners, all truth is God's truth, and the pursuit of it is a spiritual quest to understand God better. For example, in geology and astronomy scholars seek to understand more about the physical universe which God has created. In human anatomy and physiology they study with reverence how God has "fearfully and wonderfully" made his creatures. In history they seek to understand the interactions of God and humanity in the past.

For Christians, such learning is never merely theoretical. It always has an application—even a broadly vocational one. Christians learn about God to serve him more effectively and to realize his purposes in the world. Regardless of the specific career a Christian may follow, he or she becomes a better worker because the intellectual pursuit of God has given him or her an enlarged understanding of God's vocational call.[3]

Finally, the Christian college must become increasingly bold in witnessing to its secular counterpart. Christian college students sometimes suffer from a sense of inferiority when they compare their institutions with large secular universities. Their campuses are smaller, their fellow students fewer, their course offerings more limited, their professors less well paid, and their football stadiums and basketball fieldhouses seat far fewer spectators and support programs that attract much less regional and national attention. The students do not always realize that these quantitative differences come more from political preference and financial favor in receiving public funds than from a superiority in educational philosophy. In fact, in the primary task of the college, namely truth-seeking and understanding, the secular institutions fail to match the Christian colleges, and the latter should kindly but clearly remind the former of their deficiencies.

The secular view of education is limiting. It chooses not to expose its students to all of the major areas of knowledge and truth. Institutions which define their mission as that of seeking universal truth must probe man's metaphysical and religious nature as well as his empirical mind. In George Buttrick's words, "Secularism at its best is naive and at its worst is a refusal to confront life's dimension of depth." By contrast, the pursuit of truth in a Christian frame of reference is liberating in the best sense of the implied goal of a "liberal" arts education. It is free honestly and enthusiastically to follow all truth wherever it leads because of its foundational conviction that all truth is God's truth. Because the secular institution usually does not promote this degree of inclusiveness and openness in the search for truth, the Christian college views it as inadequate educationally as well as religiously.

Secular educators often accuse Christian colleges—especially fundamentalist ones—of closed-mindedness. Sometimes the charges are valid; however, by no means does one find closed-mindedness only in conservative Christian colleges. In many institutions some of the secular-minded professors proclaim their views with almost religious reverence as the final truth, not open to serious questioning. It is sad when professors or students, whether orthodox, liberal, or secular in belief, refuse to examine new information relevant to their basic intellectual positions. While such people may possess faith, they cannot legitimately call themselves truth seekers or genuine members of a college community if they are not willing to accept refinements, modifications, and even major changes in their understanding.

No necessary correlation exists between the openness of a person's mind and the frequency with which that person modifies his or her views. Such changes may reflect instability as well as openness. One can assess a person's openness, however, by the willingness, even enthusiasm, with which new light on any subject is welcomed. In some cases intellectual rigidity may come from a flaw in the person's emotional character. In other cases it may reflect a lack of willingness to respond to God who is the source of truth. Sometimes an intellectual finds it difficult to acknowledge the extent to which his or her basic worldview stems from emotions and will. If a person chooses, as a basic life decision, to serve self and as a result worships his or her own mental and other abilities, that person will not find it difficult to develop a philosophical mind set that rules out the need to be reconciled to the Creator. As Nels Ferre has insightfully observed: "Man either accepts or rejects God through whatever circuitous route. A large part of so-called secular knowledge is, in fact, due to man's sinfulness and rationalization of his disobedience. Such depth-conscience fighting of God takes place through the creation of false religions, by whatever name."[4]

The "religion" of secularism in higher education expresses itself in many forms, including relativism, scientism, and rationalism. Relativism suggests that the public university should be an ideological smorgasbord. Rather than having the institution determine the best possible intellectual diet for its students, it chooses to offer in potluck fashion whatever combination of dishes its professors happen to bring to the table. This approach possesses some merit for a governmental unit which operates and finances a limited number of institutions in a religiously pluralistic society. A major problem with the plan, however, is that it does not assure a balanced diet; indeed the most essential foods may be passed over—or not appear on the table at all.[5]

Prior to the Civil War, few institutions of higher learning assumed the name "university," because most offered only a limited range of subjects and thus did not concentrate on the whole universe of knowledge. In another sense of the word, however, the old-time colleges did operate as universities as they reflected a universal philosophical principle that saw all truth as stemming from a common source. This second meaning of the term certainly does not fit the modern secular institutions. Learning in the contemporary university emphasizes isolated parts of knowledge rather than the integral whole; it presents a fragmented view of life that suggests that there is no unity to truth and no central principle from which all truth radiates. In recognition of this reality, some students of higher education now use the term "multiversity" to describe such institutions, even though the word possesses an internal contradiction. Others use the phrase "intellectual polytheism" to suggest that the modern university promotes a worldview no less than did its nineteenth-century predecessor.[6]

With many secular professors, faith in science and its method of investigation has become the new "religion" to replace the old pre–Civil War faith in the Judeo-Christian God. At the beginning of the period of transition from one value system to another, many well-intentioned scholars decided that in their professional investigations they would concentrate on only those areas of inquiry which they could measure scientifically. Then they, or their followers, gradually forgot the assumption from which they started and began to think that those measurable things were the only realities. Finally, as applications of the new scientific knowledge allowed society to develop an advanced standard of living and to push back the frontiers of knowledge, some began to replace faith in the Creator with faith in a particular method of learning about the Creator's universe.[7]

Paralleling this developing faith in science (i.e., scientism) has been the growth of faith in the ability of the human mind to develop a variety of methods to improve the world. The mind, of course, can take us well along the road to truth and knowledge, and we must go as far as possible with this God-given gift. The unaided human mind, however, cannot lead us to complete truth. In the final analysis, the judgment on whether to place one's faith in science or in one's own mind or in the minds of the best thinkers or in God depends not upon a detached study of observable data but upon whether one wishes to use knowledge as a means to know and to do the will of the Divine Being. It may be that brilliant intellectual ability tends to inhibit the acquisition of spiritual knowledge. If, as Jesus suggests, the wealth of the rich man makes it difficult for him to enter the kingdom of God because of the great temptation to trust in his riches, so also the mental power of the intellectual, in many cases, makes it difficult to enter the kingdom of God because of the temptation to trust in his intellectual power.[8]

The Christian worldview gave unity to the old course of study; its decline contributed to the major changes which developed in the curriculum and faculty-student relations beginning in the late 1800s. To some degree the elective system worked hand-in-hand with the secularization process. The old curriculum had emphasized the inherent importance of certain bodies of knowledge. The elective system believed that few if any specific areas of study deserved such attention. Consequently, many colleges dropped the courses which most directly studied the Christian religion (e.g., moral and mental philosophy) without replacing them with required or even elective courses in biblical Christianity. By 1945, even the Harvard officials in their famous Report on General Education in a Free Society admitted that the elective system, while necessary when originally introduced, had done considerable harm because of the meaningless fragmentation it created. While Harvard once again recognized the need for a unifying purpose for higher education, it did not, however, acknowledge that once again the Christian religion might become that unifying factor.[9]

One of the great problems of contemporary higher education is that while the public universities largely promote the worldview of secularism, they actually believe that they maintain a neutral stance on religious and other types of values. One of the major tasks of the Christian college, therefore, is to remind the secular institutions that they also have an operating religious principle; as Cardinal John Newman, that great educational philosopher of the previous century, reminded his generation, "Supposing theology be not taught, its province will not simply be neglected, but will be actually usurped by other sciences."[10]

I can think of no better way to end this story of Christian higher education in America than to return to its beginning and again note the convictions of the Harvard founders. As the inscription still on the gate to Harvard Yard reminds us, these early Puritans had scarcely arrived in the howling wilderness of the New World when they believed it necessary to open a Christian college without which, in the words of John Eliot, an early missionary to the Indians, "both church and common wealth will sinke." While one might debate whether the continuance of civilization has depended upon the existence of Christian colleges as much as homes, churches, and governments, what is not contestable is the fact that from 1636 to the 1980s the Christian college has served for countless Americans as one of the most important forces in transforming mere existence in a civilization into the noble experience of enjoying the abundant life intended by God for us all.[11] May it continue to do so.

Endnotes

Notes to the Preface

1. Such studies exist, however, for the Catholic colleges in the United States and the Protestant colleges of Canada. See Edward J. Power, *Catholic Higher Education in America: A History* (New York, 1972), and Donald C. Masters, *Protestant Church Colleges in Canada* (Toronto, 1966). Also useful on Catholic colleges are the many monographs by Philip Gleason and Andrew Greeley. For Protestant seminaries, see the important recent works of Robert Handy, Robert Lynn, and Natalie Naylor.

2. Carl Henry, "Faith Affirming Colleges," *Christianity Today,* May 1971, p. 32.

3. Manning M. Pattillo and Donald M. Mackenzie, *Church Sponsored Higher Education in the United States* (Washington, 1966), p. 153.

Notes to the Introduction

1. G. R. Elton, *Political History, Principles and Practices* (1970), p. 67; as quoted by David Stevenson, *The Scottish Revolution 1637–44* (New York, 1973), p. 13.

2. In this introduction, I am treating education as the transmission of cultural values, especially values of intellectual culture. In so doing, I am dependent upon the framework of analysis offered by Bernard Bailyn, *Education in the Forming of American Society* (Chapel Hill, NC, 1960). For two fine general studies which also approach education broadly in this way, see Lawrence A. Cremin, *American Education: The Colonial Experience 1607–1783* (New York, 1970), and *American Education: The National Experience 1783–1876* (New York, 1980).

Annotations in this introduction have been kept to a minimum, especially in light of the full scholarly apparatus provided by Professor Ringenberg. I do draw attention to important general studies on themes pertinent to the Introduction and to my own work where ideas adumbrated here receive fuller attention, often with more entensive bibliographical reference.

3. Professor Ringenberg treats this first stable period, the first transitional era, and the second stable period in his first three chapters. His fourth and fifth chapters correspond to my second transitional period. His sixth chapter describes in detail what I sketch very generally for the period after 1925.

4. For the crucial works in the reconstruction of American Puritan thinking, see Perry Miller, *The New England Mind,* 2 vols. (New York and Cambridge, MA, 1939, 1953). Now, however, it is also necessary to read the two recent volumes by Norman Fiering for the best available depiction of Puritan intellectual life: *Moral Philosophy at Seventeeth-Century Harvard: A Discipline in Transition* (Chapel Hill, NC, 1981), and *Jonathan Edwards's Moral Thought and Its British Context* (Chapel Hill, NC, 1981). I have attempted to point out the importance of the Fiering books in an essay review, "Johnathan Edwards, Moral Philosophy, and the Seculariza-

tion of American Christian Thought," *Reformed Journal,* Feb. 1983, pp. 22–28.

5. Two fine studies on the continuing impact of Puritanism are Sacvan Bercovitch, *The Puritan Origins of the American Self* (New Haven, 1975), and Edmund S. Morgan, "The Puritan Ethic and the American Revolution," *William and Mary Quarterly,* 3rd ser. 24 (1967), 3–43.

6. The writings of Shepard, Cotton, and Hooker may be sampled in Perry Miller and Thomas H. Johnson, eds., *The Puritans: A Sourcebook of Their Writings,* 2 vols. (rev. ed., New York, 1963).

7. See Walter J. Ong, *Ramus: Method and the Decay of Dialogue from the Art of Discourse to the Art of Reason* (Cambridge, MA, 1958).

8. Mather, *Manductio ad Ministerium* (orig. 1726), as quoted by Fiering, *Moral Philosophy at Seventeenth-Century Harvard,* p. 40.

9. Edwards, *The Nature of True Virtue,* ed. William K. Frankena (Ann Arbor, 1960; orig. 1765), p. 26.

10. See Edwards's extraordinarily thorough interaction with especially Locke and Newton, as recorded in *The Works of Jonathan Edwards: Scientific and Philosophical Writings,* ed. Wallace E. Anderson (New Haven, 1980).

11. From "New England's First Fruits," 1643; as found in *American Christianity: An Historical Interpretation with Representative Documents,* ed. H. S. Smith, R. T. Handy, and L. A. Loetscher (New York, 1960–1963), I, p. 125.

12. Two sure guides to the ideological issues of the period are Bernard Bailyn, *The Ideological Origins of the American Revolution* (Cambridge, MA, 1967); and Gordon S. Wood, *The Creation of the American Republic, 1776–1787* (Chapel Hill, NC, 1969). I have addressed a few of the more general issues of the Revolutionary period, as they affected believers, in "Christian and Humanistic Values in Eighteenth-Century America," *Christian Scholar's Review,* 6 (1976), 114–26.

13. Morgan, "The American Revolution Considered as an Intellectual Movement," in *Paths of American Thought,* ed. Arthur M. Schlesinger, Jr., and Morton White (Boston, 1963), p. 11.

14. Figures from *Princeton University General Catalogue 1746–1906* (Princeton, 1908). A similar decline in the number of Yale students entering the ministry at about the same time has been noted by Steven J. Novak, *The Rights of Youth: American Colleges and Student Revolt, 1798–1815* (Cambridge, MA, 1977), p. 136.

15. For indications of the extent of that influence, see Nathan O. Hatch, "The Christian Movement and the Demand for a Theology of the People," *Journal of American History,* 67 (Dec. 1980), 545–67; Gordon S. Wood, "Evangelical America and Early Mormonism," *New York History,* 61 (Oct. 1980), 359–86; David Hackett Fischer, *Growing Old in America* (rev. ed., New York, 1978), especially the chapter "Transition: The Revolution in Age Relations, 1770–1820"; and Jay Fliegelman, *Prodigals and Pilgrims: The American Revolution against Patriarchal Authority, 1750–1800* (Cambridge, Eng., 1982).

16. See, as examples of a large literature, Stephen A. Marini, *Radical Sects of Revolutionary New England* (Cambridge, MA, 1982); and Frederick V. Mills, *Bishops by Ballot* (New York, 1978)

17. Henry F. May, *The Enlightenment in America* (New York, 1976), is an extraordinarily perceptive account of the various ways in which Americans appropriated Enlightenment thought. Also useful is Donald H. Meyer, *The Democratic Enlightenment* (New York, 1976).

18. The finest discussion of American "Baconianism" is by Theodore Dwight Bozeman, *Protestants in an Age of Science: The Baconian Ideal and Antebellum American Religious Thought* (Chapel Hill, NC, 1977).

19. See Varnum Lansing Collins, *President Witherspoon,* 2 vols. (Princeton, 1925); and Douglas Sloan, *The Scottish Enlightenment and the American College Ideal* (New York, 1971), chap. 4, "The Scottish Enlightenment Comes to Princeton: John Witherspoon," for authoritative biographical and intellectual accounts. I have explored Witherspoon's direct connections with the Revolution in *The Search for Christian America,* written with George M. Marsden and Nathan O. Hatch (Westchester, IL, 1983).

20. See James H. Smylie, "Madison and Witherspoon: Theological Roots of American Political Thought," *Princeton University Library Chronicle,* 22 (Spring 1961), 118-32; and Stuart C. Henry, *Unvanquished Puritan: A Portrait of Lyman Beecher* (Grand Rapids, 1973).

21. Several of the paragraphs which follow are adapted from my essays, "Christian Thinking and the Rise of the American University," *Christian Scholar's Review,* 9 (1979), 3–16; and "The Antebellum Christian-Enlightenment Synthesis and the Intellectual Response to Darwin," forthcoming in a volume edited by Morris Inch on Christianity and American Culture.

22. For excellent studies, see Timothy L. Smith, *Revivalism and Social Reform: American Protestantism on the Eve of the Civil War* (Nashville, 1957); Timothy L. Smith, "Righteousness and Hope: Christian Holiness and the Millennial Vision in America, 1800–1900," *American Quarterly,* 31 (Spring 1979), 22–45; and Donald G. Mathews, "The Second Great Awakening as an Organizing Process, 1780–1830," *American Quarterly,* 21 (Spring 1969), 23–43.

23. Quoted in George M. Marsden, *The Evangelical Mind and the New School Presbyterian Experience* (New Haven, 1970), p. 205. The general interpretation of this paragraph follows the summary in Marsden's fine study, pp. 230–49.

24. See the extensive documentation below for Professor Ringenberg's second chapter.

25. Quoted from Robert A. McCaughey, "The Transformation of American Academic Life: Harvard University 1821–1892," *Perspectives in American History,* 8 (1974), 263, 279.

26. For a recent sympathetic study of these schools, see Timothy L. Smith, *Uncommon Schools: Christian Colleges and Social Idealism in Midwestern America, 1829–1950* (Indianapolis, 1978).

27. D. H. Meyer, quoting Stow Persons, in *The Instructed Conscience: The Shaping of the American National Ethic* (Philadelphia, 1972), p. 5.

28. Meyer, pp. 65–66.

29. The following depends heavily upon the superb book by Meyer cited above.

30. For background, see Mary Latimer Gambrell, *Ministerial Training in Eighteenth-Century New England* (New York, 1937); William Warren Sweet, "The Rise of Theological Schools in America," *Church History,* 6 (1937), 260–73; and Natalie A. Naylor, "The Theological Seminary in the Configuration of American Higher Education: The Ante-Bellum Years," *History of Education Quarterly,* 17 (Spring 1977), 17–30.

31. For further reflections on the influence which the Presbyterian seminaries, and seminaries generally, exerted on American Christian thinking, see Mark Noll, "The Founding of Princeton Seminary," *Westminster*

Theological Journal, 42 (Fall 1979), 72-110; and the discussion of Princeton Seminary in the "Introduction" to Noll, *The Princeton Theology 1812–1921* (Grand Rapids, 1983).

32. "Theological Seminaries," *The New Schaff-Herzog Encyclopedia of Religious Knowledge* (1908–1912), XI.

33. A recent impressionistic survey of some 20 catalogs from evangelical seminaries showed an unusually high level of academic preparation and revealed many nearly household names; a similar survey of 15 evangelical colleges revealed competent but less sophisticated training (especially for professors of Bible) and fewer well-known authors.

34. It is even worth reflecting on how the structures of evangelical higher education, divided between college and seminary, may influence the vocabulary of what Christian scholars are about. It has been customary for some time, as an example, to speak of the "integration" of faith and learning. Yet this metaphor implies that "faith" and "learning" are somehow distinct entities needing to be brought together by something or someone which encompasses them both. But this is certainly a false picture of the Christian scholar's attempt to see the world as one entity under God, explicated in some perspectives more clearly by special revelation, in others more clearly by general revelation, and probably in most instances by a careful interweaving of the two.

35. See Richard Hofstadter, "The Revolution in Higher Education," in *Paths of American Thought;* Alexandra Oleson and John Voss, eds., *The Organization of Knowledge in Modern America, 1860 – 1920* (Baltimore, 1979); Laurence R. Veysey, *The Emergence of the American University* (Chicago, 1965); Bruce Kuklick, *The Rise of American Philosophy: Cambridge, Massachusetts, 1860 – 1930* (New Haven, 1977); and Burton J. Bledstein, *The Culture of Professionalism: The Middle Class and the Development of Higher Education in America* (New York, 1976), for stimulating accounts of this transformation. Again, the following paragraphs draw upon my essay, "Christian Thinking and the Rise of the American University."

36. Figures are from Bureau of Census, *Historical Statistics of the United States: Colonial Times to 1957* (Washington, D.C., 1960), pp. 210–11.

37. Not everyone approved the fragmentation which resulted. George Santayana, for example, commented on turn-of-the-century Harvard that it looked like "an anonymous concourse of coral insects, each secreting out one cell, and leaving that fossil legacy to enlarge the earth." McCaughey, "The Transformation of Harvard," p. 309.

38. Meyer, *Instructed Conscience,* p. 128.

39. See two important studies by George M. Marsden, *Fundamentalism and American Culture: The Shaping of Twentieth-Century Evangelicalism 1870–1925* (New York, 1980); and "The Collapse of American Evangelical Academia," forthcoming.

40. Compare, for example, the professional training of the Wheaton College faculty, as taken from three twentieth-century catalogs:

Year	Total Regular Faculty	Earned Doctorate	Bachelor's Degree Only
1928-29	33	5 (15%)	10 (30%)
1942-43	72	29 (40%)	26 (36%)
1982-83	160	107 (67%)	1 (.6%)

Notes to Chapter One

1. Walter Crosby Eells, *Degrees in Higher Education* (New York, 1963), p. 85

2. Franklin Hamlin Littell, *From State Church to Pluralism: A Protestant Interpretation of Religion in American History* (Garden City, New York, 1962), pp. xx, 32; Winthrop S. Hudson, *Religion in America* (New York, 1973), pp. 129–30.

3. Merle Curti, *The Growth of American Thought* (New York, 1951), pp. 50–53; Winthrop S. Hudson, "The Morrison Myth Concerning the Founding of Harvard," *Church History,* June 1939, pp. 154; M. Kelley Brooks, *Yale: A History* (New Haven, 1974), p. 42; Brander Matthews, ed., *A History of Columbia University* (New York, 1904), p. 444; Arthur V. Chitty, *The Episcopal Church in Education* (Cincinnati, n.d.), p. 10.

4. Hudson, "Founding of Harvard," pp. 50–51; Samuel Eliot Morison, *Three Centuries of Harvard, 1636–1936* (Cambridge, 1936), pp. 24, 44–50, 64–68, 87–88.

5. Brooks, pp. 3–4, 31–33; Richard Warch, *School of the Prophets: Yale College, 1701–1740* (New Haven, 1973), pp. 100–17.

6. See William H. Cowley, "European Influences on American Higher Education," *Educational Record,* Apr. 1939, p. 168.

7. Beverly McAnear, "College Founding in the American Colonies, 1745-1775," *Mississippi Valley Historical Review,* June 1955, pp. 24–25.

8. Douglas Sloan, "Harmony, Chaos, and Concensus: The American College Curriculum," *Teachers College Record,* Dec. 1971, p. 229; Edwin S. Gaustad, *The Great Awakening in New England* (Chicago, 1968), p. 30.

9. Thomas J. Wertenbaker, *Princeton, 1746–1896* (Princeton, 1946), pp. 10–20; Archibald Alexander, *Log College* (Philadelphia, 1851), p. 11.

10. Wilder D. Quint, *The Story of Dartmouth* (Boston, 1916), pp. 17, 55; Merle Curti and Roderick Nash, *Philanthropy in the Shaping of American Higher Education* (New Brunswick, NJ, 1965), pp. 33–35.

11. Jurgen Herbst, "From Religion to Politics: Debates and Confrontation Over American College Governance in the Mid-Eighteenth Century," *Harvard Educational Review,* Aug. 1976, pp. 273–75; Willard W. Smith, "The Relation of College and State in Colonial America," Diss. Columbia Univ. 1949, pp. 158–63.

12. Cowley, "European Influences," pp. 166–69; Kenneth S. Latourette, *A History of Christianity,* 2 vols. (New York, 1975), I, 552.

13. Wertenbaker, pp. 80–85.

14. Douglas Sloan, *The Scottish Enlightenment and the American College Ideal* (New York, 1971), pp. vii-ix, 36–39; Cowley, "European Influences," pp. 169–70.

15. Curti, p. 236; Henry May, *The Enlightenment in America* (New York, 1976), pp. 62–64, 346–50.

16. McAnear, p. 31; Wertenbaker, p. 94; W. D. Carrell, "American College Professors, 1750-1800," *History of Education Quarterly,* Fall 1968, pp. 289–90.

17. McAnear, p. 31; Wertenbaker, pp. 30, 43; Carrell, pp. 299–302; Ernest Earnest, *Academic Procession: An Informal History of the American College, 1936–1953* (New York, 1953), p. 27.

18. Carrell, pp. 292–99.

19. C. H. Cramer, *Case Western Reserve* (Boston, 1976), pp. 13–14;

Theodore Hornberger, *Scientific Thought in American Colleges, 1630–1800* (Austin, 1945), p. 36; Wertenbaker, pp. 99, 137.

20. Richard Hofstadter and Walter Metzger, *The Development of Academic Freedom in the United States* (New York, 1955), p. 155; Hudson, "Founding of Harvard," p. 154; Morison, p. 84.

21. Jurgen Herbst, *From Crisis to Crisis: American College Government, 1636–1819* (Cambridge, 1982), pp. 48ff.; John S. Brubacher and Willis Rudy, *Higher Education in Transition: A History of American Colleges and Universities, 1636–1976* (New York, 1976), pp. 26–31.

22. Curti, pp. 8–83; Wertenbaker, pp. 102–03; Morison, p. 241.

23. Hornberger, pp. 22–34.

24. Hornberger, pp. 23–60, 80–87; Stanley M. Guralnick, *Science and the Antebellum American College* (Philadelphia, 1975), pp. vii–viii.

25. Hornberger, pp. 35, 37, 67; Morison, pp. 27–28.

26. R. Freemen Butts, *The College Charts Its Course* (New York, 1939), pp. 63, 65.

27. McAnear, pp. 30, 36.

28. McAnear, pp. 32–33; James McLachlan, "The American College in the Nineteenth Century: Toward a Reappraisal," *Teachers College Record,* Dec. 1978, p. 294; Wertenbaker, pp. 116–17.

29. McAnear, pp. 32–33.

30. McAnear, pp. 33–34; Charles E. Cunningham, *Timothy Dwight, 1752–1817* (New York, 1942), pp. 10, 20; Hornberger, pp. 16, 19, 21; Richard P. McCormick, *Rutgers: A Bicentennial History* (New Brunswick, NJ, 1966), p. 20; David C. Humphrey, *From King's College to Columbia, 1746–1800* (New York, 1976), p. 163.

31. Humphrey, pp. 186–89; Henry D. Sheldon, *Student Life and Customs* (New York, 1901), pp. 85–88; Quint, pp. 68–69; McCormick, p. 20; McAnear, pp. 28–29; Wertenbaker, pp. 28–29.

32. Yale as well as Harvard suffered from significant student disorders more than did the other northern colleges. See McAnear, p. 38.

33. Kathryn M. Moore, "Freedom and Constraint in Eighteenth Century Harvard," *Journal of Higher Education,* Nov. 1976, pp. 649–51.

34. William H. Cowley, "History of Student Residential Housing," *School and Society,* 1 Dec. 1934, pp. 708–12.

35. Brooks, p. 42; Morison, p. 28; Earnest, p. 36.

36. McAnear, pp. 38–39; Herbert B. Adams, *The College of William and Mary* (Washington, 1887), pp. 15-16; Humphrey, pp. 91–96.

37. Curti and Nash, pp. 20–23.

38. Curti and Nash, pp. 4–19, 31–33; Wertenbaker, p. 3; Quint, p. 72; Chitty, p. 8.

39. Curti and Nash, pp. 28–29; Wertenbaker, pp. 31–36; Chitty, pp. 10–11.

40. McLachlan, p. 295; Donald G. Tewksbury, *The Founding of American College and Universities Before the Civil War* (New York, 1932), pp. 70, 72.

Notes to Chapter Two

1. McLachlan, p. 295; George P. Schmidt, "Colleges in Ferment," *American Historical Review,* Oct. 1953, p. 19.

2. Clarence P. Shedd, *Two Centuries of Student Christian Movements* (New York, 1934), pp. 36, 48; Cunningham, pp. 300–02.

3. Brubacher and Rudy, pp. 42–43.

4. Tewksbury, pp. 16, 69–73; David B. Potts, "College Enthusiasm As Public Response, 1800–1860," *Harvard Educational Review,* Feb. 1977, p. 41.

5. Tewksbury, pp. 104–05.

6. Tewksbury, pp. 115–16.

7. Butts, p. 118; Sloan, "American College Curriculum," p. 231; James H. Fairchild, *Oberlin: The Colony and the College, 1833 – 1883* (Oberlin, 1883), pp. 151-53; Colin B. Goodykoontz, *Home Missions on the American Frontier* (Caldwell, ID, 1939), p. 381; Earnest, p. 23.

8. N. A. Naylor, "Antebellum College Movement: Re-appraisal of Tewksbury's Founding of American Colleges and Universities," *History of Education Quarterly,* Fall 1973, p. 270; Herbst, *American College Government,* pp. xi–xii; Charles D. Johnson, *Higher Education of the Southern Baptists: An Institutional History, 1826 – 1954* (Waco, 1955), p. 47; William C. Ringenberg, "The Protestant College on the Michigan Frontier," Diss. Michigan State 1970, pp. 63, 66, 72-73.

9. David B. Potts, "American Colleges in the Nineteenth Century: From Localism to Denominationalism," *History of Education Quarterly,* Winter 1971, pp. 367–68; Potts, "College Enthusiasm," pp. 31–37; Timothy L. Smith, *Uncommon Schools: Christian Colleges and Social Idealism in Midwestern America, 1820 – 1950* (Indianapolis, 1978), pp. 3, 21–29, 59.

10. *General Catalogue of Oberlin College, 1833 – 1908,* p. 117; *Oberlin College Catalogue, 1858 – 1859,* p. 38; *Oberlin College Catalogue, 1864 – 1865,* pp. 6–34; Clyde S. Kilby, *Minority of One: The Biography of Jonathan Blanchard* (Grand Rapids, 1959), pp. 151–52; Charlie Brown Hershey, *Colorado College, 1874 – 1949* (Colorado Springs, 1952), p. 41; Smith, *Uncommon Schools,* p. 30.

11. John D. Wright, *Transylvania: Tutor to the West* (Lexington, 1975), pp. ix, x, 86, 155, 174.

12. Potts, "College Enthusiasm," pp. 37–38; David F. Allmendinger, "New England Students and the Revolution in Higher Education, 1800–1900," *History of Education Quarterly,* Winter 1971, pp. 381–86; David F. Allmendinger, *Paupers and Scholars: The Transformation of Student Life in Nineteenth-Century New England* (New York, 1975), pp. 1–22.

13. George P. Schmidt, *The Liberal Arts College* (New Brunswick, NJ, 1957), p. 274; *Beloit College Catalog, 1860 – 1861,* p. 12; *Franklin College Catalog, 1847,* pp. 5–7.

14. Albea Godbold, *The Church College of the Old South* (Durham, 1944), pp. 107–09; Walter Havighurst, *The Miami Years, 1809–1959* (New York, 1958), pp. 32–33.

15. Godbold, pp. 120–23; *Beloit College Catalog, 1860 – 61,* p. 19; Thomas LeDuc, *Piety and Intellect at Amherst College* (New York, 1946), p. 24.

16. Godbold, p. 71.

17. Hofstadter and Metzger, pp. 152, 293.

18. George P. Schmidt, *The Old Time College President* (New York, 1930), pp. 190–91; Shedd, *Student Christian Movements,* p. 122.

19. Wertenbaker, p. 165; Godbold, pp. 128–30; George B. Manhart, *DePauw Through the Years,* 2 vols. (Greencastle, IN, 1962), I, p. 138.

20. Kilby, p. 84.

21. Tewksbury, pp. 83–84; Johnson, *Higher Education of Southern Bap-*

tists, p. 10; Godbold, chapter two; William M. Glasgow, *The Geneva Book* (Philadelphia, 1908), p. 72; G. Wallace Chessman, *Denison: The Story of an Ohio College* (Granville, 1957), p. 117.

22. McLachlan, p. 297; Goodykoontz, pp. 362, 365; Shedd, *Student Christian Movements,* p. 122; Godbold, p. 196; Ringenberg, "Protestant College on the Michigan Frontier," p. 159; Claude M. Fuess, *Amherst: The Story of a New England College* (Boston, 1935), pp. 242–43. For comparative data on the late-eighteenth-century period, see Donald O. Schneider, "Education in Colonial American Colleges, 1750–1770, and the Occupation and Political Offices of Their Alumni," Diss. George Peabody Univ. 1965; and Walter C. Bronson, *The History of Brown University, 1764 – 1914* (Providence, 1914), p. 154.

23. Humphrey, p. 160.

24. Earnest, p. 40; Cunningham, p. 266.

25. Earnest, p. 41; for a vivid description of the dramatic influence of one of these powerful "old-time presidents" (Wayland), see Bronson, pp. 207ff.

26. Shedd, pp. xviii, 24–31, 40–41, 90; Morison, pp. 61–62.

27. Shedd, pp. 48–61, 69, 71–74, 80.

28. Potts, "College Enthusiasm," p. 38; Curti, p. 225; Godbold, pp. 59, 152, 198–201; Rockwell D. Hunt, *History of the College of the Pacific, 1851 – 1951* (Stockton, 1951), p. 33; McLachlan, p. 296; Kilby, p. 152; *Beloit College Catalog, 1860 – 61,* p. 20; Ringenberg, "Protestant College on the Michigan Frontier," p. 102.

29. See, for example, Johnson, *Higher Education of Southern Baptists,* pp. 11–12, 68–69, 98; and Godbold, p. 56.

30. Parker E. Lichtenstein, "Berea College," in *Struggle and Promise: A Future for Private Colleges,* ed. Conrad Hilberry and Morris Keeton (New York, 1969), pp. 52–53.

31. Warren H. Smith, *Hobart and William Smith* (Geneva, NY, 1972), p. 177; *Annual Report of the Directors of the American Education Society,* 28 May 1860 (Boston, 1860), p. 6; Naylor, p. 270; James Findlay, "Congregationalists and American Education," *History of Education,* Winter 1977, pp. 449–50; Allmendinger, "New England Students," pp. 381–86; *Wake Forest Catalog, 1978 – 1979,* p. 13.

32. Daniel T. Johnson, "Financing the Western Colleges, 1844–1862," *Journal of the Illinois State Historical Society,* Spring 1972, pp. 43–53.

33. Wertenbaker, p. 271.

34. *Ripon College Catalog, 1864 – 65,* p. 16.

35. Sloan, "American College Curriculum," pp. 240–41; Curti, p. 362; Earnest, p. 22.

36. Schmidt, *Old Time College President,* pp. 93, 104–05, 107; Sloan, "American College Curriculum," pp. 246–47; D.H. Meyer, *The Instructed Conscience: The Shaping of the American National Ethic* (Philadelphia, 1972), pp. x–xiv, 6–11.

37. Schmidt, *Old Time College President,* pp. 108–18, 144; Ralph Henry Gabriel, *Religion and Learning at Yale* (New Haven, 1958), pp. 109–13; Rufus Jones, *Haverford College* (New York, 1933), p. 69; Meyer, pp. 147–56.

38. Guralnick, pp. viii–xii, 141–42, 158–59; Potts, "College Enthusiasm," p. 39; Godbold, p. 81; Sloan, "American College Curriculum," p. 233.

39. Guralnick, pp. 153, 155; Theodore Dwight Bozeman, *Protestants in an Age of Science: The Baconian Ideal and Antebellum American*

Religious Thought (Chapel Hill, NC, 1977), pp. vi–xii, 76–81; Gabriel, pp. 113–16; Hofstadter and Metzger, p. 292; Wertenbaker, p. 95; Sloan, "American College Curriculum," p. 227.

40. Cunningham, pp. 35–39.

41. Earnest, p. 95.

42. Guy E. Snavely, *The Church and the Four-Year College: An Appraisal of Their Relation* (New York, 1955), pp. 80–81; Matthew N. Young, *A History of Colleges of the Churches of Christ* (Kansas City, 1949), p. 31; Glasgow, p. 20.

43. Wertenbaker, pp. 198–99; John Barnard, *From Evangelicalism to Progressivism at Oberlin College, 1866–1917* (Columbus, 1969), p. 25; Earnest, p. 45; Johnson, *Higher Education of Southern Baptists,* p. 10.

44. Frederick Rudolph, *The American College and University: A History* (New York, 1965), pp. 281–82.

45. McLachlan, pp. 303–04; Schmidt, *Old Time College President,* pp. 226–227.

46. Sloan, "American College Curriculum," pp. 242–48; Earnest, pp. 75–77.

47. Butts, pp. 129–31.

48. Eells, pp. 72–73.

49. Eells, pp. 73–78.

50. Schmidt, *Liberal Arts College,* pp. 70–71; Schmidt, "Colleges in Ferment," p. 19; Wertenbaker, p. 300; Charles O. Brown, MS, "Faculty of Olivet College, 1867–1876," (Olivet College archives).

51. Earnest, p. 76; Wertenbaker, p. 300; Oliphant, p. 116; Ringenberg, "Protestant College on the Michigan Frontier," pp. 92–93.

52. D. Elton Trueblood, *The Idea of a College* (New York, 1959), pp. 34–36; Kilby, p. 96.

53. Sheldon, *Student Life,* pp. 89–93, 125–35; Thomas S. Harding, *College Literary Societies, 1815–1876* (New York, 1971), p. 22; Brubacher and Rudy, pp. 46–48.

54. Sheldon, *Student Life,* pp. 125–35; Godbold, p. 88.

55. Godbold, pp. 85–88; Ringenberg, "Protestant College on the Michigan Frontier," p. 119; Earnest, p. 86; Manhart, pp. 129–30.

56. Kilby, pp. 28–29; Barnard, pp. 21–22; Wertenbaker, pp. 201–04.

57. Harding, pp. 49, 101, 132, 158, 197–98, 232, 235–36; Codman Hislop, *Eliphalet Nott* (Middletown, CT, 1971), p. 181.

58. Godbold, pp. 94, 168; Barnard, p. 21; Oliphant, p. 66; Wertenbaker, pp. 237–38.

59. The largest college library collection was the one at Harvard which numbered 13,000 volumes in 1800 and 122,000 in 1865 (Hornberger, p. 78; Brubacher and Rudy, pp. 94–95).

60. Harding, pp. 56, 67–68; Godbold, p. 79.

61. Harding, pp. 56, 83.

62. Vivian Lyon Moore, *The First Hundred Years of Hillsdale College* (Ann Arbor, 1944), p. 93; Harding, p. 1.

63. Harding, pp. 262, 296–98, 318.

64. Sheldon, *Student Life,* pp. 145–47, 192–95.

65. Earnest, pp. 125–27; John J. Shiperd, Letter to Hamilton Hill, 17 August 1844, Michigan Historical Collection, Univ. of Michigan; Butts, p. 140; also see Cramer, p. 160.

66. Sheldon, *Student Life,* p. 151; Fuess, pp. 220–22.

67. Schmidt, *Old Time College President,* pp. 204–06, 222–25; "The First Circular of Oberlin College, March 8, 1834" in Frances J. Hosford,

Father Shipherd's Magna Charta (Boston, 1937), p. 5; Gilbert Barnes, *The Antislavery Impulse, 1830–1844* (New York, 1964), pp. 64–77; Robert S. Fletcher, *A History of Oberlin from its Foundation through the Civil War,* 2 vols. (Oberlin, 1942), I, pp. 174–73, 236–53; Charles G. Finney, *Memoirs of Charles G. Finney* (New York, 1876), pp. 337–51; Godbold, pp. 29, 75, 89–90, 166.

68. Kilby, pp. 36, 118–20, 171–74, 187, 196, 207, 217–18; Earnest, p. 128.

69. Schmidt, *Old Time College President,* pp. 78–80; Kilby, p. 152; Earnest, pp. 42–43.

70. Floyd B. Streeter, "History of Prohibition Legislation in Michigan," *Michigan History,* April 1918, p. 299.

71. James C. Olson, *J. Sterling Morton* (Lincoln, 1942), p. 16; Godbold, pp. 102–03; Wertenbaker, pp. 242–43; Sheldon, *Student Life,* pp. 95–101, 106–10; Earnest, pp. 44–45.

72. Sheldon, *Student Life,* p. 113; Earnest, p. 46.

73. Herbst, "American College Governance," pp. 276–77; John T. Wahlquist and James W. Thornton, *State Colleges and Universities* (Washington, 1964), pp. 4–5.

74. Kent Sagendorph, *Michigan, the Story of the University* (New York, 1948), pp. 64, 72, 74; Erastus O. Haven, *Autobiography* (New York, 1883), p. 144; *University of Michigan Regent's Proceedings, 1837–1864* (Ann Arbor, 1915), pp. 183–84, 720–22, 919; *University of Michigan Catalog, 1843–44,* pp. 12–13; Wilfred B. Shaw, *History of the University of Michigan* (New York, 1920), p. 42.

75. Coulter, *College Life in the Old South* (New York, 1951), p. 151; Godbold, pp. 179–80.

76. Naylor, p. 269.

77. Naylor, p. 269; Coulter, p. 47; Earle D. Ross, "Religious Influences in the Development of State Colleges and Universities," *Indiana Magazine of History,* Dec. 1950, p. 354; Godbold, p. 184.

78. Ross, pp. 348–49, 353; Roger Ebert, *An Illinois Century: One Hundred Years of Campus Life* (Urbana, 1967), pp. 35–36; Sherman B. Barnes, "Learning and Piety in Ohio Colleges, 1865–1900," *Ohio Historical Quarterly,* Oct. 1960, p. 331.

79. *University of Michigan Catalog, 1852–53,* p. 25; *University of Michigan Regent's Proceedings,* pp. 720–22; Haven, p. 150; Christian Library Association of the University of Michigan, MS, Constitution and Minutes of the 1 May 1858 meeting, Michigan Historical Collection, Univ. of Michigan; Madison Kuhn, *Michigan State: The First Hundred Years* (East Lansing, 1955), p. 91.

80. Thomas N. Hoover, *The History of Ohio University* (Athens, 1954), p. 26; Godbold, pp. 172–77.

81. Wahlquist and Thornton, pp. 4–5; R. P. Thomson, "Colleges in the Revolutionary South: The Shaping of a Tradition," *Higher Education Quarterly,* Winter 1970, pp. 404–07; Curti, p. 226; Ross, pp. 348–49.

82. Hofstadter and Metzger, pp. 298–99; Wahlquist and Thornton, pp. 4–5.

83. Havighurst, p. 46.

84. Godbold, pp. 52–53, 149–53; Andrew Ten Brook, *American State Universities: Their Origin and Progress* (Cincinnati, 1875), pp. 223–24; Howard H. Peckham, *The Making of the University of Michigan* (Ann Arbor, 1967), p. 64.

85. Godbold, p. 148; Ringenberg, "Protestant College on the Michigan Frontier," p. 181.

86. Ten Brook, pp. 356, 372–74.
87. See especially the writings of Richard Hofstadter.
88. McLachlan, pp. 298–300; Naylor, pp. 261–62, 261–70; Sloan, "American College Curriculum," pp. 224–26; Potts, "College Enthusiasm," pp. 28–30; James Axtell, "The Death of the Liberal Arts College," *History of Education Quarterly,* Winter 1971, pp. 341, 346; Potts, "American Colleges in the Nineteenth Century," p. 366.

Notes to Chapter Three

1. Frank H. Bowles and Frank A. Decosta, *Between Two Worlds: A Profile of Negro Higher Education* (New York, 1971), p. 25; H. M. Bond, "Origin and Development of the Negro Church-Related College," *Journal of Negro Education,* Summer 1960, p. 219; Carter G. Woodson, *The Education of the Negro Prior to 1861* (New York, 1928), pp. 265–72.
2. Woodson, pp. 265–78; Earnest, p. 63.
3. Bowles and Decosta, pp. 12–13.
4. Bowles and Decosta, pp. 20–21; Woodson, pp. 256–64.
5. Stephen J. Wright, "The Negro College in America," *Harvard Educational Review,* Summer, 1960, pp. 272–73; Frederick A. McGinnis, *A History and an Interpretation of Wilberforce University* (Wilberforce, 1941), p. 37.
6. Dwight O. W. Holmes, *The Evolution of the Negro College* (New York, 1969), pp. 79–83.
7. Holmes, pp. 79–83; *Berea College Catalog, 1977–79,* p. 9.
8. Henry A. Bullock, *A History of Negro Education in the South* (Cambridge, 1967), pp. 18–24; Bowles and Decosta, p. 27; Daniel C. Thompson, *Private Black Colleges at the Crossroads* (Westport, CT, 1973), pp. 9–10.
9. Bowles and Decosta, p. 30; Rayford W. Logan, "Evolution of Private Colleges for Negroes," *Journal of Negro Education,* Summer 1958, pp. 213–16; Bond, pp. 222–24; August Meier and Elliott M. Rudwick, *From Plantation to Ghetto* (New York, 1966), pp. 146–47; Holmes, p. 12.
10. Bowles and Decosta, p. 33.
11. Richard I. McKinney, *Religion in Higher Education Among Negroes* (New York, 1972), pp. ix, 3; Bond, pp. 220–21; Francis G. Peabody, *Education for Life: The Story of Hampton Institute* (New York, 1919), p. xii.
12. Wilmot Carter, *Shaw's Universe* (Raleigh, 1973), pp. iv, 1–3; Elizabeth Geen, "Morehouse College," in Keeton and Hilberry, *A Future for Colleges,* pp. 370–71.
13. Woodson, p. 256; Bond, pp. 219–20, 223–24.
14. Bullock, p. 175.
15. For a shocking description of the persecution faced by teachers from the North, see Henry Lee Swint, *The Northern Teacher in the South, 1862–1870* (Nashville, 1941), pp. 96–109.
16. Holmes, pp. 11–12; Bullock, p. 24; Meier and Rudwick, pp. 146–47; Curti and Nash, p. 177; also see Jacqueline Jones, "Women Who Were More than Men: Sex and Status in Freedman's Teaching," *History of Education Quarterly,* Spring 1979, pp. 48–49.
17. Logan, pp. 217–18; Bowles and Decosta, p. 29.
18. One study conducted in the 1960s stated that the black schools which then attracted the best quality students included Fisk, Hampton, Howard, Lincoln, Morehouse, and Xavier. See A. J. Jaffe, Walter Adams, and

Sandra G. Meyers, *Negro Higher Education in the 1960s* (New York, 1968), p. 242.

19. Geen, pp. 376–77.

20. Geen, p. 370; Curti and Nash, p. 168; James P. Browley, *Two Centuries of Methodist Concern: Bondage, Freedom, and Education of Black People* (New York, 1974), p. 433.

21. Curti and Nash, pp. 168–81; Holmes, pp. 163–78.

22. Curti and Nash, p. 171; Joe M. Richardson, *A History of Fisk University, 1865–1946* (University, AL, 1980), pp. 24–32.

23. Curti and Nash, p. 175.

24. Most of the United Negro College Fund colleges are at least somewhat church-related. See Thompson, pp. 275–76.

25. Curti and Nash, p. 183; Bond, p. 226.

26. Earnest, pp. 183–202, 259; Schmidt, *Liberal Arts College,* p. 143; Liva Baker, *I'm Radcliffe; Fly Me* (New York, 1976), pp. 173–77; Arthur C. Cole, *A Hundred Years of Mount Holyoke College* (New York, 1940), pp. 103ff.; Thomas Woody, *A History of Women's Education in the United States,* 2 vols. (New York, 1974 edition), II, p. 198.

27. Mabel Newcomer, *A Century of Higher Education for American Women* (New York, 1959), pp. 6–9.

28. Newcomer, p. 9; Anne Firor Scott, "The Ever Widening Circle: The Diffusion of Feminist Values from the Troy Female Seminary, 1822–72," *History of Education Quarterly,* Spring 1979, pp. 3, 7; Elizabeth A. Green, *Mary Lyon and Mount Holyoke* (Hanover, NH, 1979), pp. xiii–xvi; Woody, I, p. 361.

29. Earnest, pp. 169–92.

30. Woody, II, pp. 151–55; Newcomer, pp. 25–32.

31. Earnest, p. 176.

32. Earnest, pp. 174–75; Woody, II, pp. 144, 149.

33. Jeanne L. Noble, *The Negro Woman's College Education* (New York, 1956), pp. 17–22.

34. Woody, II, pp. 148–49; Earnest, pp. 180–82; Baker, pp. 175–76.

35. Elaine Kendall, *Peculiar Institution: An Informal History of the Seven Sisters Colleges* (New York, 1976), p. 30; Earnest, p. 192; Jean Glasscock, ed., *Wellesley College, 1875–1975* (Wellesley, 1975), p. 132.

36. Woody, I, p. 361; Earnest, p. 192; Newcomer, pp. 171–72.

37. Woody, II, pp. 368–69; Page Smith, *Daughters of the Promised Land* (Boston, 1970), pp. 181–82.

38. Smith, *Daughters of the Promised Land,* p. 189.

39. Earnest, p. 192.

40. Earnest, p. 197; Woody, II, pp. 231–33.

41. Earnest, p. 197; Godbold, pp. 103, 171; *Texas Christian University Catalog,* 1978–79, pp. 14–15.

42. Earnest, p. 198; Woody, II, pp. 3–4, 16.

43. Edwin Mims, *History of Vanderbilt University* (Nashville, 1946), pp. 13, 84; Curti and Nash, p. 124.

44. Nora C. Chaffin, *1839–1892: The Beginnings of Duke University* (Durham, 1950), pp. 492–98; Curti and Nash, p. 125.

45. Curti and Nash, pp. 126–27.

46. Curti and Nash, pp. 127, 147; *Wake Forest College Catalog, 1926–27,* p. 10.

47. Richard J. Storr, *Harper's University* (Chicago, 1966), pp. 3–105; Thomas W. Goodspeed, *A History of the University of Chicago* (Chicago, 1916), pp. 10–11, 69, 292–93; Curti and Nash, pp. 116–17, 124.

48. Orrin L. Elliott, *Stanford University: The First Twenty-five Years* (Stanford, 1937), pp. 106, 137–41.

49. John C. French, *A History of the University Founded by Johns Hopkins* (Baltimore, 1946), pp. 64–71, 324–32; Hugh Hawkins, *Pioneer: A History of Johns Hopkins University, 1874–1889* (Ithaca, 1960), pp. 214–15.

50. Curti and Nash, pp. 158–59.

51. Curti and Nash, pp. 212–37.

52. James H. Lehman, *Beyond Anything Foreseen: A Study of the History of Higher Education in the Church of the Brethren* (n.p., n.d.), pp. 2, 6–8; Hubert R. Pellman, *Eastern Mennonite College, 1917–1967* (Harrisonburg, VI, 1967), p. 16; C. Henry Smith and E. J. Hirschler, eds., *The Story of Bluffton College* (Bluffton, 1925), p. 109.

53. David T. Nelson, *Luther College, 1861–1961* (Decorah, IA, 1961), pp. 18–20, 343; Emory Lindquist, *Bethany in Kansas* (Lindsborg, KS, 1945), p. 2; Leland H. Carlson, *A History of North Park College* (Chicago, 1941), pp. 45–46; Walter C. Schnackenberg, *The Lamp and the Cross: Pacific Lutheran University* (n.p., 1965), p. 2; Nicholas P. Wolterstorff, ed., *Christian Liberal Arts Education: Calvin College Curriculum Study* (Grand Rapids, 1970), p. 22; Willis F. Dunbar, *The Michigan Record in Higher Education* (Detroit, 1963), p. 170; Harold H. Lentz, *A History of Wittenberg College* (Wittenberg, 1946), p. 13; Wynand Wichers, *A Century of Hope, 1866–1966* (Grand Rapids, 1968), pp. 65–73.

54. Nelson, *Luther,* p. 34; also see Lehman, p. 37.

55. Conrad Bergendoff, *Augustana . . . A Profession of Faith* (Rock Island, IL, 1969), pp. 78, 97, 104–106; Lindquist, p. 282.

56. Wichers, pp. 78–79.

57. Lehman, p. 37; John S. Umble, *Goshen College: 1894–1954* (Goshen, 1955), p. 7.

58. Morison, pp. 341–46; Hislop, pp. 231–32.

59. Hofstadter and Metzger, p. 360; Rudolph, p. 246; Morison, p. 262.

60. Lehman, pp. 36–37, 43, 50; Glasscock, p. 132; Leal A. Headley and Merrill E. Jarchow, *Carleton: The Final Century* (Northfield, MN, 1966), p. 164; *Franklin College Catalog, 1896,* p. 16; Hershey, pp. 192–93; Merrimon Cunningim, *The College Seeks Religion* (New Haven, 1947), pp. 143–44; James B. Sellers, *History of the University of Alabama* (Tuscaloosa, 1953), p. 463; Alice D. Miller and Susan Myers, *Barnard College: The First Fifty Years* (New York, 1939), pp. 72–73; Barnes, "Learning and Piety in Ohio Colleges," pp. 333–34; Martha Frances Montague, *Lewis and Clark College, 1867–1967* (Portland, 1968), pp. 59, 77–78; Lawrence E. Nelson, *Redlands: Biography of a College* (Redlands, CA, 1958), p. 181.

61. Morison, pp. 384–35, 387, 446.

62. Curti, pp. 580–86. For a discussion of how the rising middle class encouraged the development of professional expertise and authority in the universities, see Burton J. Bledstein, *The Culture of Professionalism: The Middle Class and the Development of Higher Education in America* (New York, 1976), pp. x–xi, 287–90; also see Alexandra Oleson and John Voss, *The Organization of Knowledge in America, 1860–1920* (Baltimore, 1979), and Bruce Leslie, "Between Piety and Expertise: Professionalization of College Faculty in the 'Age of the University,' " *Pennsylvania History,* July 1979, pp. 245–65.

63. Barnard, pp. 65–665; also see Wertenbaker, pp. 229, 265, 310–311, 350.

64. Harold S. Wechsler, *The Qualified Student: A History of Selective College Admission in America* (New York, 1977), pp. 40–50; William K. Selden, *Accreditation* (New York, 1960), pp. 27–28.

65. Earnest, p. 220; Wertenbaker, pp. 162–63.

66. Sheldon, *Student Life,* pp. 202–03; Carter, *Shaw,* pp. 85–86; William C. Ringenberg, *Taylor University: The First 125 Years* (Grand Rapids, 1973), pp. 116–18; John R. Betts, *America's Sporting Heritage, 1850 – 1950* (Reading, MA, 1974), pp. 124, 129.

67. Earnest, pp. 137–38; Rudolph, p. 154; Wells Twombly, *200 Years of Sport in America* (New York, 1976), pp. 70–71, 74–78, 81–83; John A. Krout, *Annals of American Sport* (New Haven, 1929), p. 144.

68. Twombly, pp. 78–81; Manhart, I, pp. 142–43; Wertenbaker, p. 325.

69. Twombly, p. 78; *Albion College Standard,* Dec. 1868, p. 6.

70. Earnest, pp. 220–25; Betts, pp. 124–29.

71. Earnest, pp. 220–21, 225.

72. Twombly, p. 93; Oliphant, pp. 235–36; Betts, p. 127.

73. Between 1883 and 1901, Yale fielded nine undefeated teams and three unscored-upon teams, including the 1888 squad which outscored its opponents 700–0 (see Earnest, p. 222).

74. Twombly, pp. 93–96; Krout, p. 238.

75. James Naismith, *Basketball: Its Origin and Development* (New York, 1941), pp. 18–60, 111–24.

76. John Robson, *Baird's Manual of American College Fraternities* (Menasha, WI, 1968), p. 5; J.E. Morpurgo, *Their Majesties Royall College: William and Mary in the Seventeenth and Eighteenth Centuries* (Williamsburg, 1976), pp. 181–82.

77. Morpurgo, pp. 6–7; Hislop, p. 389; Havighurst, p. 91.

78. Hislop, p. 390; Wertenbaker, pp. 281, 322.

79. Walter Pilkington, *Hamilton College: 1812 – 1962* (Clinton, NY, 1962), pp. 131–32; Lentz, pp. 112–14.

80. Henry C. Hubbard, *Ohio Weslyan's First Hundred Years* (Delaware, OH, 1943), p. 267; David D. Wallace, *History of Wofford College, 1854-1949* (Nashville, 1951), pp. 79, 181–85.

81. Charles W. Cooper, *Whittier* (Los Angeles, 1967), p. 218.

82. Robson, p. 9; also see Charles S. Johnson, *Fraternities in Our Colleges* (New York, 1972), p. 14.

83. Johnson, *Fraternities,* p. 13.

84. This, for example, was the experience of Baptist Colgate in the 1840s. See Harold D. Williams, *A History of Colgate University, 1819 – 1969* (New York, 1969), pp. 90–91.

Notes to Chapter Four

1. Billy Graham, "Why I Believe in Christian Education," *Abundant Life,* June 1967, p. 17.

2. See Pattillo and Mackenzie, *Church Sponsored Higher Education,* p. 153; Phillip E. Jacob, *Changing Values in College* (New York, 1957), p. 204; Myron F. Wicke, *The Church Related College* (Washington, 1964), p. 7; and C. Robert Pace, *Education and Evangelism* (New York, 1972), pp. 92–93. The higher educational institutions in Canada have secularized even more completely than they have in the United States; see Masters, *Church Colleges in Canada,* pp. v, 207–11.

3. Butts, p. 395; Howard R. Bowen, *Investment in Learning: The Individual and Social Value of American Higher Education* (San Fran-

cisco, 1977), pp. 125–30; Kenneth A. Feldman and Theodore M. Newcomb, *The Impact of College on Students* (San Francisco, 1969), pp. 8, 10. Also see Dean R. Hoge, *Commitment on Campus: Changes in Religion and Values over Five Centuries* (Philadelphia, 1974), pp. 186, 190.

4. Curti, pp. 531–32. For a lucid summary of the many rapid changes in American higher education in this period, see Mark A. Noll, "Christian Thinking and the Rise of the American University," *Christian Scholar's Review,* pp. 3–16. Also see Noll's introduction to this book, pp. 24ff.

5. Curti, p. 542; Carl Diehl, *Americans and German Scholarship* (New Haven, 1978), pp. 3–4; Gabriel, pp. 197–98; also see Jerry W. Brown, *The Rise of Biblical Criticism in America, 1800 – 1870; The New England Scholars* (Middletown, CT, 1969), pp. 7–9.

6. Gabriel, pp. 183–84, 195; Lawrence R. Veysey, *The Emergence of the American University* (Chicago, 1965), p. 204.

7. William R. Hutchinson, *The Modernist Impulse in American Protestantism* (Cambridge, 1976), pp. 76–115; Veysey, p. 204; Barnard, pp. 121–32; Ross, p. 356.

8. Schmidt, "Colleges in Ferment," pp. 29–33.

9. Schmidt, "Colleges in Ferment," pp. 29–33, 37; Hofstadter and Metzger, pp. 334–35.

10. Paul A. Carter, *The Spiritual Crisis of the Gilded Age* (DeKalb, IL, 1971), p. 28; Schmidt, *Liberal Arts College,* pp. 161–66; A. Hunter Dupree, *Asa Gray* (Cambridge, 1959), pp. 358–59; Barnard, pp. 50–51.

11. Curti, p. 549; Schmidt, "Colleges in Ferment," pp. 34–35, 37; Gabriel, pp. 152, 156–58.

12. Wertenbacker, pp. 311–12; Curti, pp. 548–51; Glenn C. Altschuler, "From Religion to Ethics: Andrew D. White and the Dilemma of a Christian Rationalist," *Church History,* Sept. 1978, pp. 308–24.

13. Gabriel, pp. 180, 191–94.

14. Kuhn, p. 91; Hofstadter and Metzger, pp. 326, 345–46; *Wake Forest University Catalog, 1978–79,* p. 15.

15. Hofstadter and Metzger, pp. 330–31; Wright, *Transylvania,* pp. 240–41; Kenneth M. Plummer, *A History of West Virginia Wesleyan College* (Buckhannon, WV, 1965), pp. 19–20.

16. Interview with D. Elton Trueblood, 21 Aug. 1978; also see Earnest, p. 126.

17. Veysey, p. 48; Barnard, p. 112; Plummer, p. 132; Wicke, p. 65; Richard Solberg and Merton P. Strommen, *How Church-Related are Church-Related Colleges?* (New York, 1980), pp. 55–64, 84.

18. Cunningim, p. 139; Pattillo and MacKenzie, pp. 147–48.

19. Cunningim, p. 168.

20. John H. Timmerman, *Promises to Keep: A Centennial History of Calvin College* (Grand Rapids, 1975), p. 131.

21. Schmidt, *Liberal Arts College,* pp. 191–92; Cunningim, pp. 135, 301.

22. Earl J. McGrath, "Future of the Protestant College," *Liberal Education,* March 1961, p. 47; Pattillo and MacKenzie, pp. 138–39; Interview with Milo A. Rediger, 26 Oct. 1978.

23. Hofstadter and Metzger, p. 352; Rudolph, p. 419; E. Wilson Lyon, *The History of Pomona College, 1887 – 1969* (Claremont, CA, 1977), p. 289.

24. Butts, p. 61; Morison, pp. 189–90, 195, 242–45, 257, 259.

25. Morison, p. 218; Cunningham, pp. 224–32; Brown, p. 46.

26. Barrett Wendell, *A Literary History of American Criticism* (New York, 1931), pp. 407–08, 421.

27. Bronson, pp. 186–92; Louis Hatch, *The History of Bowdoin College* (Portland, ME, 1927), pp. 289–90.

28. Harold Bolce, "Blasting at the Rock of Ages," in James C. Stone and Donald P. DeNeve, *Portraits of the American University, 1890–1910* (San Francisco, 1971), pp. 269–80.

29. Lee A. Dew, *A History of Arkansas State University, 1909 – 1967* (Jonesboro, AK, 1968), p. 113; Clifford S. Griffin, *The University of Kansas* (Lawrence, 1974), pp. 224–25. For an able and largely representative study of the role of religion in the state university in the transitional late nineteenth century, see Winton U. Solberg, "The Conflict Between Religion and Secularism at the University of Illinois, 1867–1894," *American Quarterly,* Summer 1966, pp. 183–99.

30. Cedric Cummins, *The University of South Dakota, 1862 – 1966* (Vermillion, 1975), p. 226; John K. Bettersworth, *People's College: A History of Mississippi State* (Birmingham, 1953), p. 372; McKinney, pp. 46, 63–65.

31. Gabriel, pp. 163–65.

32. *Geneva College Catalog, 1878–80,* p. 24; Barnes, "Learning and Piety in Ohio Colleges," pp. 343–44; Kilby, p. 200.

33. Morris Bishop, *A History of Cornell* (Ithaca, 1962), pp. 190–94, 213–15; Hugh Hawkins, "The University-Builders Observe the Colleges," *History of Education Quarterly,* Winter 1971, pp. 353–58; Hopkins, p. 220.

34. Henry D. Sheldon, *History of University of Oregon* (Portland, 1940), pp. 63, 115, 227.

35. Cunningim, pp. 1, 14, 80–89, 298–300; Edgar M. Carlson, *Church Sponsored Higher Education and the Lutheran Church in America* (New York, 1967), p. 37.

36. William F. Buckley, Jr., *God and Man at Yale* (Chicago, 1951), pp. xiii, 4–5, 9–11, 14–16.

37. Potts, "American Colleges in the Nineteenth Century," p. 373; John D. Millett, *Strengthening Community in Higher Education* (New York, 1974), p. 1.

38. Cornelius H. Patton and Walter T. Field, *Eight O'Clock Chapel: A Study of New England College Life in the Eighties* (Boston, 1927), pp. 199–212.

39. Potts, "American Colleges in the Nineteenth Century," pp. 369–73.

40. Wicke, p. v; McGrath, "Future of the Protestant College," p. 45; George A. Buttrick, *Biblical Thought and the Secular University* (Baton Rouge, 1960), p. 4; Pattillo and MacKenzie, p. 153; Pace, pp. 92–93; Christopher Jencks and David Riesman, *The Academic Revolution* (Garden City, NY, 1969), p. 332.

41. Pattillo and Mackenzie, pp. 140–41.

42. *Christianity Today,* 29 June 1979, p. 45; Richard G. Hutcheson, Jr., *Mainline Churches and the Evangelicals* (Atlanta, 1981), pp. 15–17.

43. Barnard, pp. 50–51, 67, 77, 110–13, 127; for another excellent study of the secularization process in a specific institution, Knox, see Thomas A. Askew, "The Liberal Arts College Encounters Intellectual Change: A Comparative Study of Education at Knox and Wheaton Colleges, 1837–1925," Diss. Northwestern 1969.

44. *Franklin College Catalog, 1900 – 01,* pp. 16, 40.

45. *Franklin College Catalog, 1921 – 22,* pp. 25–26, 45, 50–52.

46. *Franklin College Catalog, 1950 – 51,* pp. 27, 129–30.

47. *Franklin College Catalog, 1978,* pp. 94, 119; Interview with John Shelly, 17 Oct. 1978; Byron E. Waterman, "A Study of the Purposes of

a Private Liberal Arts College: Franklin College," M.A. Thesis Indiana Univ. 1977, pp. 4, 8.

48. *Ripon College Catalog, 1883,* p. 24; *Ripon College Catalog, 1904,* p. 35; *Ripon College Catalog, 1926,* pp. 8–9, 77.

49. *Ripon College Catalog, 1950–51,* pp. 18, 76.

50. *Ripon College Catalog, 1978–79,* pp. 4–5, 11–12, 93, 108.

51. Kendall, pp. 178–79, 211; Thompson, pp. 100, 249–50; McKinney, pp. 109–11.

52. Pattillo and Mackenzie, p. 21.

53. For a discussion of the origins of the contemporary evangelical Friends movement, see Jones, *Haverford,* p. 28.

54. Chitty, pp. 22–24; "Academies, Colleges and Seminaries Related to the United Church of Christ," *Journal of Current Social Issues, 1976–77* (supplement), pp. 30–31; *Wake Forest College Catalog, 1978–79,* pp. 18–19, 25, 122–23.

55. Wicke, pp. 30, 41; W. A. Geier, "A New Trail in Methodist Higher Education," *School and Society,* 14 Sept. 1957, p. 250.

56. Earnest C. Marriner, *The History of Colby College* (Waterville, ME, 1963), p. 578.

57. Pattillo and Mackenzie, pp. vii, 20–21, 248; Safara A. Witmer, *Bible-College Story: Education with Dimension* (New York, 1962), pp. 15, 44.

58. Pattillo and Mackenzie, pp. 27–29, 295; National Center for Education Statistics, *1980 Digest of Education Statistics* (Washington, 1980), pp. 82, 88.

59. Pattillo and Mackenzie, pp. 26–29, 102–10; Wicke, p. 98.

60. Alexander W. Astin and Calvin B. T. Lee, *The Invisible Colleges: A Profile of Small Private Colleges with Limited Resources* (New York, 1972), p. 99; S. A. Clark and R. F. Larson, "Mobility, Productivity, and Inbreeding at Small Colleges: A Comparative Study," *Sociology of Education,* Fall 1972, pp. 426, 432.

61. See Merrimon Cunningim, "Categories of Church-Relatedness," in Robert Parsonage, ed., *Church-Related Higher Education* (Valley Forge, PA, 1978), chapter two.

62. Ferre, p. 155; Averill, p. 589; Havighurst, p. 252; *Miami University Catalog, 1980–81,* pp. 68, 74.

63. *Pomona College Catalog, 1977–78,* pp. 5, 23, 78, 199–202.

64. *Wellesley College Catalog, 1974–75,* pp. 10, 30, 42, 166–69.

65. *Texas Christian University Catalog, 1978–79,* pp. 5, 53, 66.

66. Commission of Higher Education, National Council of Churches, *What is a Christian College?* (New York, 1958), pp. 9–10, 14, 27, 33, 37, 39, 45.

67. N.F.S. Ferre, "Place of the Chapel in a Christian College," *Journal of Higher Education,* Apr. 1967, p. 177; G.A. Buttrick et al., "Toward a Philosophy of the Church-Related University," *Christian Scholar,* Summer 1962, pp. 95–96; L. A. King, "A Fable About a Slanted Education," *Eternity,* Aug. 1978, pp. 22–25, 37.

Notes to Chapter Five

1. Louis G. Geiger, *University of the Northern Plains: A History of the University of North Dakota* (Grand Forks, 1958), p. 256; Harold F. Williamson and Payson S. Wild, *Northwestern Univeristy: A History,*

1850–1975 (Evanston, 1976), p. 90; Shedd, *Student Christian Movements,* p. 9.

2. Shedd, *Student Christian Movements,* p. 9.

3. See, for example, George H. Callcott, *A History of the University of Maryland* (Baltimore, 1966), p. 242; Smith and Hirschler, pp. 246–50; *University of Wisconsin Catalog, 1920–21,* p. 87.

4. Shedd, *Student Christian Movements,* pp. 167; Robert N. Daniel, *Furman University: A History* (Greenville, SC, 1951), p. 130; Bettersworth, p. 371; James B. Sellers, *History of the University of Alabama* (Tuscaloosa, 1953), p. 462; Dunaway, *Pennsylvania State,* pp. 382–85.

5. McKinney, pp. 87–88.

6. Shedd, *Student Christian Movements,* pp. 92–94, 103–04, 118–20, 123–26, 152; C. Howard Hopkins, *A History of the YMCA in North America* (New York, 1951), p. 274; C. Howard Hopkins, *John R. Mott, 1865–1955* (Grand Rapids, 1979), p. 53.

7. Shedd, *Student Christian Movements,* pp. 188–97, 206–10.

8. Shedd, *Student Christian Movements,* pp. 120, 167; Hopkins, *YMCA,* pp. 282–83, 625–27, 646, 655–56.

9. Hopkins, *YMCA,* pp. 625–27; Franklin H. Littell, *From State Church to Pluralism: A Protestant Interpretation of Religion in American History* (New York, 1971), pp. 155–57; Hopkins, *Mott,* pp. 21, 24, 44, 210, 225.

10. Shedd, *Student Christian Movements,* pp. 92, 100–04, 119.

11. Sheldon, *Student Life,* pp. 271–81; Sheldon, *Oregon,* p. 130.

12. Hopkins, *YMCA,* pp. 274, 284–86; Sheldon, *Student Life,* p. 281.

13. Shedd, *Student Christian Movements,* pp. 167–68.

14. Shedd, *Student Christian Movements,* pp. 166–67, 248; Hopkins, *YMCA,* pp. 282–86, 628; Sheldon, *Student Life,* p. 281.

15. Sheldon, *Student Life,* pp. 271–74; Hopkins, *YMCA,* pp. 288–89.

16. Shedd, *Student Christian Movements,* pp. 238–67, 289, 405; Hopkins, *YMCA,* p. 295; Watson A. Omulogoli, "The Student Volunteer Movement," M.A. Thesis Wheaton College 1967, pp. 123–25.

17. Sheldon, *Student Life,* pp. 283–85.

18. Omulogoli, p. 104; Hopkins, *YMCA,* pp. 282–83; Shedd, *Student Christian Movements,* pp. 381–93, 422.

19. Omulogoli, pp. 108, 117.

20. Omulogoli, pp. 125–26.

21. Hopkins, *YMCA,* pp. 646, 655–56.

22. Clarence P. Shedd, *The Church Follows Its Students* (New Haven, 1938), pp. xiii–xviii, 9–32, 281–82; John Strietelmeier, *Valparaiso's First Century* (Valparaiso, IN, 1959), p. 78.

23. Charles E. Hummel, *Campus Christian Witness* (Chicago, 1958), pp. 1–11.

24. Hummel, pp. 191–94; also see David M. Howard, *Student Power in World Evangelism* (Downers Grove, IL, 1970), chapter nine.

25. Richard Quebedeaux, *I Found It: The Story of Bill Bright and Campus Crusade* (New York, 1979), pp. 52–66, 125–29, 142–46.

26. Ringenberg, *Taylor,* pp. 163–67; Quebedeaux, p. 142.

27. Quebedeaux, pp. xii, 58.

28. Nomenclature is a problem in Bible college history. Later in this section I will discuss the evolution from Bible training schools and Bible institutes to Bible colleges; however, to minimize confusion and misunderstanding, throughout the text I will usually use the term "Bible college" and "Bible colleges" except when referring exclusively to the

pre-1940 period. While this may be generous, it probably compares favorably with the generally accepted practice of using the term "college" to describe the many nineteenth-century liberal arts institutions that enrolled primarily preparatory students.

29. Virginia L. Brereton, "Education and Evangelism: Protestant Fundamentalist Bible Schools, 1880-1940," paper presented at the Conference on Urban Education, Columbia Univ., New York City, 12 Dec. 1980, pp. 20ff.; Safara A. Witmer, "A New Form of American Education," in Frank E. Gaebelein, ed., *Christian Education in a Democracy* (New York, 1951), pp. 165-67; H. Richard Niebuhr, Daniel D. Williams, and James Gustafson, *The Advancement of Theological Education* (New York, 1957), p. 5; Louis Gasper, *The Fundamentalist Movement* (Paris, 1963), pp. 11-12; William S. McBirnie, Jr., "A Study of the Bible Institute Movement," Diss. Southwestern Baptist Theological Seminary 1952, p. 6; Harold W. Boon, "The Development of the Bible College or Institute in the United States and Canada Since 1880," Diss. New York Univ. 1950, pp. 2-3, 30-34, 41. Also see Virginia L. Brereton, "Protestant Fundamentalist Bible Schools," Diss. Columbia Univ. 1981.

30. Ernest Sandeen, *The Roots of Fundamentalism: British and American Millenarianism, 1800 – 1930* (Chicago, 1970), pp. 183, 241-42; Gene A. Getz, *MBI: The Story of Moody Bible Institute* (Chicago, 1969), pp. 22, 28, 48; S. A. Witmer, *The Bible College Story: Education with Dimension* (Wheaton, IL, 1970), pp. 53-66; Don Gray, "A Critical Analysis of the Academic Evolutionary Development Within the Assemblies of God Higher Education Movement, 1914-1975," Diss. Southwestern Baptist Theological Seminary 1976, pp. 57, 97-101; McBirnie, p. 37; Johnson, *Higher Education of Southern Baptists,* pp. 401-04. Also see Gerald C. Tiffin, "The Interaction Between the Bible College Movement and the Independent Disciples of Christ Denomination," Diss. Stanford 1968.

31. George Dollar, *A History of Fundamentalism in America* (Greenville, SC, 1973), pp. 113-17, 199-200; William Bell Riley, *The Menace of Modernism* (New York, 1917), p. 115.

32. McBirnie, pp. 11-12, 16, 19-23; Witmer, *Bible College Story,* p. 33; Boon, pp. 26-29.

33. Boon, pp. 30-36, 40-41; James Findlay, "Moody, 'Gapmen,' and the Gospel: The Early Days of Moody Bible Institute," *Church History,* Sept. 1962, pp. 325-26; Stanley N. Gundry, *Love Them In: The Proclamation Theology of D. L. Moody* (Chicago, 1976), pp. 55-56, 166-68.

34. Getz, *MBI,* pp. 90-91; Findlay, "*Moody Bible Institute,* " p. 323; Witmer, *Bible College Story,* p. 36.

35. Getz, pp. 21, 24, 47-55, 346.

36. Nathan R. Wood, *A School of Christ: Gordon College* (Boston, 1953), pp. 17-18; Witmer, *Bible College Story,* pp. 38, 73; Charles B. Eavey, *History of Christian Education* (Chicago, 1964), pp. 338-41.

37. Boon, pp. 50-51; Wood, pp. 10-20.

38. Witmer, *Bible College Story,* p. 35; Findlay, "Moody Bible Institute," p. 326.

39. Witmer, *Bible College Story,* p. 89; *Montana Institute of the Bible Catalog, 1980-82,* p. 24.

40. S. A. Witmer, "If J. E. Ramseyer Had Lived In Days Like These," *The Missionary Worker,* 15 June 1962, p. 6.

41. Getz, pp. 45-46; *Fort Wayne Bible Training School Catalog 1906-07,*

p. 10; Harry M. Shuman et al., *After Fifty Years: A Record of God's Working Through the Christian and Missionary Alliance* (Harrisburg, PA, 1939), pp. 87–97.

42. Kenneth S. Latourette, *A History of Christianity*, 2 vols. (New York, 1975), II, p. 1046; Witmer, "New Form of Education," pp. 164–65; Witmer, *Bible College Story*, pp. 77–83, 111; *American Association of Bible Colleges Manual, 1975,* p. 7; Getz, pp. 352–53; Kenneth Gangel, "The Bible College: Past, Present, and Future," *Christianity Today*, 7 Nov. 1980, p. 35.

43. Byron O. Osborne, *The Malone Story* (Newton, KS, 1970), p. 233; Boon, p. 92; "Educational Experiences and Career Patterns of Bible College Graduates," survey conducted by the American Association of Bible Colleges, 1980, p. 5.

44. Witmer, "New Form of Education," pp. 163–66; Boon, p. 66; Getz, pp. 114–16; *Gordon Bible Institute Catalog, 1914,* p. 42.

45. *Liberty Baptist College Catalog, 1978–79,* pp. 6, 37; Conrad Hilberry, "Wheaton College," in *A Future for Private Colleges*, ed. Hilberry and Keeton, p. 35; Melton Wright, *Fortress of Faith: The Story of Bob Jones University* (Grand Rapids, 1960), p. 214.

46. McBirnie, pp. 82–83; Boon, pp. 75–76; Witmer, *Bible College Story*, pp. 42–44; Gangel, p. 35.

47. McBirnie, p. 88; Witmer, *Bible College Story*, p. 44; Osborne, pp. 206-07; Eavey, p. 344.

48. Witmer, "New Form of Education," pp. 158–62, 176; S. A. Witmer, "Bible College Education," *School and Society*, 16 Oct. 1954, pp. 113–15.

49. Interview with Samuel D. Sutherland, 20 Oct. 1978; Witmer, *Bible College Story*, p. 74; *Biola Catalog, 1978–79,* p. 25; *Northwestern College Catalog, 1979–81,* pp. 37, 40–41.

50. Witmer, *Bible College Story*, p. 45; Lenice F. Redd, "The Bible Institute Movement in America," M.A. Thesis Wheaton College 1947, pp. 55–57; Boon, pp.19–22; Robert W. Lynn and Elliott Wright, *The Big Little School: 200 Years of the Sunday School* (Nashville, 1971), pp. 40ff.

51. Interview with Samuel D. Sutherland, 20 Oct. 1978; Witmer, *Bible College Story*, pp. 45–47; McBirnie, p. 115; *American Association of Bible Colleges Manual, 1975*, pp. 7–8.

52. S. A. Witmer, "The Paradox in Bible College Education," in Timothy M. Warner, ed., *S. A. Witmer: Beloved Educator* (Wheaton, IL, 1970), pp. 33–35; *The Missionary Worker*, 15 June 1962, p. 2; Warner, p. 5.

53. Witmer, *Bible College Story*, p. 46; *American Association of Bible Colleges Manual, 1975*, pp. 45–46, 75–76; *American Association of Bible Colleges Manual, 1979–80*, pp. 3–17.

54. Witmer, *Bible College Story*, p. 44; Getz, pp. 11–12, 21.

55. *American Association of Bible Colleges Directory, 1979–1980*, p. 3–17.

56. Boon, pp. 99–101; *Baptist Bible College Catalog, 1978–79*, pp. 33-36.

57. Witmer, *Bible College Story*, pp. 40, 55–56; McBirnie, p. 2; *American Association of Bible Colleges Manual, 1975*, p. 22; *American Association of Bible Colleges Directory, 1979–80*, pp. 3–17; Gangel, p. 35; Letter from R. E. Bell, 24 Nov. 1980; *AABC Newsletter,* Fall 1974, p. 7; *Fact Book on Theological Education, 1980–81*, p. 66.

58. Letter from R. E. Bell, 9 Apr. 1981; *AABC Newsletter*, Winter 1975, p. 1; *AABC Newsletter*, Winter 1980, p. 6; R. E. Bell, ed., "Student Recruitment in the Bible College," (study conducted by the American Association of Bible Colleges, 1975), pp. 8, 10, 15–16.

Notes to pages 173-86   241

59. Hilberry, "Wheaton," p. 35.

60. Askew, pp. 235-48.

61. If Redlands was reluctant to be known as "the Wheaton of the West," another California school, Westmont, gladly accepted that label following its beginning in Santa Barbara in 1940.

62. Lawrence E. Nelson, *Redlands: Biography of a College* (Redlands, 1958), pp. 247-48.

63. *Bryan College Catalog, 1977-79*, pp. 7-8.

64. William Jennings Bryan, *Darwin's Confession* (Upland, IN, n.d.), pp. 1-4.

65. Percival A. Wesche, *Henry Clay Morrison; Crusader and Saint* (n.p., n.d.), pp. 72, 93-94, 169, 187.

66. See Ronald H. Nash, *The New Evangelicalism* (Grand Rapids, 1963); George M. Marsden, *Fundamentalism and American Culture* (New York, 1980), p. 228.

67. Dollar, pp. 283-85.

68. Roger C. Ellison, "A Foundation Study of the Development of Tennessee Temple Schools," Diss. Bob Jones 1973, pp. 13-15, 61-80, 163; Dollar, pp. 195, 242-43.

69. Billy Vick Bartlett, *The History of Baptist Separatism* (Springfield, MO, 1972), pp. 2-7, 32-33, 50-51, 60-65, 79; Dollar, pp. 197-98, 271-72; *Baptist Bible College Catalog, 1978-79*, pp. 9, 14, 16.

70. "Man With Vision," *Christian Life*, March 1978, pp. 20-21, 59-63; "A Tide of Born-Again Politics," *Newsweek*, 15 Sept. 1980, pp. 28-35.

71. Wright, *Bob Jones University*, pp. 24-51; Dollar, pp. 270-71.

72. *Bob Jones University Catalog, 1978-79*, pp. 184, 189; "Tax Troubles," *Christianity Today*, 7 June 1974, p. 50; Larry King, "The Buckle on the Bible Belt," *Harper's Magazine*, June 1966, p. 55; R. Behenson, "Ars Sacra in the Peruna Belt," *National Review*, 20 July 1973, p. 792; R. G. Sherrill, "Bob Jones University, New Curricula for Bigotry," *Nation*, 29 March 1965, pp. 326-27.

73. *Bob Jones University Catalog, 1978-79*, pp. 2, 8, 190, 197-204.

74. See, for example, Gasper, pp. 105-06.

75. Dollar, p. 270; "World's Most Unusual," *Time*, 16 June 1952, p. 74; *Bob Jones University Catalog, 1978-79*, pp. 5, 45; *Liberty Baptist College Catalog, 1978-79*, pp. 3, 37.

76. Wright, *Bob Jones University*, p. 213.

77. Ellison, pp. 51, 198; *Baptist Bible College Catalog, 1978-79*, pp. 5, 45; *Liberty Baptist College Catalog, 1978-79*, pp. 3, 37.

78. Dollar, p. 259; Ellison, p. 199; *Liberty Baptist College Catalog, 1978-79*, p. 55; Wolterstorff, pp. 25-26; Gasper, p. 114; R. Drummand Ayres, "Private Schools Provoking Church-State Conflict," *New York Times*, 28 Apr. 1978, pp. 1, 23.

79. Ellison, p. 92; King, pp. 53, 56; "The Sins of Billy James," *Time*, 16 Feb. 1976, p. 52; "Personalia," *Christianity Today*, 5 Sept. 1980, p. 79.

80. "Sunday Schools of the Decade," *Christian Life*, Oct. 1977, pp. 30-34.

81. Sherrill, p. 328; John Pollack, *Billy Graham: The Authorized Biography* (New York, 1966), p. 11; Ellison, p. 174.

82. Ellison, pp. 44-46; Sherrill, pp. 327-28; Bartlett, pp. 62-69; Wright, *Bob Jones University*, p. 73.

83. Sherrill, pp. 327-29; "Born-Again Politics," pp. 28-32.

84. Adlai S. Croom, *The Early History of Harding College* (n.p., 1954), pp. 128-31; also see Marsden, pp. 206-07.

85. By contrast, before the Civil War a significant number of evangelical colleges and leaders promoted a radical brand of social activism. See Donald W. Dayton, *Discovering An Evangelical Heritage* (New York, 1976); and David R. Huehner, "Reform and the Pre–Civil War American College," Diss. Univ. of Illinois 1972.

86. Hilberry, "Wheaton," p. 37.

Notes to Chapter Six

1. Young, p. 186; Mary A. Tenney, *Still Abides the Memory* (Greenville, IL, 1942), pp. 282-83; Stanley High, "Pity the Poor Collegian," *Saturday Evening Post*, 3 June 1939, p. 71.

2. Brigham Young University with its 28,000 students is the largest of the seriously religious colleges, but few Mormons or non-Mormons would wish to classify it as Protestant.

3. Bernard Cochran, "Southern Baptist Dilemma in Higher Education," *Christian Century*, 28 Dec. 1966, p. 1600; Earl J. McGrath et al., *Study of Southern Baptist Colleges and Universities, 1976-77* (Nashville, 1977), pp. 18-20, 63; *Baylor University Catalog, 1978-79*, pp. i, 15, 22, 126-32.

4. Carlson, *Church Sponsored Higher Education*, pp. 12-13; *Lutheran Higher Education Directory, 1980-82*, pp. 10-59; interview with Gary Greinke, 29 June 1981. For a helpful explanation of the complex denominational genealogy from which the Lutheran colleges developed, see Arthur L. Olsen, "Unpacking Luther's Heritage—American Style," in J. Victor Hahn, ed., *Lutheran Higher Education in the 1980s: Heritage and Challenge* (Washington, D.C., 1980).

5. Pattillo and Mackenzie, pp. 253-54, 256-60; interview with Gary Greinke, 29 June 1981; McGrath, *Southern Baptist Colleges*, pp. 84, 96; Education Commission of the Southern Baptist Convention, *Baptist Education Study Task* (Nashville, 1978), p. 62; Letter from Charles J. Miller, 18 Sept. 1978.

6. Pattillo and MacKenzie, pp. 15-16.

7. Some of the more aggressively separatist of these were discussed in the section on fundamentalist higher education in chapter five.

8. Vinson Synan, *The Holiness-Pentecostal Movement in the United States* (Grand Rapids, 1971), pp. 51, 209; William W. Menzies, *Annointed to Serve: The Story of the Assemblies of God* (Springfield, MO, 1971), pp. 362-64; also see Klaude Kendrick, *The Promise Fulfilled: A History of the Modern Pentecostal Movement* (Springfield, MO, 1961), and Timothy L. Smith, *Called Unto Holiness: The Story of the Nazarenes* (Kansas City, 1962). Synan and Kendrick emphasize the similar origins of the Holiness and Pentecostal movements.

9. Oral Roberts, *The Call* (New York, 1971), pp. 198-99; "Oral Roberts College Has Grown in Seven Years," *New York Times*, 13 June 1972, sec. 2, p. 1; *ORU News Bulletin*, Sept. 1976; *Oral Roberts University Catalog, 1978-79*, p. 16.

10. Roberts, ch. 10; *ORU News Bulletin*, Sept. 1976; "Oral Roberts College," p. 1; *Oral Roberts University School of Medicine Catalog, 1980-81*, p. 45; "When God Talks, Oral Listens," *Time*, 16 Nov. 1981, p. 64.

11. "Oral Roberts College," p. 1; *Oral Roberts University Student Handbook, 1978-79*, pp. 46-47, 50: *ORU News Bulletin*, Sept. 1976.

12. *ORU News Bulletin*, Sept. 1976.

13. *ORU News Bulletin*, Sept. 1976.

14. Roberts, pp. 177–96; Pollack, pp. 41–46; Philip Yancey, "The Ironies and Impact of PTL," *Christianity Today*, 21 Sept. 1979, p. 30.

15. Donald F. Ackland, *Moving Heaven and Earth: R. G. LeTourneau* (New York, 1949), pp. 155–56; *LeTourneau College Catalog, 1979–80*, pp. 7–8, 14–15.

16. *The Story of America's Most Unique College: The School of the Ozarks* (n.p., n.d.); *School of the Ozarks Catalog, 1981–83*, pp. 10–12, 22–26.

17. John W. Snyder, "Why Not a Christian College on a University Campus?" *Christianity Today*, 17 Feb. 1967, pp. 14–17; Frank C. Nelsen, "Evangelical Living and Learning Centers: A Proposal," *Christianity Today*, 26 May 1972, pp. 7–8; Ron Sider, "Christian Cluster Colleges off to a Good Start," *Christianity Today,* 24 May 1974, pp. 12–16; *Conrad Grebel College Catalog, 1981–82*, pp. 8–12, 30, 33–34; Shedd, *Church Follows Its Students*, p. 21; Geiger, pp. 144, 163–65, 336; Johnson, *Higher Education of Southern Baptists*, pp. 405–06; *Northwest Christian College Catalog, 1978–1980*, pp. 12–13, 36–37.

18. A similar enrollment pattern is occurring in seminary education where the conservative Protestant institutions—especially the Southern Baptist and independent ones—are experiencing the sharpest growth. A clear majority of the following twenty-five largest seminaries (Fall 1980) are evangelical or orthodox in nature:

1. Southwestern (Southern Baptist), 3,684
2. Fuller, 2,394
3. Southern (Southern Baptist), 2,068
4. New Orleans (Southern Baptist), 1,242
5. Southeastern (Southern Baptist), 1,055
6. San Francisco (United Presbyterian), 962
7. Trinity (Evangelical Free), 833
8. Princeton, 810
9. Dallas, 777
10. Asbury, 742
11. Concordia of St. Louis (Lutheran Church Missouri Synod), 724
12. Talbot, 720
13. Drew (United Methodist), 705
14. Gordon-Conwell, 693
15. Luther (American Lutheran Church), 643
16. McCormick (United Presbyterian), 618
17. Candler (United Methodist), 608
18. Golden Gate Baptist (Southern Baptist), 587
19. Concordia of Ft. Wayne (Lutheran Church Missouri Synod), 571
20. Nazarene, 499
21. Boston (United Methodist), 486
22. Yale, 473
23. Andover-Newton, 463
24. Bethel (Baptist General Conference), 443
25. Perkins (United Methodist), 438

This enrollment data appears in the January, 1981, *Bulletin of the Association of Theological Schools* and the 1980–81 *Yearbook of Higher Education*. Also see Kenneth S. Kantzer, "Documenting the Dramatic Shift in

Seminaries from Liberal to Conservative," *Christianity Today*, 4 Feb. 1983, pp. 10–11.

19. Kenneth Briggs, "Evangelical Colleges Reborn," *New York Times Magazine,* 14 Dec. 1980, pp. 140–44; Pace, *Education and Evangelism,* pp. xii, 2; Carl Henry, *Evangelicals in Search of Identity* (Waco, TX, 1976), p. 62; *Christian College News,* 8 Aug. 1980, p. 3; David Riesman, "The Evangelical College: Untouched by the Academic Revolution," *Change,* Jan./Feb. 1981, p. 15; Pattillo and MacKenzie, p. 114.

20. For the philosophy and history of CASC in its early years, see Alfred T. Hill, *The Small College Meets the Challenge: The Story of CASC* (New York, 1959).

21. "Dean's List Top Ten," *Christianity Today*, 30 Jan. 1970, p. 36; "Evaluating Christian Colleges," *Christianity Today,* 27 March 1970, p. 23; Conrad Hilberry, "Wheaton College," in Morris Keeton and Conrad Hilberry, eds., *Struggle and Promise: A Future for Colleges* (New York, 1969), pp. 21, 40, 73; "All That and Billy Graham, Too," *Time*, 22 Sept. 1980, p. 83.

22. "Graham Center," *Christianity Today*, 10 Oct. 1980, pp. 74–75; interview with William Shoemaker, 3 July 1980.

23. Askew, p. 231; Harold W. Berk, "The Christian College Consortium in Social Context," Diss. Univ. of Toledo 1974, pp. 64–74.

24. Paul Ramsay and John F. Wilson, eds., *The Study of Religion in Colleges and Universities* (Princeton, 1970), p. 11; Jack Haas and Richard Wright, "What Christian Colleges Teach About Creation," *Christianity Today*, 17 June 1977, pp. 8–11; Hilberry, "Wheaton," p. 33; James O. Buswell III, "Creationist Views on Human Origin," *Christianity Today*, 8 Aug. 1975, pp. 4–6.

25. Bernard M. Loomer, "Religion and the Mind of the University," in Amos N. Wilder, ed., *Liberal Learning and Religion* (New York, 1951), pp. 159–63; Ernest L. Boyer and Martin Kaplan, *Education for Survival* (Washington, 1977), p. 11.

26. Nicholas P. Wolterstorff et al., pp. 23–26; Bernard Ramm, *The Christian College in the Twentieth Century* (Grand Rapids, 1963), pp. 76–80.

27. *Christian College News*, 31 Oct. 1980, pp. 2a–4a, 14 Nov. 1980, pp. 1a, 5, 28 Nov. 1980, p. 2a, 26 Dec. 1980, p. 8, 30 Jan. 1981, p. 6, 13 Feb. 1981, p. 8; *Goshen College Catalog, 1980–82*, pp. 45–46, 75–78; Kenneth A. Briggs, "Evangelical Institute Preaches Ecology," *New York Times*, 29 June 1981, p. B12. For an excellent institutional self-study promoting the integration idea, see St. Olaf's Henry Hong, ed., *Integration in the Christian Liberal Arts College* (Northfield, MN, 1956). Also note Frank E. Gaebelein, *The Pattern of God's Truth* (New York, 1954), and the very influential writings of Arthur F. Holmes, especially *The Idea of a Christian College* (Grand Rapids, 1975), chapter four; and *All Truth is God's Truth* (Grand Rapids, 1977).

28. James R. Cameron, *Eastern Nazarene College, 1900–1950* (Kansas City, 1968), p. 287.

29. Jay B. Kenyon, *Ten College Generations* (New York, 1956), p. 125.

30. Kenyon, pp. 130–31; "42 Hours of Repentance," *Time*, 20 Feb. 1950, pp. 56, 58; "Wheaton Repents," *Newsweek,* 20 Feb. 1950, pp. 82–83; "College Revival Becomes Confession Marathon," *Life*, 20 Feb, 1950, pp. 40–41.

31. "Asbury Revival Blazes Cross-Country Trail," *Christianity Today*, 13 March 1970, pp. 46-50.

32. Kenyon, pp. 124-25; Pattillo and MacKenzie, pp. 111-13.

33. Pace, *Education and Evangelism*, p. xii; John H. Furbay, "Undergraduates in a Group of Evangelical Christian Colleges," Diss. Yale 1931, pp. 141, 184; Hilberry, "Wheaton," p. 36.

34. *ORU News Bulletin, 1972.*

35. Part of this section originally appeared in the essay "Why Did Christian Colleges Remain Calm?" *Taylor University Magazine*, Fall 1972.

36. *Houghton College Catalog, 1926-27*, p. 13.

37. "Evangelical Colleges Plan Consortium," *Christianity Today*, 9 April 1971, pp. 44-45; Berk, pp. 1, 79, 289; Christian College Consortium Articles of Incorporation, 24 June 1971.

38. Gordon R. Werkema, "Description of the Christian College Consortium," unpublished letter, 4 Feb. 1976. Also, see *A Guide to Christian Colleges* (Grand Rapids, 1982).

39. Carnegie Foundation for the Advancement of Teaching, *The States and Higher Education* (San Francisco, 1976), p. 41.

40. George N. Rainsford, *Congress and Higher Education in the Nineteenth Century* (Knoxville, 1972), pp. 96, 130-31, 135.

41. Carnegie Foundation, *States and Higher Education*, p. 28; Richard G. Axt, *The Federal Government and Financing Higher Education* (New York, 1952), pp. 79-81, 122-43, 156-57; Alice M. Rivlin, *The Role of the Federal Government in Financing Higher Education* (Washington, 1961), pp. 61-97.

42. W. H. McFarlane, "Patterns of State Aid to Private Higher Education," *College and University Journal*, May 1972, pp. 19-20; Carnegie Foundation, *States and Higher Education*, pp. 80-81; Paul Hardin et al., *Endangered Service: Independent Colleges, Public Policy, and the First Amendment* (Nashville, 1976), pp. 83-84.

43. C. Stanley Lowell, "Will Churches Give Up Their Colleges?" *Church and State*, Jul.-Aug. 1971, pp. 10-11; "Public Aid to Church-related Colleges and Universities," *School and Society*, 30 Oct. 1965, pp. 404-05; Frank J. Sorauf, *The Wall of Separation* (Princeton, 1976), pp. 52-53; H. I. Hester, *Southern Baptists in Christian Education*, (n.p., 1968), pp. 58, 86; *Baptist Education Study Task Report*, p. 63; Luther J. Carter, "Facilities Grants Forbidden to Baptist Colleges," *Science*, 29 Apr. 1966, pp. 626-29; Cochran, p. 1600; "Baptists in a Bind," *Christian Century*, 8 Dec. 1965, p. 1502.

44. Carnegie Council on Policy Studies in Higher Education, *The Federal Role in Postsecondary Education* (San Francisco, 1975), pp. 36-39; Peggy Heim et al., *A National Policy for Private Higher Education* (Washington D.C., 1974), p. 19; Hardin, pp. 30, 82; "Packwood-Moynihan Parochial Bill Introduced," *Church and State*, Apr. 1981, p. 3; "Senate Holds Parochial Hearings," *Church and State*, Jul.-Aug. 1981, pp. 5-10; interview with John Dellenback, 24 Dec. 1980.

45. "Church Colleges and the Scramble for Public Funds," *Christian Century*, 20 Oct. 1976, pp. 883-85.

46. *Baptist Bible College Catalog, 1978-79*, p. 41.

47. Sorauf, pp. 361-69; Edward N. Leavy and Eric A. Raps, "The Judicial Double Standard for State Aid to Church-Affiliated Educational Institutions," *Journal of Church and State*, Spring 1979, pp. 209-22; Hardin, pp. 93ff.

48. Hardin, pp. 93ff.; *Christian College News*, 19 Oct. 1979, p. 3.

49. "Grove City in Legal Thicket," *Christianity Today,* 16 Nov. 1979, pp. 45–46; *Christian College News*, 11 Jul. 1980, p. 2, and 8 Aug. 1980, pp. 3–4; "ORU Takes Offensive over Law School Accreditation," *Christianity Today*, 4 Sept. 1981, pp. 73–74; "The Bar Association Does Accreditation About-face," *Christianity Today*, 18 Sept. 1981, pp. 47.

50. For an interesting explanation of the reasons for these mixed results, see Walfred H. Peterson, "The Thwarted Opportunity for Judicial Activism in Church-State Relations: Separation and Accommodation in Precarious Balance," *Journal of Church and State,* Fall 1980, pp. 437–58.

51. Hardin, pp. 20, 62; Gary A. Greinke, *Survival with a Purpose: A Master Plan Revisited* (n.p., 1977), pp. 9–10; Carol van Alstyne, "The Costs to Colleges and Universities of Implementing Federally Mandated Social Programs," in Sidney Hook et al., *The University and the State* (Buffalo, 1978), pp. 116–19; Advisory Commission on Intergovernmental Relations, *The Evolution of a Problematic Partnership: The Feds and Higher Ed* (Washington, 1981), pp. 33–45.

Notes to the Epilogue

1. Robert C. Baptista, "The Christian College: An Endangered Species," *Christianity Today*, 7 Nov. 1980, pp. 30–33; W. Richard Stephens, "Statement Before the House Subcommittee on Postsecondary Education" (Washington, D.C., 24 Feb. 1981), p. 2.

2. Trueblood, *The Idea of a College*, pp. 24, 31–32.

3. See Howard Lowry, *The Mind's Adventure* (Philadelphia, 1950), pp. 102–05; D. Elton Trueblood, "The Redemption of the College," in Elizabeth Newby, ed., *A Philosopher's Way* (Nashville, 1978), pp. 112–14; Gaebelein, p. 23.

4. Part of this section on the witness of the Christian college originally appeared as "A Critique of Secular Higher Education," *Taylor University Magazine*, Winter 1982, pp. 2–5. Also see Lowry, p. 7; George A. Buttrick, *Biblical Thought and the Secular University* (Baton Rouge, 1960), p. 7; N.F.S. Ferre, "Church-Related Colleges and a Mature Faith," *Religious Education,* March 1959, pp. 149–53.

5. Buttrick, *Biblical Thought and the Secular University*, p. 19.

6. Holmes, *Idea of a Christian College*, pp. 19, 57–58; Jacques Barzun, *The American University* (New York, 1970), p. 240.

7. Herbert Butterfield, *Christianity and History* (New York, 1949), p. 21.

8. Butterfield, pp. 60, 113–14; Buttrick, *Biblical Thought and the Secular University*, pp. 38–41, 57–58.

9. Cunningim, *College Seeks Religion,* pp. 10–11; Lowry, pp. 51–54.

10. E. J. McGrath, "Future of the Protestant College," *Liberal Education*, March 1961, p. 50.

11. Richard Hofstadter and Wilson Smith, *American Higher Education: A Documentary History* (Chicago, 1962), pp. 1, 5–7.

Index